# Design Thinking

by Christian Müller-Roterberg

## Design Thinking For Dummies®

Published by: **John Wiley & Sons, Inc.,** 111 River Street, Hoboken, NJ 07030-5774, www.wiley.com

Copyright © 2020 by John Wiley & Sons, Inc., Hoboken, New Jersey

Published simultaneously in Canada

For general information on our other products and services, please contact our Customer Care Department within the U.S. at 877-762-2974, outside the U.S. at 317-572-3993, or fax 317-572-4002. For technical support, please visit www.wiley.com/techsupport.

Wiley publishes in a variety of print and electronic formats and by print-on-demand. Some material included with standard print versions of this book may not be included in e-books or in print-on-demand. If this book refers to media such as a CD or DVD that is not included in the version you purchased, you may download this material at http://booksupport.wiley.com. For more information about Wiley products, visit www.wiley.com.

Library of Congress Control Number: 2020934428

ISBN: 978-1-119-59392-8; 978-1-119-59395-9 (ebk); 978-1-119-59412-3 (ebk)

Manufactured in the United States of America

SKY10044266_030923

# Contents at a Glance

**Introduction** .................................................... 1

**Part 1: Getting Started with Design Thinking** ................ 7
CHAPTER 1: Everything You Need to Know About Design Thinking. .............. 9
CHAPTER 2: Understanding the Principles of Design Thinking. ................ 29
CHAPTER 3: Creating Ideal Conditions ...................................... 43
CHAPTER 4: Planning a Design Thinking Project ............................. 59
CHAPTER 5: Supporting Teamwork in the Project. ........................... 77

**Part 2: The Problem Phases** ................................. 93
CHAPTER 6: Understanding the Task. ....................................... 95
CHAPTER 7: Putting Yourself in the Roles of Others. ....................... 117
CHAPTER 8: Observing People in Action. ................................... 137
CHAPTER 9: Redefining the Problem. ....................................... 159

**Part 3: The Solution Phases** ............................... 177
CHAPTER 10: Finding Ideas ................................................ 179
CHAPTER 11: Developing Ideas Intuitively and Creatively ................... 195
CHAPTER 12: Evaluating Ideas ............................................. 211
CHAPTER 13: Designing Prototypes. ........................................ 227
CHAPTER 14: Testing Ideas and Assumptions ............................... 241

**Part 4: The Part of Tens** .................................. 255
CHAPTER 15: Ten Success Factors for Interviews ........................... 257
CHAPTER 16: Ten Success Factors for Implementing Your Idea. .............. 263

**Index** .................................................... 275

# Table of Contents

**INTRODUCTION** . . . . . . . . . . . . . . . . . . . . . . . . . . . . . . . . . . . . . . . . 1

About This Book. . . . . . . . . . . . . . . . . . . . . . . . . . . . . . . . . . . . . . . . . . . 1

Conventions Used in This Book. . . . . . . . . . . . . . . . . . . . . . . . . . . . . . . 2

Foolish Assumptions. . . . . . . . . . . . . . . . . . . . . . . . . . . . . . . . . . . . . . . . 2

What You Don't Have to Read . . . . . . . . . . . . . . . . . . . . . . . . . . . . . . . . 3

How This Book Is Organized . . . . . . . . . . . . . . . . . . . . . . . . . . . . . . . . . 3

    Part 1: Getting Started with Design Thinking. . . . . . . . . . . . . . . . . 3

    Part 2: The Problem Phases. . . . . . . . . . . . . . . . . . . . . . . . . . . . . . . . 4

    Part 3: The Solution Phases . . . . . . . . . . . . . . . . . . . . . . . . . . . . . . . 4

    Part 4: The Part of Tens . . . . . . . . . . . . . . . . . . . . . . . . . . . . . . . . . . 4

Icons Used in This Book . . . . . . . . . . . . . . . . . . . . . . . . . . . . . . . . . . . . . 4

Beyond the Book . . . . . . . . . . . . . . . . . . . . . . . . . . . . . . . . . . . . . . . . . . . 5

Where to Go from Here . . . . . . . . . . . . . . . . . . . . . . . . . . . . . . . . . . . . . . 5

**PART 1: GETTING STARTED WITH DESIGN THINKING** . . . . . . 7

CHAPTER 1: **Everything You Need to Know About Design Thinking** . . . . . . . . . . . . . . . . . . . . . . . . . . . . . . . . . . . . . 9

This Is Design Thinking . . . . . . . . . . . . . . . . . . . . . . . . . . . . . . . . . . . . . . 9

    More than just design. . . . . . . . . . . . . . . . . . . . . . . . . . . . . . . . . . . 10

    More than just a workshop . . . . . . . . . . . . . . . . . . . . . . . . . . . . . . 10

    More than just brainstorming . . . . . . . . . . . . . . . . . . . . . . . . . . . . 11

    More than just methods. . . . . . . . . . . . . . . . . . . . . . . . . . . . . . . . . 11

Seeing What Design Thinking Can Do . . . . . . . . . . . . . . . . . . . . . . . . . 12

    Developing new products . . . . . . . . . . . . . . . . . . . . . . . . . . . . . . . 12

    Creating new services. . . . . . . . . . . . . . . . . . . . . . . . . . . . . . . . . . . 12

    Designing new business models. . . . . . . . . . . . . . . . . . . . . . . . . . 13

    Designing social and organizational innovations . . . . . . . . . . . . 13

    Establishing a culture of innovation . . . . . . . . . . . . . . . . . . . . . . . 14

Understanding the Basics of Design Thinking. . . . . . . . . . . . . . . . . . . 14

    Following and communicating the principles . . . . . . . . . . . . . . . . 14

    Getting an overview of the whole process. . . . . . . . . . . . . . . . . . 15

    Going through the process in detail . . . . . . . . . . . . . . . . . . . . . . . 17

Start Design Thinking Right Away . . . . . . . . . . . . . . . . . . . . . . . . . . . . 24

    Assembling the team . . . . . . . . . . . . . . . . . . . . . . . . . . . . . . . . . . . 24

    Defining team roles and communication practices . . . . . . . . . . . 25

    Planning the project work . . . . . . . . . . . . . . . . . . . . . . . . . . . . . . . 25

    Furnishing the work environment . . . . . . . . . . . . . . . . . . . . . . . . 26

    Asking for support. . . . . . . . . . . . . . . . . . . . . . . . . . . . . . . . . . . . . . 27

CHAPTER 2: **Understanding the Principles of Design Thinking** . . . . . . . . . . . . . . . . . . . . . . . . . . . . 29

    Focusing on People Early On . . . . . . . . . . . . . . . . . . . . . . . . . . . . . . . 30
    More than Traditional Market Research . . . . . . . . . . . . . . . . . . . . . . 31
    Finding the Lead User . . . . . . . . . . . . . . . . . . . . . . . . . . . . . . . . . . . . 32
    Actively Involving the Lead User . . . . . . . . . . . . . . . . . . . . . . . . . . . 35
    Developing Empathy . . . . . . . . . . . . . . . . . . . . . . . . . . . . . . . . . . . . . 36
    Illustrating Ideas . . . . . . . . . . . . . . . . . . . . . . . . . . . . . . . . . . . . . . . 37
    Failing in Order to Learn . . . . . . . . . . . . . . . . . . . . . . . . . . . . . . . . . 38
    Ensuring Diversity on the Team . . . . . . . . . . . . . . . . . . . . . . . . . . . 39
    Offering Team-Oriented and Creative Workspaces . . . . . . . . . . . . . . 39
    Making the Process Flexible Yet Focused . . . . . . . . . . . . . . . . . . . . . 40

CHAPTER 3: **Creating Ideal Conditions** . . . . . . . . . . . . . . . . . . . . . . . . 43

    Ensuring a Positive Attitude . . . . . . . . . . . . . . . . . . . . . . . . . . . . . . 43
        Creating the vision for the project . . . . . . . . . . . . . . . . . . . . . 44
        Communicating the vision . . . . . . . . . . . . . . . . . . . . . . . . . . . . 44
    Encouraging the Willingness to Change . . . . . . . . . . . . . . . . . . . . . 45
    Arousing Curiosity . . . . . . . . . . . . . . . . . . . . . . . . . . . . . . . . . . . . . . 45
        Presenting the task as a challenge . . . . . . . . . . . . . . . . . . . . . 46
        Presenting the task as a reward . . . . . . . . . . . . . . . . . . . . . . . 46
        Presenting the task in a comprehensible fashion . . . . . . . . . . . . 47
        Training curiosity . . . . . . . . . . . . . . . . . . . . . . . . . . . . . . . . . . . 47
    Asking For (and Receiving) Support from the Top . . . . . . . . . . . . . . 48
    Asking For (and Receiving) Creative Freedom . . . . . . . . . . . . . . . . . 49
    Enabling Fast Decisions in the Design Thinking Process . . . . . . . . . . 49
        Setting up the steering committee . . . . . . . . . . . . . . . . . . . . . 50
        Clarifying responsibilities . . . . . . . . . . . . . . . . . . . . . . . . . . . . 50
        Preparing the decision in an efficient manner . . . . . . . . . . . . . . 50
        Conducting the decision-making process in an
        efficient manner . . . . . . . . . . . . . . . . . . . . . . . . . . . . . . . . . . . 51
        Following up on decisions . . . . . . . . . . . . . . . . . . . . . . . . . . . . 52
    Tolerating Mistakes During Design Thinking . . . . . . . . . . . . . . . . . . 52
        Defining mistakes . . . . . . . . . . . . . . . . . . . . . . . . . . . . . . . . . . 53
        Looking at mistakes in a differentiated way . . . . . . . . . . . . . . . 54
    Find the Competencies You Need for the Task at Hand . . . . . . . . . . 54
        Determining the target competencies . . . . . . . . . . . . . . . . . . . 55
        Taking stock of the actual competencies . . . . . . . . . . . . . . . . . 55
        Comparing the target and actual competencies
        and coming up with the next steps . . . . . . . . . . . . . . . . . . . . . . 56
        Checking the competencies on an ongoing basis . . . . . . . . . . . . 56
        Ensuring that the work is appreciated . . . . . . . . . . . . . . . . . . . 57

CHAPTER 4: **Planning a Design Thinking Project** . . . . . . . . . . . . . . . . . 59

Defining the Project Goals . . . . . . . . . . . . . . . . . . . . . . . . . . . . . . . . . . .60
Compiling goals and determining their order . . . . . . . . . . . . . . . . .61
Clearly formulating goals . . . . . . . . . . . . . . . . . . . . . . . . . . . . . . . . . .62
Communicating goals . . . . . . . . . . . . . . . . . . . . . . . . . . . . . . . . . . . . .63
Planning Work Packages . . . . . . . . . . . . . . . . . . . . . . . . . . . . . . . . . . . .64
Planning work packages for incremental progress
at just the right time . . . . . . . . . . . . . . . . . . . . . . . . . . . . . . . . . . . . .65
Formulating and determining the work package
order from the user's perspective . . . . . . . . . . . . . . . . . . . . . . . . . .66
Using a task board . . . . . . . . . . . . . . . . . . . . . . . . . . . . . . . . . . . . . . .67
Correctly Planning for the Sequence . . . . . . . . . . . . . . . . . . . . . . . . . .70
Estimating the required time . . . . . . . . . . . . . . . . . . . . . . . . . . . . . .71
Creating a bar graph for a better overview . . . . . . . . . . . . . . . . . . .71
Correctly Planning for Your Resources . . . . . . . . . . . . . . . . . . . . . . . . .72
Correctly Planning for the Project Budget . . . . . . . . . . . . . . . . . . . . . .74

CHAPTER 5: **Supporting Teamwork in the Project** . . . . . . . . . . . . . . 77

Assembling the Team . . . . . . . . . . . . . . . . . . . . . . . . . . . . . . . . . . . . . . .78
Relying on variety in team makeup . . . . . . . . . . . . . . . . . . . . . . . . .78
Defining roles on the team . . . . . . . . . . . . . . . . . . . . . . . . . . . . . . . .80
Creating a matrix of responsibility . . . . . . . . . . . . . . . . . . . . . . . . . .80
Applying the principle of self-organization . . . . . . . . . . . . . . . . . . .81
Clarifying Communication within the Team . . . . . . . . . . . . . . . . . . . . .81
Determining the project reporting format . . . . . . . . . . . . . . . . . . . .82
Communicating is more important than documenting . . . . . . . . . .83
Setting up communication rules . . . . . . . . . . . . . . . . . . . . . . . . . . . .83
Arranging Workshops . . . . . . . . . . . . . . . . . . . . . . . . . . . . . . . . . . . . . . .85
Preparing a workshop . . . . . . . . . . . . . . . . . . . . . . . . . . . . . . . . . . . .85
Holding workshops correctly . . . . . . . . . . . . . . . . . . . . . . . . . . . . . . .86
Providing equipment and materials . . . . . . . . . . . . . . . . . . . . . . . . .88
Designing Common Spaces . . . . . . . . . . . . . . . . . . . . . . . . . . . . . . . . . .89
The right rooms promote communication and creativity . . . . . . . .89
A flexible environment promotes flexible work . . . . . . . . . . . . . . . .90

PART 2: THE PROBLEM PHASES . . . . . . . . . . . . . . . . . . . . . . . . . . . . . . . 93

CHAPTER 6: **Understanding the Task** . . . . . . . . . . . . . . . . . . . . . . . . . 95

Finding the Right Search Area . . . . . . . . . . . . . . . . . . . . . . . . . . . . . . . .95
Searching in the market segment . . . . . . . . . . . . . . . . . . . . . . . . . . .96
Searching in the area of technology . . . . . . . . . . . . . . . . . . . . . . . . .98
Searching in your own area of competence . . . . . . . . . . . . . . . . . . .98
A Well-Defined Task Is a Task Half-Solved . . . . . . . . . . . . . . . . . . . . . .99
Clarifying what the task is and how it manifests itself . . . . . . . . .100
Clarifying who has the problem or wish . . . . . . . . . . . . . . . . . . . . .101

Clarifying where and when the problem or wish occurs. . . . . . . . .103
Clarifying why the problem or wish occurs . . . . . . . . . . . . . . . . .103
Identifying Knowledge Gaps . . . . . . . . . . . . . . . . . . . . . . . . . . . . . . .106
Systematically Closing Knowledge Gaps . . . . . . . . . . . . . . . . . . . . .107
Estimating Influences on the Task . . . . . . . . . . . . . . . . . . . . . . . . . .108
Evaluating environmental influences . . . . . . . . . . . . . . . . . . . . .108
Identifying stakeholder influences . . . . . . . . . . . . . . . . . . . . . . .111
Reformulating the Task . . . . . . . . . . . . . . . . . . . . . . . . . . . . . . . . . . .114

CHAPTER 7: **Putting Yourself in the Roles of Others**. . . . . . . . . . . . .117
Recognizing Empathy as a Key to Success. . . . . . . . . . . . . . . . . . . .117
Proceeding with Empathy . . . . . . . . . . . . . . . . . . . . . . . . . . . . . . . . .118
Create openness . . . . . . . . . . . . . . . . . . . . . . . . . . . . . . . . . . . . . .118
Discount your own ideas/Tamp down your own biases . . . . . . . .119
Share results . . . . . . . . . . . . . . . . . . . . . . . . . . . . . . . . . . . . . . . . .120
Proceed methodically . . . . . . . . . . . . . . . . . . . . . . . . . . . . . . . . . .120
Collecting Information . . . . . . . . . . . . . . . . . . . . . . . . . . . . . . . . . . . .120
Evaluating Information. . . . . . . . . . . . . . . . . . . . . . . . . . . . . . . . . . . .121
Characterizing a customer using the Persona method . . . . . . . .122
Understanding the situation with the help of an
empathy map. . . . . . . . . . . . . . . . . . . . . . . . . . . . . . . . . . . . . . . . .125
Exploring the process with the customer journey . . . . . . . . . . . .129
Describing the phases of the customer journey. . . . . . . . . . . . . .130
Discovering the problems (and improvements)
in the customer journey. . . . . . . . . . . . . . . . . . . . . . . . . . . . . . . . .131

CHAPTER 8: **Observing People in Action** . . . . . . . . . . . . . . . . . . . . . . .137
Putting Observations to Proper Use. . . . . . . . . . . . . . . . . . . . . . . . .137
Thoroughly Preparing Your Observations. . . . . . . . . . . . . . . . . . . . .139
Determine who should be observed . . . . . . . . . . . . . . . . . . . . . .139
Determine what you should observe, whom you
should observe, and when you should observe. . . . . . . . . . . . . .140
Determine how you want to observe. . . . . . . . . . . . . . . . . . . . . .142
Determine who should do the observing . . . . . . . . . . . . . . . . . . .144
Your Observations in a Systematic Fashion . . . . . . . . . . . . . . . . . . .145
Observing the right thing. . . . . . . . . . . . . . . . . . . . . . . . . . . . . . . .146
Observing correctly. . . . . . . . . . . . . . . . . . . . . . . . . . . . . . . . . . . .148
Avoiding observation errors . . . . . . . . . . . . . . . . . . . . . . . . . . . . .151
Applying Consistent Observational Methodologies. . . . . . . . . . . . .153
Artifacts analysis: Analyzing the customer's objects . . . . . . . . . .154
Behavioral mapping and tracking: Documenting the
customer's movements and activities . . . . . . . . . . . . . . . . . . . . .155
Mental models: Describing the real behavior of
the customer . . . . . . . . . . . . . . . . . . . . . . . . . . . . . . . . . . . . . . . . .156
Mystery shopping: Detecting shopping behavior. . . . . . . . . . . . .156

CHAPTER 9: **Redefining the Problem** . . . . . . . . . . . . . . . . . . . . . . . . . . . . .159

Finding the Task. . . . . . . . . . . . . . . . . . . . . . . . . . . . . . . . . . . . . . . . .159

Preventing a search field that's too broad or too narrow . . . . . . .160

Avoiding the temptation to prescribe solutions . . . . . . . . . . . . . .161

Formulating a meaningful and challenging question. . . . . . . . . .161

Writing clearly from a user's perspective. . . . . . . . . . . . . . . . . . . .162

Formulating tasks clearly and comprehensibly . . . . . . . . . . . . . .162

Focusing On the Right People . . . . . . . . . . . . . . . . . . . . . . . . . . . . . .163

Recognizing the Needs of Your Target Users . . . . . . . . . . . . . . . . . .165

Analyzing Needs as Tasks. . . . . . . . . . . . . . . . . . . . . . . . . . . . . . . . . .166

Determining the problems of the target person . . . . . . . . . . . . .168

Identifying the target person's wishes . . . . . . . . . . . . . . . . . . . . . .169

Comprehending the reasons for particular
problems and wishes . . . . . . . . . . . . . . . . . . . . . . . . . . . . . . . . . . . .170

Selecting the Most Important Wishes and Problems. . . . . . . . . . . .172

Determining the Right Point of View . . . . . . . . . . . . . . . . . . . . . . . .175

**PART 3: THE SOLUTION PHASES** . . . . . . . . . . . . . . . . . . . . . . . . . . . . .177

CHAPTER 10: **Finding Ideas** . . . . . . . . . . . . . . . . . . . . . . . . . . . . . . . . . . . .179

Mastering the Creative Process. . . . . . . . . . . . . . . . . . . . . . . . . . . . .179

Opening Up Sources of New Ideas . . . . . . . . . . . . . . . . . . . . . . . . . .181

Taking advantage of employee skills and knowledge
at your own company . . . . . . . . . . . . . . . . . . . . . . . . . . . . . . . . . . . .181

Surveying and observing customers and involving
them in developing solutions . . . . . . . . . . . . . . . . . . . . . . . . . . . . .182

Surveying and working with suppliers . . . . . . . . . . . . . . . . . . . . . .182

Keeping up with what the competitors are doing . . . . . . . . . . . .182

Evaluating publications and patent information . . . . . . . . . . . . .183

Participating in trade fairs and conferences . . . . . . . . . . . . . . . . .183

Collaborating with experts. . . . . . . . . . . . . . . . . . . . . . . . . . . . . . . .183

Understanding the Creative Principles. . . . . . . . . . . . . . . . . . . . . . .184

The decomposition principle. . . . . . . . . . . . . . . . . . . . . . . . . . . . . .184

The associative principle . . . . . . . . . . . . . . . . . . . . . . . . . . . . . . . . .184

The analogy and confrontation principles. . . . . . . . . . . . . . . . . . .184

The abstraction and imagination principles . . . . . . . . . . . . . . . . .185

Know the Success Factors for Increasing Creativity . . . . . . . . . . . .185

Questioning the conventional wisdom. . . . . . . . . . . . . . . . . . . . . .185

Simplifying products and processes. . . . . . . . . . . . . . . . . . . . . . . .186

Starting where others left off. . . . . . . . . . . . . . . . . . . . . . . . . . . . . .186

Observing everything and everyone in every possible place . . . .187

Experimenting with ideas. . . . . . . . . . . . . . . . . . . . . . . . . . . . . . . . .187

Networking. . . . . . . . . . . . . . . . . . . . . . . . . . . . . . . . . . . . . . . . . . . . .188

Overcoming obstacles to creativity. . . . . . . . . . . . . . . . . . . . . . . . .188

Selecting the Appropriate Creativity Techniques . . . . . . . . . . . . . . . .190
    Structuring the topic with mind-mapping . . . . . . . . . . . . . . . . . . . .191
    Systematically finding solutions with a morphological box . . . . .192

CHAPTER 11: **Developing Ideas Intuitively and Creatively** . . . . . . .195
Solving Difficult Problems Intuitively and Creatively . . . . . . . . . . . . .195
Generating Ideas by Brainstorming . . . . . . . . . . . . . . . . . . . . . . . . . . . .196
    Giving the flow of ideas a new boost . . . . . . . . . . . . . . . . . . . . . . .197
    Getting to know the different brainstorming variants . . . . . . . . .199
    Written brainstorming . . . . . . . . . . . . . . . . . . . . . . . . . . . . . . . . . . .201
Inspiring with Random Words . . . . . . . . . . . . . . . . . . . . . . . . . . . . . . . . .204
Getting New Stimuli through Provocations . . . . . . . . . . . . . . . . . . . . . .205
Changing Perspectives with the Walt Disney Method . . . . . . . . . . . .205
Assuming Different Mindsets with the Six Hats Method . . . . . . . . . .207

CHAPTER 12: **Evaluating Ideas** . . . . . . . . . . . . . . . . . . . . . . . . . . . . . . . . .211
Selecting the Right Evaluation Method . . . . . . . . . . . . . . . . . . . . . . . .211
Relying on Diversity in the Team for Your Evaluations . . . . . . . . . . .212
Quickly Selecting Ideas . . . . . . . . . . . . . . . . . . . . . . . . . . . . . . . . . . . . . .212
Evaluating the Advantages of (and Barriers to) Ideas . . . . . . . . . . . .213
Evaluating Ideas with Checklists . . . . . . . . . . . . . . . . . . . . . . . . . . . . . .215
    Determining feasibility . . . . . . . . . . . . . . . . . . . . . . . . . . . . . . . . . . .215
    Estimating the fit . . . . . . . . . . . . . . . . . . . . . . . . . . . . . . . . . . . . . . . .217
    Testing your idea's desirability from the customers'
    perspective . . . . . . . . . . . . . . . . . . . . . . . . . . . . . . . . . . . . . . . . . . . .217
    Considering the economic viability and scalability
    of your idea . . . . . . . . . . . . . . . . . . . . . . . . . . . . . . . . . . . . . . . . . . . .218
    Ensuring sustainability . . . . . . . . . . . . . . . . . . . . . . . . . . . . . . . . . . .220
    Determining adaptability . . . . . . . . . . . . . . . . . . . . . . . . . . . . . . . . .220
Making the Chances for Success Measurable . . . . . . . . . . . . . . . . . . .221
    Finding and weighting appropriate evaluation criteria . . . . . . . .222
    Weighing criteria against each other . . . . . . . . . . . . . . . . . . . . . . .225
    Evaluating and selecting ideas . . . . . . . . . . . . . . . . . . . . . . . . . . . . .226

CHAPTER 13: **Designing Prototypes** . . . . . . . . . . . . . . . . . . . . . . . . . . . .227
Understanding the Benefit of Experiments . . . . . . . . . . . . . . . . . . . . .228
Clarifying Tasks in the Prototype Phase . . . . . . . . . . . . . . . . . . . . . . . .228
Developing and Using Prototypes Efficiently . . . . . . . . . . . . . . . . . . .229
    Plan less, experiment more . . . . . . . . . . . . . . . . . . . . . . . . . . . . . . .230
    Minimize effort . . . . . . . . . . . . . . . . . . . . . . . . . . . . . . . . . . . . . . . . .230
    Correct at an early stage . . . . . . . . . . . . . . . . . . . . . . . . . . . . . . . . .231
    Tolerate errors . . . . . . . . . . . . . . . . . . . . . . . . . . . . . . . . . . . . . . . . . .232
Using Different Prototypes . . . . . . . . . . . . . . . . . . . . . . . . . . . . . . . . . . .232

Making Ideas Clear and Tangible . . . . . . . . . . . . . . . . . . . . . . . . . . . .233
    Telling stories. . . . . . . . . . . . . . . . . . . . . . . . . . . . . . . . . . . . . . . .233
    Visualizing stories . . . . . . . . . . . . . . . . . . . . . . . . . . . . . . . . . . . . .235
    Performing stories. . . . . . . . . . . . . . . . . . . . . . . . . . . . . . . . . . . . .236
    Using digital prototypes . . . . . . . . . . . . . . . . . . . . . . . . . . . . . . . .237
    Demonstrating instead of presenting . . . . . . . . . . . . . . . . . . . . .238

CHAPTER 14: **Testing Ideas and Assumptions**. . . . . . . . . . . . . . . . . . . . . 241
Clarifying Tasks in the Test Phase. . . . . . . . . . . . . . . . . . . . . . . . . . . . .241
    Checking assumptions about the target users . . . . . . . . . . . . . .242
    Checking assumptions about problems and needs. . . . . . . . . . .243
    Testing assumptions about the benefits of the idea . . . . . . . . . .245
Testing with Interviews. . . . . . . . . . . . . . . . . . . . . . . . . . . . . . . . . . . . .247
    Asking the right people. . . . . . . . . . . . . . . . . . . . . . . . . . . . . . . . .247
    Asking the right questions . . . . . . . . . . . . . . . . . . . . . . . . . . . . . .248
    Asking the questions correctly . . . . . . . . . . . . . . . . . . . . . . . . . .249
Testing with Online Studies . . . . . . . . . . . . . . . . . . . . . . . . . . . . . . . . .250
    Comparing user behavior. . . . . . . . . . . . . . . . . . . . . . . . . . . . . . .250
    Evaluating user behavior with key figures . . . . . . . . . . . . . . . . .251
Learning from Test Results . . . . . . . . . . . . . . . . . . . . . . . . . . . . . . . . . .252

PART 4: THE PART OF TENS. . . . . . . . . . . . . . . . . . . . . . . . . . . . . . . . . . . .255

CHAPTER 15: **Ten Success Factors for Interviews**. . . . . . . . . . . . . . . . . 257
Ensuring Good Preparation. . . . . . . . . . . . . . . . . . . . . . . . . . . . . . . . . .257
Finding the Right Entry . . . . . . . . . . . . . . . . . . . . . . . . . . . . . . . . . . . . .258
Taking Notes Correctly . . . . . . . . . . . . . . . . . . . . . . . . . . . . . . . . . . . . .258
Listening Actively. . . . . . . . . . . . . . . . . . . . . . . . . . . . . . . . . . . . . . . . . .259
Paying Attention to Emotions . . . . . . . . . . . . . . . . . . . . . . . . . . . . . . .259
Always Following Up . . . . . . . . . . . . . . . . . . . . . . . . . . . . . . . . . . . . . . .259
Concluding Discussions Successfully . . . . . . . . . . . . . . . . . . . . . . . . . .260
Completing a Sufficient Number of Interviews. . . . . . . . . . . . . . . . . .260
Postprocessing Interviews . . . . . . . . . . . . . . . . . . . . . . . . . . . . . . . . . .261
Using Every Opportunity . . . . . . . . . . . . . . . . . . . . . . . . . . . . . . . . . . .261

CHAPTER 16: **Ten Success Factors for Implementing Your Idea**. . . . . . . . . . . . . . . . . . . . . . . . . . . . . . . . . . . . . . . . . . . . . . 263
Prepare the Structures . . . . . . . . . . . . . . . . . . . . . . . . . . . . . . . . . . . . .263
Encourage Collaboration and Communicate Openly. . . . . . . . . . . . .264
    Complete the forming phase in a positive way. . . . . . . . . . . . . .265
    Master the storming phase . . . . . . . . . . . . . . . . . . . . . . . . . . . . .265
    Support the norming phase. . . . . . . . . . . . . . . . . . . . . . . . . . . . .266
    Use the performing phase efficiently . . . . . . . . . . . . . . . . . . . . .266
    Successfully prepare the adjourning phase . . . . . . . . . . . . . . . .267

Create a Sense of Urgency....................................267
Establish a Leadership Coalition..............................268
Communicate a Vision for the Culture of Innovation ...........269
Establish a Company Culture Tolerant of Mistakes..............269
Broadly Empower Employees ...................................270
Overcome Resistance.........................................271
Counter Objections..........................................272
Curb Euphoria ..............................................273

INDEX......................................................275

# Introduction

Ready for an adventure? That's where design thinking will take you. You'll learn a lot, cope with a lot of uncertainties, and discover many new things. Design thinking offers you a method to develop innovative products, services, business models, and concepts. With design thinking, you can use the obstacles in your path to create something new, learn to think outside the box, and still move straight to your goal. Design thinking lets you answer questions that your customers never thought they would have, and later your customers will say: "This is exactly the solution I was always waiting for."

Developing innovative ideas always takes some effort. Compared to traditional product development processes, this effort is manageable. Asking yourself whether you can afford design thinking is the wrong way to start. Ask yourself instead whether you can afford to skip design thinking. Yes, design thinking costs money, but not investing in design thinking costs you more in the long run.

## About This Book

The book you're holding in your hands is a guide for practitioners with a 360-degree view of the innovative approach known as design thinking. It

>> **Takes a look at the entire process, from beginning to end:** You start with the customer's problem and end with a solution for the customer.

>> **Examines all significant success factors for design thinking — the five Ps:**

- Practices
- People
- Principles
- Processes
- Places

>> **Follows different perspectives on design thinking:** You learn which steps you must take in order to succeed with design thinking, from these perspectives:

- The company

- The project

- The employee

- The customer

This book answers your questions about what design thinking is, which conditions must be created at your company in order for it to succeed, how you can plan a project, and how to implement it successfully. This book can be used in myriad ways and is a Swiss army knife in paper form. It is

>> A step-by-step manual for using design thinking to identify a problem and come up with a solution

>> A guidebook with practical suggestions for the implementation of a design thinking strategy

>> A reference book divided into parts, chapters, and sections so that you can quickly find the content you're looking for when you need it

This book, which is designed so that you can swiftly get a grasp on everything, features many examples, instructions, checklists, illustrations, and tables. It's also structured systematically according to the design thinking process.

# Conventions Used in This Book

This book doesn't have many rules. The entire book is structured so that you can quickly find everything you need and get a grasp on the contents. The detailed table of contents helps you jump right to the information you need, and each chapter begins with a brief and succinct description of the chapter's main topics. Whenever topics overlap or other chapters are mentioned, cross-references help you conveniently jump back and forth between the chapters. If you're interested in a particular term, you can look it up in the index.

# Foolish Assumptions

This book is not (only) for designers. Design thinking is too important for you to let only designers develop attractive products. Whether you work at a company, an educational institution, a research institute, a public agency, or a nonprofit organization, you can benefit from the people-based approach that is at the heart of design thinking. Whether you have an education in the technical, economic, or social field, this creative approach gives you new stimuli and ideas.

On an individual level, I make the following assumptions about you:

>> You're working in a department at a company and want to see the bigger picture.

>> You want to apply design thinking at your organization and need to know how to implement it.

>> Your company is already working with some design thinking methods. You want to enhance your previous work with new methods, tips, and tricks for its implementation, and you want a set of comprehensive instructions.

You don't need to have any specific skills for this book — you only have to be curious.

# What You Don't Have to Read

It's worth your time to read the entire book. You can find important tips everywhere in it. Even if you can use only a few of its suggestions, the time and money you invest will be worth it. I guarantee that you'll be able to use more than just a few of the tips, regardless of whether you're a novice or an expert. Some of the text in this book appears in a gray box, in order to highlight background information. You don't absolutely need this info, but it's always helpful.

# How This Book Is Organized

To make things easier for you, I've arranged this book into four distinct parts, as described in this section.

## Part 1: Getting Started with Design Thinking

This section gives you an overview of the principles and methods of design thinking. You'll find out how to create the necessary conditions for design thinking in order for it to succeed at your company, how to plan a project, and how to organize teamwork.

## Part 2: The Problem Phases

The first phase of the design thinking process is all about giving you an in-depth understanding of what your target users need. Observations and interviews give you a better grasp of your customers' perspective. At the conclusion of the problem phase, you summarize your task in the form of a defined problem.

## Part 3: The Solution Phases

Only when you reach the solution phase do you develop new ideas. After implementing creative principles and techniques, you evaluate your ideas and make a selection. Customers can use prototypes to tangibly test your selected ideas, and you can benefit from their feedback.

## Part 4: The Part of Tens

No *For Dummies* book exists without The Part of Tens. In this part, you learn about ten (or so) success factors for interviews and ten (or so) success factors for implementing design thinking projects.

# Icons Used in This Book

Now and then you'll find symbols in in the margins of this book. Their purpose is to make you aware of important information.

**TIP**

This icon points to tips and tricks that should be helpful when you apply and implement an idea. They show you how you can improve your project.

This icon highlights illustrative examples from practical experience. They should offer inspiration for your project.

**EXAMPLE**

**WARNING**

This icon makes you aware of potential stumbling blocks and shows you how to *not* do something. If you avoid errors that others have made before you, you'll save time, money, and effort.

# Beyond the Book

In addition to what you're reading right now, this publication comes with a free, access-anywhere Cheat Sheet that offers a number of tips, techniques, and resources related to data science. To view this Cheat Sheet, visit www.dummies.com and type **"Design Thinking For Dummies Cheat Sheet"** in the Search box.

# Where to Go from Here

You can start immediately, by choosing one of these two strategies:

>> Read the book straight through, from cover to cover.

>> Find individual chapters that you want to read first. (Each chapter covers an entire subject area so that you can read and understand it independently of the other chapters.) If you have no experience with design thinking yet, I recommend starting with Chapter 1, which offers a crash course in design thinking principles.

My advice to you: Read the way design thinkers would do it. Experiment with the reading strategy that works best for you. Jump to different sections while you read the book, if that makes sense to you. If necessary, reread a chapter multiple times or look up individual terms in the index. The idea here is for you to come up with your own way to read this book effectively.

# 1

# Getting Started with Design Thinking

Get to know design thinking with its advantages and principles.

Examine the individual steps in the design thinking process.

Create the foundation for success and prepare your organization for the project.

Define the goals, plan workflows, and resources for the project work.

Assemble a powerful team, arrange team-appropriate rooms, and manage team responsibilities as well as team communication.

Chapter **1**

# Everything You Need to Know About Design Thinking

D o you want to invent something, design something, or implement something new? Design thinking offers you a method to develop innovative products, services, methods, business models, and concepts. This chapter gives you an overview of the potential, the basics, and the principles of this approach to innovation. You'll learn how to proceed with design thinking and what you must consider when carrying out the individual steps. You'll form a team and manage the collaboration; organize the project work by structuring a logical order for the tasks; assign resources; and respond flexibly to changes. You'll even learn about the importance of your work environment — from office floor plans to furnishings — when it comes to supporting the creativity of your team members.

## This Is Design Thinking

*Design thinking* is a human-based approach to innovation that aims to establish creative ideas and effective business models by focusing on the needs of people. The basic idea behind design thinking is that you apply the approaches and methods of designers to the development of innovations (this is what the word *design* stands for) while also engaging in a systematic, fact-based analysis of the feasibility and economic viability of these innovations — just like what a researcher does (this is what the *thinking* part of the term stands for).

Designers start with their customers' problems or wishes and consider them from the perspective of their target users. With this knowledge, designers develop the first user-oriented ideas, visualize their creative solutions at an early stage, and then design prototypes. They quickly request their customers' feedback and change their concept on this basis. Step by step, the designers approach the best solution for their target users. The approach and individual methods of the design are supplemented by a mindset that purposefully analyzes the feasibility and economic viability of the product during development. Like a researcher, you set verifiable goals for each step, make assumptions, and test these assumptions with the help of observations and surveys regarding their validity.

## More than just design

The shaping and design of material products is just one application area. You can use this approach for all areas in life and business. Maybe you want to enhance your customer service, introduce new ways of executing your business processes, or change the corporate culture. Then you're dealing with many-layered issues. When you have no simple solutions, design thinking helps you find an innovative solution.

## More than just a workshop

Design thinking is a process consisting of various steps — individual steps you complete multiple times. During the process, you rely on group work in the form of workshops as well as individual work.

TIP

Provide variety. Complete individual work after a workshop phase. This increases motivation, and you can more easily tap into your team members' different kinds of potential. When it comes to individual work, you can utilize the expertise of team members who don't feel comfortable with group work.

You complete various forms of group work and supplement them with results from the individual work. The team members work individually to conduct interviews with potential customers, and then everyone presents their results in a workshop. The group evaluates the results together. This leads to the creation of new assumptions about your target users or potential solutions, which the individual team members can then test in surveys.

# More than just brainstorming

Brainstorming for the creative idea is just one phase in the design thinking process. The idea here is to fully comprehend the problem and understand your target users. Analyze the starting situation and make assumptions that you investigate with observations and surveys with potential customers. Creative phases with a lot of design freedom alternate with phases in which you summarize your results and focus on the priorities.

# More than just methods

Different methods can help you during the individual phases of the design thinking process. You can describe your target users with the Persona method, where you come up with a profile of your target audience, made up of the most important characteristics, modes of behavior, problems, and preferences of that audience. With the Customer Journey method, you can analyze the individual steps that the customer experiences while using a product. However, you must apply creative techniques that have assisted you when searching for a new idea as well as the various methods you may have made use of during the creation of the prototype. You can test your assumptions and ideas by applying methods from experimental research. The right application of the right methods is crucial for the success of the project.

The methods are just one factor. In design thinking, you have to keep the 5 Ps in mind:

>> **Practices:** You apply proven methods from various disciplines, such as design, market research, ethnology, psychology, engineering sciences, and strategic management.

>> **People:** You assemble a team that contributes different competencies and perspectives.

>> **Principles:** You follow principles that determine the team's approach and position — mindset, in other words — and that serve as a guideline for the team's collaboration.

>> **Processes:** You're flexible and you handle the different work and decision-making processes in an agile manner.

>> **Places:** You offer places for group and individual work that encourage creativity and also enable focused work.

# Seeing What Design Thinking Can Do

It takes new ideas to handle social challenges such as climate change, population growth, food security, health, mobility, or energy supply. These ideas are the foundation for economic growth. Some ideas develop into worldwide standards, and others cover niches in local and regional markets. Design thinking supports you in your creative work regardless of whether your question deals with a big or small problem, and it provides you with possible solutions. The approach can be used for all kinds of questions. These might be new products, services, business models, or social and organizational concepts.

## Developing new products

New technologies such as artificial intelligence or nanotechnology definitely offer opportunities for new products. When it comes to product development in these areas, however, the difficulties don't necessarily lie in the limitations of the new technologies themselves. Difficulties arise when you have to recognize the right application areas of technologies in order to present the greatest benefit for a large number of people. You have to know who might be the product's target users and which of your potential customers' needs you might satisfy. Design thinking can help you find applications that promise success.

**EXAMPLE**

New ideas don't have to come from the high-tech area. At General Electric Healthcare, people noticed that children were afraid of the high-tech equipment, such as the magnetic resonance image scanners (MRI) used for diagnostic imaging procedures. Some of the children had to be sedated before the examination. Engineers subsequently tried to view the entire examination process through the eyes of a child, which led them to completely redesign the equipment and spatial environment. The walls in a children's hospital were painted to look like a pirate ship, and the exam table like a shipwreck. The exam procedure was designed as a child-friendly, role-playing game, in which the even the equipment's background sounds were integrated as an adventure game.

## Creating new services

Service innovations involve changes in how the services are delivered — a new service for customer consultations, the automation and digitization of business processes, or new payment options for customers, for example. The potential of service innovations is often underestimated. Services involve particularly in-depth exchanges with customers so that a human-based approach like design thinking can offer numerous ideas when it comes to improving and redesigning services.

As early as the 1940s, the brothers Dick and Mac McDonald already used an approach similar to design thinking. While observing their customers, they realized that the truck drivers who made up a significant portion of their customer base wanted to have simple food served quickly and often ordered the same meals. The brothers limited their meal selection and offered mainly the bestselling hamburgers and French fries. At the same time, they improved the processes in the kitchen and service area. They also redesigned the dining spaces in their restaurant, with the result that only 30 seconds passed between the order and the food delivery.

## Designing new business models

With a business model, you describe the way in which a company creates added value for certain customers, how it produces this value, and how it generates permanently growing revenue from it. The introduction of the *freemium* principle (a combination of *free* and pre*mium*), in which a basic version is offered for free and a premium version is based on charges, was initially a business model innovation and is now widespread even outside of online offers.

## Designing social and organizational innovations

Social innovations are solutions for social problems and challenges that aren't driven by the goal of making profits. Design thinking starts with the problems and wishes of people and makes them the top priority. With design thinking, you can systematically solve tasks in the social domain. The solution can be a product, a service, or a concept of how to solve a social problem.

Students at Stanford University applied design thinking to develop a simply designed lamp to be used in developing countries — a lamp that could illuminate a room in a cheap, maintenance-free, and ecofriendly manner. Equipped with a mobile solar system that can function off the grid as well as LED lights and rechargeable batteries, the lamps are designed particularly for the needs of people in developing countries.

Examples of organizational innovations include new decision-making processes at a company or a new organizational form.

The Swiss web app company Liip has changed its organizational structure so that it eliminates hierarchies — individual teams at the company now organize themselves. Each team decides on its strategy, the type of customer acquisition it means to employ, and the applied techniques it feels are necessary for success.

Each team also handles the recruitment of new employees on its own. (If you think this means anarchy, know that there are clear rules on how to coordinate among the equal teams.)

## Establishing a culture of innovation

In a dynamically changing environment, some companies continue to achieve competitive advantages through the agile, creative, and flexible recognition and utilization of entrepreneurial opportunities. They develop new markets and successfully position themselves as global players. These companies have a culture of innovation that promotes their employees' creativity and successfully turns it into new products, services, processes, or business models. With these principles and approaches, they set the foundation for a corporate culture that promotes innovation.

# Understanding the Basics of Design Thinking

Before you try some of the methods of design thinking in a workshop, you should become familiar with the basics. The principles and methods of this approach to innovation are probably unfamiliar to many in your organization. New ideas are always met with skepticism, reservations, or resistance. Overcome your reservations and foster your curiosity.

## Following and communicating the principles

In design thinking, you should observe a few principles that will guide you toward success:

>> **Align yourself with people and their needs at an early stage:** You start with people by either taking up a problem your target users have pointed out or a wish they may have expressed. Look for *lead users* — the ones who are ahead of their time and anticipate future needs of the target market. They are especially useful because their needs precede those of all other customers in the market and they have a strong incentive to resolve the need. Actively involve these customers in the development of your idea.

- **Develop empathy:** Put yourself in the position of your target users and explore these users' emotions, thoughts, intentions, and actions.

- **Illustrate ideas:** Visualize your idea and demonstrate it with a prototype for potential users to experiment with. Prototypes can be hardware of various kinds, drawings, stories, role-playing games, model designs, or online applications in the form of Internet pages or apps.

- **Learning from failure:** Establish a culture that welcomes the value of mistakes at your company so that errors are tolerated as well as learned from. Make sure that mistakes are understood as a fixed component in the design thinking process and perceived as opportunities to learn.

- **Ensure diversity in the team:** Rely on diversity in the team so that you offer different perspectives. Diversity is shown in age, gender, education, cultural background, and personality type.

- **Offer team-oriented and creative workspaces:** The workspaces for individual and group work as well as spaces for the group as a whole must have a flexible and inspiring design. You should choose different locations, rooms, or furniture arrangements for the different design thinking phases.

- **Make the process flexible:** The design thinking process promotes a gradual approach. Analyze the problem, use it to formulate a task, develop initial possible solutions, test them, and learn from the feedback.

TIP

You don't strictly go through these phases in sequence. Whenever you get information that you have to analyze in detail, jump back to a previous step.

Consider and observe these principles during the entire innovation process. Discuss the principles in each workshop, write them down, and display them in communal spaces so that they're easily visible. As a team, check whether you've consistently adhered to the principles after each phase.

## Getting an overview of the whole process

In the first part of the design thinking process, you analyze the problem. This is the *problem space*, where you address the What and Why. (What is the problem? Why is it a problem?) Only in the second part, the *solution space*, are specific solutions developed and tested: Here you ask about the How. (How can something be solved?)

In this process, you combine two phases. In the *divergent* (dispersing) phase, you collect information or develop numerous ideas that result in expanding your perspectives. In the convergent (combining) phase, you sharpen the field-of-view and compile the results or decide on choices.

These divergent and convergent phases alternate. According to the British Design Council, the change between expanding and focusing resembles the image of a double diamond (Double Diamond Process Model), as shown in Figure 1-1.

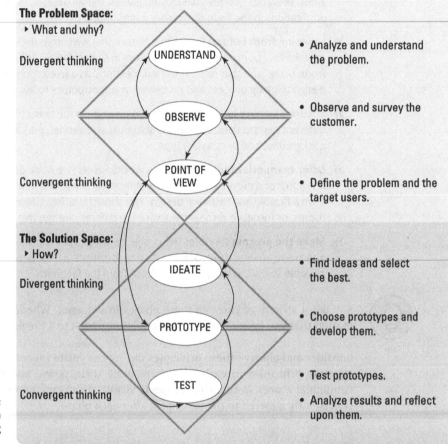

**The Problem Space:**
▸ What and why?

Divergent thinking

UNDERSTAND

- Analyze and understand the problem.

OBSERVE

- Observe and survey the customer.

Convergent thinking

POINT OF VIEW

- Define the problem and the target users.

**The Solution Space:**
▸ How?

Divergent thinking

IDEATE

- Find ideas and select the best.

PROTOTYPE

- Choose prototypes and develop them.

TEST

- Test prototypes.

Convergent thinking

- Analyze results and reflect upon them.

FIGURE 1-1: The design thinking process.

The design thinking process is similar to the approach of members of the Hasso Plattner Institute of Design at Stanford University (commonly known as the "d.school"). They spell out these six distinct phases:

1. **Understanding the problem:** In the first phase, you create an in-depth understanding of your target users' problem or need. You have to clarify which information you're still lacking about the target users, their needs, and their problems.

2. **Observing customers:** This phase consists of detailed research and on-site observations about the customer's need or problem. It utilizes observations and surveys so that you can put yourself in the customer's shoes.

3. **Defining the question:** After the observations and surveys, you should focus the insights on a selected group of customers or users and summarize their problems and needs in a defined question.

4. **Finding and selecting ideas:** Only in this phase do you actually find ideas. You need to employ creative principles and techniques so that you prepare multiple possible solutions. Evaluate the usefulness, economic viability, and feasibility of your ideas and make a selection.

5. **Developing prototypes:** In this phase, you should visualize the ideas, make them tangible, and then outline, design, model, or simulate them so that the potential customer understands your idea and can test it.

6. **Testing assumptions:** In this concluding phase, you test your assumptions or ideas with systematic customer feedback. You receive responses, learn from them, and continue developing your idea.

Even if the phases are shown in sequence, as shown in Figure 1-1, there are numerous feedback locations between the phases. You can skip phases (at first). If you already find interesting solutions while researching the problem, you can design initial prototypes and test them with the help of customer surveys. If you see that the customer doesn't care for the idea, take a few steps back and analyze the needs of your target users again. Critically ask yourself whether you chose the right target users.

TIP

Run through the individual phases quickly. The principle is to fail early and often so that you can learn from the failure. The feedback between the process phases helps you learn.

If necessary, terminate the process if the customer doesn't give you positive feedback. This saves you time and money that you would have spent on something that flops in the market.

## Going through the process in detail

The path toward creating an attractive solution for your target users' needs can be complex and can carry great uncertainties regarding its success. In situations of uncertainty and complexity, there's often little information available about the best solution. The best way to achieve your goal is to proceed gradually: Collect information about your task so that you can accumulate knowledge.

## Collecting and evaluating information about the task

In the first phase, you have to understand the task you want to solve. Take enough time for the task analysis, which can be presented as a problem brought up by your target users or a wish expressed by them. When analyzing your task, it's helpful to systematically answer the six "W" questions:

>> What is the need of your target users?

>> Who has this need?

>> In what way is this need of your user group revealed?

>> Where is this need evident?

>> When does this need show?

>> Why do your target users have this need?

Compile all the information and describe what you know about your target users and the problem. A problem or wish can refer to a service, a design, user friendliness, usage period, price, or environmental or social compatibility. Focus on just a few significant characteristics of the need.

**TIP**

You need convincing and up-to-date information to close the gaps in your knowledge. You can use the following sources:

>> Publications and patent databases

>> Customers surveys or direct customer observations

>> Supplier surveys

>> Joint workshops with customers or suppliers

Search online and offline for studies, articles, and newspaper reports about your target users, and be sure to collect statements, contact details, or other relevant information in social networks. Finally, don't forget to search for blogs by or about your target users.

## Observing the target users

Collect important impressions and information about the problems and needs of your target users through observations in real environments. Only through observations can you capture the authentic and spontaneous behavior of people in their natural environment.

TIP

Don't immediately evaluate the people and situations you encounter. Ask yourself what kinds of actions are underway and which situations are being created. Don't immediately categorize it. The focus should be on the respondent's actions instead of on their disposition, values, and norms. You can better get to the bottom of those aspects through interviews.

Observations aren't just about the specific superficial activities — the persons and situations must be considered as a whole. Capture the surroundings, including all relevant objects, the situation itself, and all actions and interactions of the people as well as their emotions.

TIP

Link the observation with a survey, for example, by asking the target users about their motivations behind specific actions. You can perform a survey before, during, or after the observed situation.

When you start recognizing patterns in the observations, you have invested enough time. Write down as much as necessary — but as little as possible.

## Defining the task

The analytical phases are followed by the consolidation — the *synthesis* — of the gained information in a concise form. The question or problem is your task — the design challenge that you and your team want to master.

The information must answer two basic questions that are important for solving the problem:

>> Who are the target users that matter here?

>> What is the specific need that you want to satisfy?

TIP

In this phase, don't offer any indication of what a possible solution might look like. Always separate the wording of the challenge from finding the solution.

The Persona method is the best way to summarize the relevant information when it comes to describing the target users. A *persona* is a real or fictitious person with individual characteristics that represent the target users (or at least some of them). Describe the characteristics of this person (age, gender, education level, opinions, hobbies, and modes of behavior) with keywords or in short sentences. (For more on the Persona method, check out Chapter 7.)

When you describe customer needs, ignore the fact that your target users want to get a certain product or specific service. Ask yourself what and why your target user wants to achieve something in a particular situation. The problems and frustrations of your target user when handling a task are often the starting points for the subsequent solution. In addition to the problems, consider the (unstated) wishes of the target user. These wishes enable you to find new offers for the target user. Ask your target user about the motivations behind the needs.

## Finding solutions

Based on how you define your task, your goal must be to develop as many ideas as possible for potential solutions. For the initial search for ideas, you can use these sources:

>> General Internet research in the area of your task

>> Articles in trade magazines

>> Descriptions of patents in databases

>> Participation in specialized presentations or discussions at trade shows and conferences

>> Surveys and observations of lead users or suppliers who have already found initial possible solutions

TIP

Be sure to integrate experts with a scientific background as well as those with practical experience into your design thinking process. Organize joint workshops, execute your projects together, or ask experts about your assumptions and ideas. Many years of experience with creative processes have yielded some general prin-ciples regarding the search for problem-solving ideas:

>> **The decomposition principle:** The idea here is to disassemble the problem, task, process steps, or redesigned product into its various parts and then vary or combine these parts in a new way.

>> **The association principle:** Here, you want to link together ideas, information, perceptions, and emotions. One example is brainstorming and its variants.

Brainstorming is common enough, and probably doesn't need defining here. The idea is for participants to spontaneously express ideas, leading to many ideas being produced in a short amount of time. The participants give their imagination free reign to find new and original ideas — even the craziest ideas are welcome. The free expression of ideas also stipulates that only one person speaks at a time. Ideas by others can and should be picked up, modified, or refined. The most important rule to follow is to focus just on finding ideas — actually evaluating the ideas you find should wait until later. (For more on brainstorming, see Chapter 11.)

>> **Analogy and confrontation:** These involve specific methods for adopting a new perspective on a problem. With analogies, you compare your task with a task from a completely different area and then use the commonalities and differences you discover as a stimulus for new ideas.

TIP

Use the principle of analogy to put yourself in the situation of another person or another company. Ask yourself what would happen if you were another person or a company. One example is, "What if I were a billionaire?" A billionaire symbolizes infinite riches that would be available for the solution to the problem. This analogy method, known as the *what-if* technique, allows you to overcome your own mental barriers.

As for confrontations, the selected area you choose is intentionally posed as a counterpart to your task. Setting the two areas side-by-side forces you to change perspective and thus get new ideas.

>> **Provocation:** With the Provocation technique, you formulate the solution as provocative statements in order to get new stimuli from exaggerations, contradictions, or wishful thinking. Consider how you might make the customer's problem more extreme.

>> **Abstraction and imagination:** The idea here is to move out from your problem so that you can view it from a higher, more abstract, or pictorial level. Get as much distance from the problem as possible so that you can understand the problem from a "helicopter perspective" and get ideas for solutions. Use your imagination to create a more image-based view of the problem, abstracting out even further.

>> **Simplification:** As with abstraction, the simplification of products and processes is a successful formula for innovative solutions. The idea here is to remove or decrease process steps, characteristics, or functions that aren't relevant for the customer or aren't perceived and acknowledged as relevant. Instead, you should focus on the necessary functions, streamline your products, and standardize and automate your processes.

The greatest potential of creative principles and techniques lies in their combination. Test the various principles and techniques in a team, and then go with what works best.

TIP

Remove all obstacles to your creativity. Avoid stress and unhealthy behavior — it can influence your creativity. Renovate non-ergonomic workplaces, replace inadequate work equipment, reduce noise levels, and fix rooms that are too cold or hot. On an organizational level, rigid and strict controls, numerous regulations, and a dry formalism result in a bureaucracy that limits the flourishing of creativity. Scrutinize the regulations and formalities. Create breathing spaces where no regulations apply.

## Selecting solutions that work

If you pursue every possible solution, you'll soon reach your limits because you probably aren't working with an unlimited budget. Admittedly, people want to see quick results — usually, a newly developed product poised for great success — but despite such pressures, you should avoid initiating multiple developments simultaneously. Have the team make a selection at an early stage.

There is no single correct evaluation method. If you employ several kinds of evaluations, you will develop a comprehensive picture of your idea. *Dot-voting* — where you have every participant distribute five adhesive dots to the various individual ideas, including giving multiple dots to one idea — is a great way to make a rough selection. Just sort the ideas according to the number of dots received.

TIP

Employees from different departments often assess the opportunities and risks of the same potential solutions in different ways. Utilize the range of perspectives and rely on variety in the evaluation. This makes the idea easier to implement later, when you integrate persons from different departments during the decision.

When the rough selection is completed, look at the advantages, opportunities, and implementation barriers of your proposed solutions. Use checklists like the following to review whether the ideas can meet the stipulated criteria:

>> **Feasibility:** You must check whether the idea is feasible.

>> **Fit (strategic and cultural fit):** The idea must fit the vision, strategy, and culture of the company.

>> **Desirability:** Your idea must have a customer benefit.

>> **Business viability:** An idea with business viability is one where the income is higher than the expenses.

>> **Scalability:** This refers to the idea's ability to accomplish high growth with relatively little effort.

>> **Sustainability:** Your idea must be successful in the long run; it must have a long-lasting economic, social, and ecological benefit.

>> **Adaptability:** In a dynamically changing environment, your idea must be adaptable.

## Developing prototypes

With a prototype, you can vividly present and test the essential functions and characteristics of your idea. Create a prototype early on, without elaborate planning and with little effort. You can choose from different types, and the selection depends on the maturity of your idea and whether you want to develop an innovative product, a service, or a business model.

>> **Drawings and photo collages:** You can easily and quickly create a prototype of your idea on paper, a whiteboard, or an electronic device with a drawing or an image made of collaged photos. Outline the product design or create drawings from the individual functions and characteristics of your idea.

>> **Model constructions:** Use paper, cardboard, modeling clay, or Styrofoam to illustrate certain functions or characteristics of your idea. A 3D printer makes it possible to create realistic models.

>> **Stories and role-playing games:** Tell a story about the use of a product so that you get feedback about its usefulness and ease of use. With storytelling, describe the advantages or the use of your idea as a real or fictitious story. You can also act out the story in the form of a video or role-playing game or with toy building blocks.

>> **Digital prototypes:** You can prepare initial visual representations of control elements and buttons with wireframes. Create a web page on which you present your ideas and evaluate the user behavior on this web page.

TIP

If the creation of a prototype involves a significant amount of effort, you can also simulate how a prototype functions in an experiment for test subjects. For example, if you want to test whether customers accept the use of artificial intelligence by a consulting service, you can offer an entry screen on a computer and explain that the answers to the test subject's questions are provided by a computer. Simulate this for the test subjects, and have an employee answer the questions. Check whether customers generally accept such a consulting service. You will also find out how to design artificial intelligence for the consultation. This is a *Wizard of Oz* prototype. Just as in the classic movie *The Wizard of Oz*, something happens behind a screen, and it's not necessarily what the customers expect. Tell the test subjects that this is an experiment.

## Testing solutions

Design thinking lives off early feedback from potential customers about ideas and assumptions. You can learn from this and adapt your assumptions and solutions. The idea here is to formulate and check various assumptions about the behavior and needs of your target users as well as your ideas for a solution. Ask the customers for an evaluation based on a single characteristic that the customers can most easily test on a prototype. If you get negative feedback from a customer, you have to respond quickly and flexibly. Use what you learn to design a new prototype and test it again.

TIP

You can gain respondents in various ways. Use your friends and your contacts in the social networks, ask friends of friends for recommendations, or create emails describing your project for others to forward, along with a note that you're looking for contacts to test your assumptions or ideas. You can approach your employees or colleagues at your own company and survey them in the role of the customer.

Always be thinking about where you might find potential customers. The place might be understood as a real location (cafés, shops, trade shows) or a virtual place (social networks, trade forums). Research where your customers shop, work, or spend their time off. During the first contact with anybody from a new pool of potential customers, emphasize that this is not a sales pitch but that you're looking for advice and need that person's evaluation.

Conduct personal interviews, if at all possible. During each interview, don't just consider content-specific claims — pay particular attention to statements that have some emotion behind them or that come as a surprise. You know that you have conducted enough interviews when you recognize a clear response pattern. When you create an online prototype in the form of a web page or an app, you examine the visitor behavior on this page. With this online prototype, you can test individual functions or the user friendliness of these online offers.

If your assumptions aren't confirmed or if your observations and surveys show ambiguous results, you might need to return to an earlier stage in the design thinking process. You learn from the failure, change the idea according to the feedback from your target users, create an improved prototype, and perform new tests. With this approach, you'll gradually reach a promising product, service. or business model innovation.

# Start Design Thinking Right Away

After you know the principles behind design thinking and the approach you need to take, you can start immediately. Form a team, define the roles and communication channels, plan the first steps, and prepare the technical setup and work environment.

## Assembling the team

You should form a team with at least five, and no more than nine, people for the design thinking project. When approaching individuals, keep in mind that you want the final makeup of the team to be as diverse as possible. Don't just consider characteristics such as age, gender, or ethnic affiliation. Look at the professional and personal experiences and values so that you can utilize the various perspectives, methods, and knowledge of the team members for the project's success.

## Defining team roles and communication practices

At the beginning of a design thinking phase, discuss the individual tasks the team will take, and then have each member independently select their tasks. Settle the responsibilities within the project team as well as with internal organizational units and external partners. Who is responsible? Who performs the work? With whom does a task need to be coordinated, and who must be informed?

Avoid extensive documentation in the form of reports. Your preferred communication method should be spontaneous talks and project discussions face-to-face. Hold daily status meetings in the form of a daily scrum, which follows these rules:

>> Meetings occur daily and always in the same place.

>> Meetings should never last more than 15 minutes.

>> Always stand during meetings. (No chairs!)

In design thinking, group work and focused individual work alternate. One element is the workshop format, which is designed to promote an in-depth exchange between team members. Arrange workshops in each phase of a design thinking project so that you can complete the tasks while working together. The goal of the workshop can be that you develop a shared understanding of the task, characterize the target users more precisely, compile the results of observations and surveys, find ideas, or create prototypes.

TIP

Vary the composition and type of group and individual work in the scope of a workshop so that it continues to be diverse and inspiring. You can change work times and break times, switch rooms and furnishings, recruit external moderators, and apply different methods during the workshops, for example.

## Planning the project work

For a design thinking initiative, you plan and execute the project according to an agile method. First, write down all necessary set tasks in any order. (In project management terms, these set tasks are referred to as *work packages*.) Then ask yourselves what you have to do to reach the selected goal. Make a detailed plan for the next steps that need to be carried out. When a step has been completed, that progress as well as any developments outside of the confines of the project will have worked to improve the knowledge base. Then you can make a better plan for the next step. With this agile approach, you can quickly and flexibly integrate emerging changes — ideally, in the form of customer feedback — into your planning at an early stage.

TIP

The form your planning takes can be illustrated with the pencil-and-pen rule: Write down the next steps permanently with a pen, and then outline the later steps with a pencil so that they can be easily changed.

With sequence planning, you determine the logical succession of the tasks. A rough outline consists of the phases of the design thinking process:

>> Understand the task.

>> Search for solutions.

>> Create the prototype.

>> Test the proposed solution with the customer.

In addition to planning the sequence, you should define interim goals, where the progress of the project can be reviewed and a decision can be made about how to proceed (with Go to continue or Kill to terminate the project).

Use buffer times if only particular time slots are available for the employees or the tasks. Take into account a particular time requirement (5 to 15 percent of the total time needed) for the coordination of your design thinking project. A bar graph is the best way to illustrate the timeline.

You have to know the type and amount of materials needed to complete any set task. When estimating the projected required amount of work, each set task is considered in detail so that you can reach the task's goal. All members initially estimate their own required effort for each individual activity. Then the estimated results are compared with each other and the group reaches an agreement when it comes to the shared value.

## Furnishing the work environment

You have to make communal workspaces and separate individual spaces available. These are referred to, on one hand, as *we spaces* for groups or as meeting rooms for everyone to communicate openly and, on the other hand, as *me spaces* for quiet individual work.

TIP

Because of the distribution into small groups, the use of bulky partitions, the communal nature of the work on prototypes, and the desired movement of the participants, design thinking workshops require a lot of space.

During design thinking, you switch between group and individual work within just a few minutes. The rooms and furnishings have to support flexibility. It should be possible to spontaneously divide large work areas that can support team work according to the work requirements (type of work, group size) by means of sliding doors or easily movable partitions. You can also establish small groups that don't want their work to be disturbed by using sliding whiteboards, pin boards, or metaplan walls as room dividers. Make sure that the participants relax during the breaks, and encourage informal exchanges.

TIP

Furnish the group work areas with upright tables and movable stools so that new groups that encourage movement can form. Movement promotes creativity. Don't hesitate to post sticky notes on windows, doors, and white walls.

Depending on the product area or industry, the technical equipment for the workshop rooms can vary. In addition to the standard office and telecommunication equipment, you can include 3D printers, scanners, crayons, smartboards, or virtual reality devices in rooms for design thinking. These devices simplify the communication and visualization of work results. You initially have to provide paper and transparencies in various sizes and colors, presentation cards, sticky notes, different types of pens, and magnets and adhesives to cover the basic supplies.

Remember the important role of the moderator when you plan a workshop. Find an appropriate person. A moderator brings the participants together, structures the process, summarizes the results, and keeps an eye on the goal and time span of the workshop. An external moderator can help you overcome the operational blindness and divergent interests of the participants.

## Asking for support

Request support for your project, especially from your supervisors. Look for allies at your company who know or want to know about design thinking. Make employees at the company curious about this innovative approach. Point out the need for innovation in order to achieve sustainable corporate success. Explain the use, principles, and methods of design thinking. Counter objections by suggesting that you start on a project with limited duration and a manageable budget. At the same time, ask for freedom to design the contents of the project. This is how you can create ideal conditions for the successful implementation of your design thinking project.

IN THIS CHAPTER

» **Focusing on people**

» **Visualizing and demonstrating ideas**

» **Understanding mistakes as opportunities to learn**

» **Integrating different perspectives on the team**

» **Designing workspaces and establishing processes for success**

Chapter **2**

# Understanding the Principles of Design Thinking

I n this chapter, you get to find out more about the principles of design think-ing and come to understand the significant role these principles play in your project's success. In design thinking, everything revolves around people. You learn that you must focus on people's needs early on and that, above all, you have to work with your lead users. By using this strategy, you can establish proxim-ity to your target users so that you can better analyze their emotions, goals, and activities. Design thinking follows the principle that you make the results of your analysis and proposed solutions visible and comprehensible. As a result, you ena-ble another tenet — namely, that you learn from mistakes as you develop the solution. Keep in mind that design thinking is based at the bottom on teamwork and that effective teamwork requires appropriate workspaces. As a team endeavor, design thinking also forces you to learn about and appreciate the potential ben-efits of various perspectives. After all, you have to make the process both flexible and goal-oriented.

# Focusing on People Early On

Consistent customer orientation in the generation and development of new products and services has long been acknowledged as a significant factor in a company's success. With design thinking, you actually go one step further. Design thinking is more than just customer orientation — it is centered on people. People are the beginning, middle, and end for every consideration. You begin with people by taking up a problem faced by your target users or a wish expressed by them. Your task in design thinking is not to pursue a technology or business goal — it's to satisfy the expressed needs of customers.

**TIP**

With design thinking, you don't ask the question "How can we apply XY technology?" Neither do you ask the question "How can we impress the customer with our new product?" Instead, you ask, "How can we solve the problem of our target users in such a way that it's less of an effort for them to use our solution?"

Your target users should have a substantial influence on the go/stop decisions in the process. If a potential customer group responds that the identified problem is relevant, you can start your activities. However, if you get feedback that the problem is an insignificant one in the eyes of the customer, you stop further activities and identify another problem. If the target users don't consider the solution that you found attractive, change your approach at an early stage.

The principle of creating an early focus on people offers you numerous advantages and opportunities:

>> You focus, right from the start, on the most important wishes and problems of your target users.

>> You gain detailed impressions of the user market.

>> You prevent your development from bypassing the market.

>> You prevent *overengineering* — another word for "excessive perfectionism." You avoid overreaching in a technical sense when regarded from the customer's perspective. One example is a product that has too many features and thus becomes complicated to use.

**EXAMPLE**

The US-based company Juicero originally wanted to sell, for $700, a juice press that took prepackaged bags of fruits and vegetables and squeezed out the juice with greater or less strength, depending on the contents of the plastic bags. The appliance was connected to the Internet so that the juice ingredients could be shown and the plastic bags could be reordered. Ultimately, users figured out that it was quicker to just crush the prepackaged fruit and veggies by hand rather than with the help of the juice press — and it was a lot cheaper.

>> You save time in terms of product development and subsequent marketing.

>> You cut development and marketing costs.

>> You lower the marketing risk.

>> You accelerate the market launch.

# More than Traditional Market Research

In traditional market research, you ask the customers about their wishes and needs and what they think about a specific product. With these kinds of direct questions, traditional market research methods such as customer surveys often yield, for numerous reasons, disappointing results when it comes to the search for innovation.

The methods of traditional market research are focused on the average customer — the one who is supposed to represent target users. Average customers are often too focused on current needs, on product selections, and on product features — a state of affairs often referred to as *functional fixedness.* The customer's own (product) experiences act like a mental restraint. This often prevents thinking in unconventional, innovative directions. Likewise, companies that turn today's customers' wishes into a benchmark for innovations of tomorrow are just focusing on small improvements. Over time, these companies lose their capacity for creating the groundbreaking innovations referred to as radical or disruptive. The average customer has no urgent need for new products for now.

**WARNING**

Imagine that the co-founder of Facebook, Mark Zuckerberg, had conducted a customer survey shortly before Facebook's launch in 2003. He would have asked many potential users in writing or online whether they would need a social network. With such a question at that time, you can expect that the results would have been disappointing. Customers must be able to develop an idea of what is behind a product or service and what kind of benefit they could get from it. The idea here is to analyze the needs of people *without* immediately asking about their preferences for certain product features.

Furthermore, the average customer can barely articulate new needs. In this context, one often hears a quote attributed to Henry Ford: "If I had asked people what they wanted, they would have said faster horses." Whether Ford actually said this is doubtful. Aside from that, this sentence is also misleading. Never expect customers to immediately provide you with solutions. When starting with design thinking, the focus is intentionally not on solutions but on an understanding of the person and their problems, desires, motives, goals and opinions.

Don't just analyze the average customers, which is what traditional market research often concentrates on exclusively. Be sure as well to research the behavior of people who aren't among your target users. Ask yourself the following questions:

>> In what ways are my potential customers and those who are not my target users the same? In what ways are they different?

>> Why do these differences and commonalities exist?

Keep in mind that customer surveys at companies are still usually driven by departments. Marketing determines needs and comes up with ideas for product improvements. Research and development works out technical and product specifications. Often, there's no coordination with internal and external partners. Generally speaking, customers are included only selectively at the start of the innovation process and at its end, when the final prototype gets tested. There's no consistent, partnership-based cooperation with the customers throughout the innovation process.

The customer's needs are too important to leave them to marketing alone, so make sure that employees from research, development, and production are brought in contact with the customer. This can happen in joint workshops or even by visiting the customer.

# Finding the Lead User

Because average customers can offer only a limited number of new ideas when it comes to product development, you should look instead for *lead users* — the ones whose need precedes that of all other customers in the market and who have a strong incentive to resolve this need. These people are the first to recognize and track a market trend before all other possible users have identified this trend. Their interest in satisfying their need is so strong that they often develop their own prototypes and sometimes launch them in the market on their own. Some of these people even start their own businesses based on this motivation *(user entrepreneurs)*. In other words, lead users aren't your average customers or pilot customers, and they don't necessarily represent customer needs in the current market. They aren't even necessarily previous customers; they can also come from entirely different market segments and even from outside industries.

The Internet is a lead-user product. The inventor of the World Wide Web, Tim Berners-Lee, was a lead user. As an employee of the European Organization for Nuclear Research (CERN), he saw that using different network infrastructures was causing communication problems between the various laboratory sites. He initially established the basis for the World Wide Web just so that he could communicate more easily with colleagues.

Mountain bikes are also a lead-user product. Back in the 1970s, Gary Fisher and a bunch of other old-school hippies recognized the deficits of the current sports bikes for their own demanding needs. They used bicycles in the open country and felt compelled to modify the wheels to fit those needs. This perspective resulted in the first mountain bikes.

The systematic integration of lead users promises a high potential for innovations when generating ideas for new products and services. Identifying these users and integrating their creative potential into the innovation process is the function of the lead-user method, which was already developed by Professor Eric von Hippel at the Massachusetts Institute of Technology (MIT) back in 1986.

You can find lead users for your design thinking process by first looking at dominant market and technology trends. Search online or offline for new trends in technologies and market developments (new developments of needs, new competitors). You can find tons of resources to turn to for help:

>> Publication and patent databases

>> Newspapers and trade magazines

>> Technology, market, and industry studies by trade associations, service providers, consulting companies, scientific establishments (colleges, research institutes), or national and international institutions

>> Statistics (government sites like the US Bureau of Economic Analysis [www.bea.gov] as well as private sites)

>> Trend or market research reports

>> The annual reports, sustainability reports, presentations, press releases, and websites of other companies (competitors, suppliers, startups)

>> General Internet research, forums, blogs, and social networks

>> Conferences and trade shows

>> Customer surveys, supplier surveys, workshops with customers or suppliers

>> Personal networks of your own employees

>> Expert talks

>> Cooperative work with scientific institutes or other companies

>> Employee surveys

After collecting the necessary information about technology and market trends, you should come up with possible selection criteria for lead users. Here's a list I came up with:

>> They are trendsetters.

>> They have specific knowledge about relevant technologies or about the problem you're trying to address.

>> They often face the same problem or are forced to deal with it intensively.

>> They have to deal with special (extreme) conditions.

>> They expect a great benefit from finding a solution to the problem you've identified.

>> They already have initial ideas or even prototypes for the solution or have developed their own modifications of existing solutions.

You shouldn't define these criteria too narrowly; otherwise, you might exclude lead users from other areas. Furthermore, not all of the listed selection criteria must be met, nor do they have to be satisfied 100 percent.

TIP

Be sure to analyze analogous areas. It can be helpful to take a look at other industries that either use similar technologies or face similar challenges. Ask yourself which application areas have the same problems on an abstract level and which areas use other technologies.

Based on these selection criteria, you have a number of different approaches for identifying lead users: You can send a questionnaire to a large pool of preselected individuals derived from the criteria and ask them to voluntarily disclose some of their personal information so that you can determine their suitability as lead users. You can then use these individuals as resources when identifying market and technology trends. (*Note:* You can also integrate as starting points existing customers, suppliers, and company contacts into the survey. With the help of the selection criteria mentioned above, you can distinguish between average customers and lead users among your existing customers.)

You can also just contact a limited amount of people at the outset and ask them if they in turn know potential lead users. You could start by asking them the following kinds of questions:

>> Do you know anyone who has special expertise in the areas of *XY*?

>> Do you know anyone who has already started developing their own solution to this particular problem?

>> Do you know anyone in analogous areas who has experienced similar problems or uses similar technologies?

>> Do you know anyone who is facing this problem in special circumstances or is highly motivated to find a solution to the problem?

If you're lucky, you can use the social networks of the individuals you contacted to forward your questions and concerns from person to person with the snowball effect so that you ultimately end up with a potential lead user.

To conclude the search, you have to decide whether

>> The identified persons are suitable as lead users

>> These persons are motivated and willing to participate in a workshop

>> The desired mix of people for this workshop is appropriate

Of course, there is no "perfect" lead user who can satisfy all criteria for the selection.

# Actively Involving the Lead User

You should actively involve lead users in the search for potential solutions and invite them to a creative workshop. To prepare the workshop, you have to clarify a few basic conditions, such as the available times, confidentiality aspects, remuneration, and expense reimbursements.

**WARNING**

Clarifying the inventor rights of lead users continues to be a challenging issue for companies. This calls for creative solutions that also take the legitimate interests of the lead users into account. You should avoid a wholesale transfer of inventor rights without fair compensation. You can grant exclusive usage rights to the lead user in certain areas. You could arrange remuneration in the form of a one-time, lump-sum payment, milestone payments, and/or a revenue share. In-kind benefits are also possible. You could then provide the resulting product to the lead user without charge or on reduced terms. Or, you could ensure that the lead user is one of the first customers to receive the product.

Lead users, with the help of the latest presentation and creative techniques, should work on concrete solutions together with in-house representatives from various departments, such as research and development, production, marketing, and sales. You should plan for a maximum of 12 to 16 people (half internal experts and half external lead users) and a moderator (preferably, external) for the workshop. Such a workshop can last from one to three days, depending on the topic and focus. (You can find out more about the planning and execution of workshops in Chapter 5.)

# Developing Empathy

A key principle of design thinking is *empathy* — putting yourself in the position of the customer or user so that you can explore that person's feelings, emotions, thoughts, intentions, and actions. With empathy, you not only establish distance to yourself but also build up proximity to the potential customers. You can then better orient new products and services toward the customers to the degree to which such products and services can meet their needs. In this automated, digitized, and partially dehumanized world, where decisions are often made solely on the basis of hard facts, figures, and data and where efficiency increases are a priority, this approach is promising.

**EXAMPLE**

A lack of empathy was one reason for the failure of Google Glass, which was introduced in 2012 and then dropped from the market a mere three years later. The Google Glass pitch was that it could show the user emails, calls, text messages, instructions, or videos directly in the user's field-of-view. One mark against it right out of the box was that it was voice-controlled, a feature many users ended up disliking intensely, especially when the data glasses were used in public. An even bigger factor in the flop was the sense others had, when they interacted with data glass wearers, that their privacy was being invaded — a perception that Google had not reckoned with. Numerous people felt they were being permanently filmed by the wearer of the data glasses and even threatened the users with violence. Google didn't adequately address the needs of the users and, getting back to empathy, had not placed itself in the position of users faced with actually using its product.

Analyzing the feelings and emotions of your target users makes it possible for you to not only identify the still unspoken and undiscovered needs of your customers but also understand the motivations behind such needs. Products and services influence feelings and create emotions. Feelings and emotions can also show you the motivations behind the use of applications. You check your email more often when you happen to feel depressed. You use social networks more often when you feel alone. You resort to Internet search engines when you feel uncertain. You watch videos when you get bored. People frequently use products or services for more than just one reason. There's actually a network of emotions that explains the actions of people. Only when you correctly identify and understand the feelings and emotions of users can you use this as a basis for solving the problems of your target users or for making their wishes come true. (For more on the importance of feelings and emotions, see Chapter 7.)

Feelings and emotions can be divided into basic forms that can be found among all people across all cultures. These basic forms (and, in parentheses, their variations) include anxiety (fear, panic), anger (annoyance), sadness, joy (happiness), curiosity (surprise), disgust (boredom, revulsion), and contempt.

**TIP**

Pay attention to people's feelings when they do or don't do something. Ask yourself the following questions:

>> Which feelings do you recognize when you look at their gestures and facial expressions?

>> Which feelings do you identify when you hear a person's statements and their tone of voice?

Take the time to analyze the underlying emotions. Name them and assign them to the basic forms. For practice, you can start with yourself: Pay attention to your feelings for a week and explore them. Before going to sleep at night, name and describe them in a journal of emotions. Divide these feelings into positive, neutral, and negative. Ask yourself why the situations you encountered during the course of the day led to these emotions.

# Illustrating Ideas

In design thinking, your goal is to make your ideas comprehensible and attainable at an early stage. You visualize your ideas and preferably demonstrate them with a prototype for potential users to experiment with. Prototypes don't necessarily have to be pieces of hardware; they can also be drawings, images, role-playing games, model constructions, or videos. (For more on prototypes, see Chapter 13.) It's not about giving your target users a finished and perfect product. Quite the contrary. Initially, your target user should only review individual functions, features, characteristics, or activities of a product or service offer. A prototype helps you make something that is difficult to describe more tangible. When creating and selecting a prototype, the guiding principle is this: As simple as possible, as meaningful as possible.

EXAMPLE On its website, Dropbox showed a short video that explained the benefits of its product idea in a simple and original way. The interesting part: This software solution didn't exist yet at that time. The video was a huge success, and more than 100,000 people registered to find out more about the software. The founders thus received positive feedback about their idea and began with the implementation.

# Failing in Order to Learn

Another important principle in design thinking involves learning from mistakes. Make sure that mistakes are understood as a fixed component in the design thinking process and are considered to be opportunities for learning. The tasks you deal with in design thinking are always accompanied by uncertainties. You have to acknowledge that a Zero Defects approach is impossible in the scope of innovation and that this shouldn't be the goal. Even just the attempt to reach something perfect with the first draft, concept, prototype, or product is often doomed to fail when it comes to innovation and it works to stifle groundbreaking new concepts.

TIP Quickly learn from mistakes and establish a culture of experimentation at the company. Just like successes, mistakes offer learning opportunities. To learn successfully, you should answer the following questions in the design team:

>> What caused the mistake?

>> What do we now have to do together to remedy or reduce the damaging effect of the mistake?

>> How did the mistake show up first?

>> What do we have to do in the future to prevent the mistake from happening?

>> What can we learn from the mistake as a company?

Address the issue that mistakes (must) always occur and are to be expected. For that reason, allow — better yet, encourage — errors. The development of innovation consists of *two-legged* learning — learning from successes as well as from mistakes. The best way to get this point across is to use examples from your own company, showing how mistakes led to specific improvements or even innovations. (For more on learning from mistakes, see Chapter 3.)

EXAMPLE Teflon was discovered because a chemist experimented with refrigerants and stored them for too long. Penicillin was discovered by the bacteriologist Alexander Fleming when, over the summer holiday, he accidentally left out a Petri dish, leading to the formation of a mold that prevented the growth of bacterial cultures.

Popsicles were invented when the 11-year-old Frank Epperson left homemade lemonade with a stick inside on the patio during a freeze. The teabag was invented after the tea merchant filled tea into silk pouches for cost reasons and customers accidentally immersed those in boiling water.

# Ensuring Diversity on the Team

An important success factor in design thinking is the right composition of the team. There are good reasons why you should rely on diversity in the team structure. Design thinking puts people in the spotlight. Look at the people for whom you want to find a solution or whose wishes you want to fulfill. More likely than not, these people come from various age groups, consist of both women and men, or have different cultural backgrounds. It helps when your team reflects this diversity. This makes it easier for your team to put itself in the position and situation of the target users.

Another reason for the positive effect of diversity lies in how you approach the tasks facing you. In design thinking, you deal with tasks that aren't easy to solve. You need the knowledge, creativity, experience, and perspectives from different disciplines. Design thinking combines interdisciplinary broadness and technical depth. The process relies on the knowledge, experience, and perspectives of a team of engineers and scientists in the fields of the natural sciences, engineering, the humanities, and the social and economic sciences who are capable of multi-disciplinary collaboration. (For more on the importance of prioritizing diversity when it comes to team building, see Chapter 5.)

TIP

Don't just rely on diversity when it comes to the age, gender, education, or cultural background of your team members. Affiliation with the company (for a long time or a recent hire), experience with the topic (in-depth, low, none) or the personality type (introverted or extroverted) are additional factors that you can take into account.

# Offering Team-Oriented and Creative Workspaces

The room design and its furnishings have an often underestimated impact on an organization's innovation capacity. For innovative work, you have to create a balance between concentration, communication, and creativity when it comes to workspaces. At the same time, the architecture and workplace design must leave room for flexibility. That's why the "innovation factory" has to look different from the usual "production factory," which is designed purely in accordance with efficiency concerns.

The workspaces for individual and group work as well as assemblies of the whole group must have a flexible and inspiring design. I highly recommend choosing different locations, rooms, or furniture arrangements for the different design thinking phases. This lets you create a new work atmosphere on the fly — one that is appropriate for the work being carried out.

Design thinking is a communal process that not only takes place in-house but also integrates external partners. The room design should simplify and encourage the communal work with short distances. Buildings and rooms connected with walkways and covered bridges link different disciplines together in an optimal spatial design. (You can learn more about this topic in Chapter 5.)

EXAMPLE

Airbnb designed some of its corporate rooms the way its own customers originally offered them as vacation homes all over the world on its website. Google equips its workplaces with couches, gaming areas, fitness equipment, hammocks, pool tables, table tennis, massage chairs, or yoga rooms. The Lego office in Denmark also has many playfully designed work areas, such as miniature golf courses. Rather than take the stairs, the employees can use a slide. The Kickstarter office in New York City is inside an old pencil factory and includes spaces such as a theater, library, gallery, and roof garden. Trees grow in the garden, and fruits and vegetables are planted for the employees.

# Making the Process Flexible Yet Focused

In design thinking, the path to your goal is filled with uncertainties. In situations with high uncertainty, there is often little information on which to base the best approach. Forecasts for developments in the future tend to be vague in these situations when it comes to their explanatory power — or lack thereof. You can reduce uncertainty and complexity if you proceed step-by-step and respond flexibly to changes.

The design thinking process encourages this gradual approach. First, you thoroughly analyze the problem, use the results of your analysis to formulate a task, develop the first possible solutions, test them, and learn from the feedback. You don't strictly complete the phases one after another. Whenever you get information that you first have to analyze in detail, jump back to a previous step. Changes in the process are expected and desired. Each step can pose a new challenge for you. This is why part of the principle is that you make the course flexible and change it when needed. (For more on flexibility when it comes to workflows, see Chapter 4.)

Accept the fact that you won't have all the information you need right at the start and that you aren't immediately doing everything correctly. Understand that knowledge and information are the greatest enemy of uncertainty. The design thinking process will give you the relevant knowledge and required information. Uncertainty is based on a fear of failure. Think realistically about what it is you might actually lose if your project failed. From that perspective, it's usually the case that the benefits outweigh the risks.

You should be focused during the design thinking process. The principle that you should make the process focus-oriented initially seems to contradict the need for flexibility. My experience with creative processes has shown that the definition of clear boundaries or limitations is helpful for the design thinking process. Within these boundaries, you can, in turn, act flexibly. These boundaries can consist of a rough orientation based on the company strategy, a special regional focus, a certain amount of new features, the compliance with regulatory restrictions, or resources with limited availability.

Your continued focus also relates to the design thinking process. Boundaries can mean that you set yourself clear time budgets for the individual phases or specify for whom, how, and where the solution should be used. When these limitations are applied and communicated properly, they can boost creativity and have a motivating and inspiring effect on the design thinking team. Stay true to the principle "Necessity is the mother of invention."

# Chapter **3**

# Creating Ideal Conditions

My advice? Don't rush into things and immediately start with your design thinking task. Invest enough time to prepare your employees and your entourage for design thinking. In this chapter, you'll find out how to create the conditions for success when it comes to your design thinking project. First and foremost, people must be able to see the rationale behind your task. Together with your team and other involved parties at the company, you need to develop a vision for your project by describing the long-term benefit of your work. You'll find out how important it is to get support from top management, and you'll be in a position to demand creative freedom. Lastly, I'll show you how to make decisions at your company more efficiently. You'll find out how to identify the required skills for your task and how to motivate your employees for the project with both praise and appreciation.

## Ensuring a Positive Attitude

Before you start with your task, you have to answer two basic questions for yourself and all other potential participants:

>> What do you want to achieve with the task?

>> Why do you want to achieve it?

The answer to these questions is the vision of your task — the *design challenge* that you want to solve with design thinking.

## Creating the vision for the project

This is your description of the long-term vision for the future that is intended to improve the current situation. The vision provides meaning and motivation for the participants. The focus is more on the Why and What and less on the How. The vision relates to the future and integrates social developments that allow for the formation of a more personal, more human frame of reference when it comes to focusing on the customer orientation. Your product should create added value for the customers. Your design challenge should offer a benefit for people as well as for their environment.

Take the necessary time on the team and discuss the shared vision for your task. This way, you create a positive attitude and evoke a spirit of optimism in your team. One example of such a strong vision was John F. Kennedy's goal, set in 1961, for the United States to send someone to the moon within the next ten years. (That's why we use the phrase *moonshot thinking* when talking about the power of a shared vision.)

Your vision should create pressure to change, strongly push for immediate implementation, and be easily communicable in images. Consider this example of a vision: "We want to increase our market share by 20 percent among pharmaceutical products against neurodegenerative diseases." It's company-related, technically rational, and not particularly motivating. Try this one instead: "Within ten years, humans will no longer suffer from Alzheimer's." This is human-related, illustrative, and inspiring.

## Communicating the vision

Repeatedly talk about your vision with all participants, taking advantage of every opportunity to keep the conversation going. Talk about your design challenge during every team meeting, every workshop, and every lecture as well as during informal discussions with previously uninvolved employees at the company or with your business partners. Make use of every opportunity for an exchange of ideas about your vision; doing so means you'll get much-needed feedback from each exchange and thus be able to sharpen the focus of your task. Your vision, and the task derived from it, should be permanently visible and ever-present at your company. Put your design challenge on the intranet, display a poster with your task in the common spaces, write an article about your goals in the company magazine, and distribute flyers and stickers about your project at the company.

**TIP**

Write up your design challenge as though it were a story and give it a meaningful name. Talk entertainingly and emotionally about the challenges that you want to solve using design thinking. Use the fictional elements of storytelling to tell the very real story of your vision — especially when it comes to the benefits your solution can achieve for people. The plot of the story must answer the questions of why you want to master the task and what you'll use to master it. (You can find out more about storytelling in Chapter 13.)

# Encouraging the Willingness to Change

During the execution of the design thinking process and the later implementation of the results, you depend on many employees and external cooperative partners, such as suppliers. The approach, as well as the actual result of design thinking, is probably unfamiliar and new to them. New ideas are always met with skepticism, reservations, or resistance. You're forcing your employees to change their habits, assigned tasks, or workflows.

With an inspiring vision, you can create the foundations necessary for change. It helps if you generate a sense of the importance, necessity, and urgency for something new among your allies and within the company. This requires an analysis of both the current situation as well as future challenges.

A "do-nothing" scenario can act as an eye-opener. Ask the team or the company as a whole what would happen if they were to suddenly stop all efforts to create something new from one day to the next. Ask the following questions:

>> What would happen if we don't solve this task as a company?

>> What would our competitors do?

>> How would our customers react over the long term?

>> What risks does this create?

>> Which opportunities would be missed without this task?

# Arousing Curiosity

Curiosity is an emotional assessment telling you that you find something interesting. People are born with curiosity. However, with advancing age, they lose this inborn curiosity. In scientific studies, it has been proven that curiosity has positive effects. People who are curious make social contacts more quickly and easily, seem more interesting and likeable, and are more self-confident and happier. This leads to more satisfaction in life and a higher life expectancy. In addition to the personal benefit, curiosity is the foundation of openness and creativity, so that new things can be discovered and progress can be made. You have to arouse curiosity for your task at the company so that you can successfully master it with design thinking.

People become curious when they find the topic interesting. Something is interesting if the task is challenging, if it's worthwhile, and if it's also comprehensible. You therefore have to present to the company the problem and the question you want to work on using design thinking as challenging, rewarding, and comprehensible.

## Presenting the task as a challenge

You can communicate the challenging nature of the task to your team or company by demonstrating how all previous solutions to the problem proved inadequate. Go on to explain that many fuzzy correlations and unclear relationships need to be examined or that the cause of the problem is unknown. A complex task generates curiosity.

**EXAMPLE**

Constructing a wind energy system is a technical challenge as well as an economic one. In addition to the technical tasks involved in improving the rotor blades, gears, and generators, it's important to find a location that is economical, eco-friendly, and accepted by the local population. These tasks can only be resolved together. From a technical as well as an economic perspective, this task is highly interesting and is certain to arouse curiosity.

## Presenting the task as a reward

You should emphasize the fact that certain entrepreneurial and personal benefits are associated with solving the task. Explain why it's important to solve the task. Entrepreneurial benefits might be that your customers are happier, the image of the company improves, your company's market share increases, you generate greater profits, or the company's sustainability is ensured after the task is completed. In addition to the financial and career-promoting benefits resulting from the task, point out that you can also gain a personal reward by finding out how something functions or by knowing that you helped resolve a thorny problem. Learning something is often perceived as a reward. Emphasize these forms of rewards when you want to arouse curiosity for your design thinking process on the team and at the company.

# Presenting the task in a comprehensible fashion

Three aspects of the task — the challenge, the reward, and the task's comprehensibility — help generate curiosity. Design thinking is structured so that you develop a better understanding of the task step-by-step. First you have to put yourself in the shoes of the people involved as they face a specific situation. Gaining this understanding amplifies your curiosity. The nice thing about it is that understanding is self-reinforcing and is proven to create feelings of happiness. You keep wanting to know more, and you experience this knowledge as satisfying. You're personally interested in solving the task. Explain the task, the principles of design thinking, and the design thinking approach to your team and other involved parties at the company. The more the employees at the company find out about it, the more curious they will become. (For more on design thinking principles, check out Chapter 2; for more on the design thinking approach, see Chapter 1.)

## Training curiosity

Here's another positive aspect to curiosity: You can supercharge your own curiosity levels all on your own.

**EXAMPLE**

Before you visit a museum that features work by an artist you're unfamiliar with, find out more about the artist. Read something about the artist's personality, hers or his life's journey, particular style and most famous works, either in books from the library or on the Internet. You'll see that you will become much more curious about the artwork you plan to see and will want to know many more details. With this in mind — have you heard of the sport called *tamburello?* Do some research on it and get curious.

Here's what I recommend that you do to get your curiosity in shape:

>> **Overcome fear:** If the topic or the task you're facing strikes you as incomprehensible, this will only serve to confuse and unsettle you. Uncertainty causes blockages and fear. Fear inhibits curiosity. You can only break through this vicious circle if you engage with the task and acquire knowledge about it. Analyze how you react to something new or unfamiliar. Think back to a daunting situation in your past and describe your uncertainties, your fears, and why you approached the task with such reluctance. Ask yourself whether, in hindsight, your reaction was justified, objectively speaking.

>> **Try a new task:** Make an effort to try something new more often, and then take the time to describe your feelings and ask yourself why you perceived this new thing this way. For example, you could draw a picture showing the

results of your meetings instead of writing them down in words. Do something that you've never been able to do. Over time, you'll lose the fear of the new. Reading new material also encourages curiosity. Plan to read a book on a regular basis — preferably, by an author you don't know yet. If you like historical romances, read a science fiction book or a thriller. You will discover new perspectives, gain new knowledge, and learn from it.

>> **Scrutinize everything:** Frequently ask why something is the way it is. Ask why toasters have to look the way they do. Question why a couch has to be comfortable. Or, have you already asked yourself why 5-year-olds ask the question "Why?" an average of 50 times a day, whereas you as an adult ask it only 4 times, if at all?

# Asking For (and Receiving) Support from the Top

A significant success factor in design thinking is that the company or department management supports you in your project. Ask for this support. Support can reveal itself in different forms. Design thinking requires collaboration across departmental and, often, corporate boundaries. The company and department management can pave the way for these kinds of collaborations by making the support of your design thinking project mandatory at a higher hierarchical level. It helps when the company and department managers know the advantages and opportunities of design thinking and work to highlight the significance, necessity, and urgency of your design challenge whenever appropriate.

TIP

During meetings at the level of company and department management, the design challenge should be a regular item on the agenda. Other opportunities for getting the word out include presentations from managers or talks with employees and business partners in which the significance of your task is communicated.

Ultimately, support is also shown when the necessary resources are made available to you in the form of employees, devices, materials, machines, or capital. Because design thinking is a process that involves baby steps, the financing can be arranged according to milestones. (You can find out more about milestones in Chapter 5.) In my experience, having milestones speeds the approval process when it comes to releasing resources.

# Asking For (and Receiving) Creative Freedom

When you execute a design thinking project, demand that you be given the ability to make as many decisions as possible within the project team itself. Creative freedom among employees boosts their sense of responsibility, serves to motivate employees, and frees up the management team so that they can focus their energies on strategic decisions.

This freedom can initially refer to the approach that's taken. If the What was coordinated with the company and department management ("What should the design challenge achieve?"), then the responsibility for the How ("How should the task be solved?") lies with the project team. Clarify who at the company is responsible for what in the design thinking project. This is best done in writing with a *design brief,* where you summarize the task and goals, the target users, the time span, and the financial scope — just try keep it to one page or, at most, three pages. (For more on design brief, check out Chapter 5.)

The freedom can also refer to working hours. Here, the employees get time quotas they can pick and choose, where they may engage in creative tasks from a design thinking approach — nondirected time.

TIP

For the project's design brief, plan to free up about 15 percent of a team member's working hours from specific work packages. Without setting any preconditions, have your employees use this time in any way they consider meaningful. Make financial resources available at the same percentage level so that the employees can access them. (You can find out more in Chapter 16 about establishing creative freedom at the company in order to foster a culture of innovation.)

# Enabling Fast Decisions in the Design Thinking Process

During a design thinking project, you have to make numerous decisions — how to define the specific task, for example, or how the project should be executed, with which resources, and in which time frame. Not everything will be decided by you alone. Depending on the content, scope, and significance of the project and the company size, you may have to involve people from other departments and on different hierarchy levels in order to make the required decisions.

# Setting up the steering committee

Most of the time, when you want to get a project off the ground, you start out by convening a steering committee. That's fine, but you must set down a number of preconditions so that this steering committee can act quickly. Initially, the steering committee should be assembled in such a way that the design thinking project draws meaningful and dedicated support. Make sure that all relevant decision-makers are represented. Often, you can master the tasks in design thinking only on an interdisciplinary and interdepartmental level. You must involve representatives in research, development, production, marketing, and sales — and in some cases even from legal and patents — because they provide needed context and will either play decisive roles in the subsequent implementation of the idea or be responsible for releasing resources. The makeup of the group of participants can change as long as a certain staff continuity is maintained in the course of a design thinking project. The number of members on the steering committee should be limited to five to nine people; otherwise, it will be difficult to make effective and efficient decisions.

# Clarifying responsibilities

After you have clarified the composition of the steering committee, define the committee's responsibilities and procedures. The committee should do one of the following:

>> Concentrate on ensuring that the employees in the design thinking project share information with the relevant departments

>> Take on advisory functions

>> Be responsible for releasing the required resources (personnel, material, machines, capital)

Clarify which of these responsibilities belongs to the steering panel.

TIP

Schedule specific times for the steering committee sessions early on and set time limits. The meeting should take place only if there's an agenda with a decision paper to discuss or important information that needs to be disseminated.

# Preparing the decision in an efficient manner

A week before the meeting, ask for the submission of the decision paper. You have to determine who gets sent this document, with which maximum scope, and through which medium (in paper form or electronically). Prepare this paper according to the criteria for the decision to be made and with the language and level of detail appropriate for the decision-making individuals.

EXAMPLE

Suppose that you want to get resources so that your team can create a prototype by way of a 3D printing process. Without much technical detail, explain that the prototype will be able to give you qualified customer feedback about the product's user friendliness. If you want to perform an extensive observational study of the customers and need a new job position for this task, describe the benefit of this action and the concrete tasks for this job.

TIP

It helps if you define standard templates and guidelines for the reports at the company level in order to reduce the reporting effort and ensure that the decision-makers can immediately receive the information they need. If necessary, clarify any questions about the results verbally with the project manager beforehand.

## Conducting the decision-making process in an efficient manner

All authorized decision-makers need to be at the table during meetings so that decisions can be made without further consultations. Anyone who either doesn't care to or can't participate either tacitly agrees to whatever decision is made or has to send an authorized representative to express their views.

WARNING

Avoid virtual meetings. Make sure that all participants are physically present during the meetings. A meeting where some of the participants are connected via video or even a completely virtual meeting should be an alternative only when quick decisions have to be made. Video conferences require extensive preparation and should be used only — if at all — during less-extensive design thinking projects.

TIP

For the steering committee meeting, appoint a discussion leader or moderator who doesn't necessarily have the highest rank and isn't a primary decision-maker. The team leader of the design thinking project must be present for the entire discussion.

During the steering committee meeting, the project manager should present for 15 minutes without interruption, though the number of slides should be limited. The presentation must focus on critical (new) aspects and on the main results. It's not helpful if you repeat something already stated in the project report. Limit the number of questions and comments as well as their duration.

Clearly structure the decision-making process during the meeting. The decision must be made in the steering committee. It should be unambiguous for everyone.

Clear go-and-stop decisions are helpful. *Go* means that all requested resources will be available promptly. A Go can also be associated with conditions. For example, your team might still have to perform technical tests about the feasibility of the product or prove the potential customer acceptance with a customer survey. *Stop* means the end of the project and thus the dissolution of the project team.

## Following up on decisions

To ensure continuous improvement, there should be a critical review of the degree to which the meetings were effective and efficient. This is the purpose of the following questions, which the chairperson or moderator should answer for themselves after every meeting:

» Is the composition of the steering committee appropriate for the task of the design thinking project?

» Were the preparation and organization optimal?

» Was the process expedient, and was there enough time to complete the tasks specified in the decision paper?

Learn from the answers to these questions, and continue to improve the decision-making process.

# Tolerating Mistakes During Design Thinking

Design thinking doesn't work without mistakes, and without mistakes, you won't get design thinking to work. The tasks of design thinking carry a high level of uncertainty and complexity — an uncertainty and complexity that results in mistakes when it comes to planning the costs and time spent, for example. The thing is, you can definitely learn from mistakes during design thinking. Analyze why potential customers reject a function of your new product's prototype, for example. With that information in hand, you can improve the functions, completely redesign them, or eliminate them entirely.

TIP

Make sure that mistakes are recognized as a fixed component in the design thinking process and are considered learning opportunities. The best way to communicate examples is from your own company, showing how mistakes led to specific improvements or even innovations. The development of new products, services, procedures and business models is a double learning process, in that they result from successes as well as mistakes.

When mistakes are recognized as an integral part of reality and as a learning opportunity, dealing with them becomes easier. Mistakes can then be considered "supposed mistakes," meaning you see them as normal events that you have to analyze objectively and rationally so that you can gain new knowledge from them and derive measures to resolve them.

# Defining mistakes

Clarifying what you actually consider a mistake at the company creates an understanding among all employees involved in the design thinking process, eliminates their fear of mistakes, and is the foundation for further analyses that lead to learning. The following questions should be answered here:

>> What is actually called a mistake? What is not a mistake?

>> How is a mistake evaluated?

>> Who gets to call something a mistake?

Because the term *mistake* usually has a negative connotation, feel free to use other, more neutral expressions, such as these:

>> Change

>> Deviation

>> Difference

>> Discovery or learning achievement

>> Discrepancy

>> Divergence

>> Improvement or optimization potential

>> ...onformity

...press it, everyone should know what is understood by it.

# Looking at mistakes in a differentiated way

Not all mistakes are the same and not all cause the same amount of pain. Although the definition of a mistake ultimately depends on the observer, it's also possible to define *intelligent mistakes* — ones that are not only not penalized but are also desirable. You can characterize intelligent mistakes this way:

>> **The task was well-planned, and a calculable risk was taken.** You took the time to thoroughly plan the design thinking project. (You can find out more about planning in Chapter 4.) Part of this planning process involved your estimating the risk of potential deviations from the goals, schedules, and costs of the project. You knew that estimating the risk always means that you quantify the probability that the deviation will occur and that you describe the potential consequences from it. You estimated the technical risk by assessing the occurrence of technical-quality defects at less than 10 percent and evaluated consequences in case the development time was extended by six months.

>> **The task was important.** Assumptions about the customer played a key role in the project. (There's no need to discuss mistakes made in unimportant tasks.)

>> **It wasn't possible to foresee the results.** You planned the specific task with your team (you can find more info about this topic in Chapter 9) and then compared the result with your planning.

>> **Fast feedback about the mistake was provided.** You encouraged the team members to report a possible mistake or deviation promptly. Keep in mind that the sooner you find out about the mistake, the better you can react to it. If the employees don't have to worry about drawbacks, they will communicate the mistakes quickly and comprehensively.

TIP

It helps if you delineate the characteristics of intelligent mistakes in advance in a task-specific way and communicate this to everyone involved. (What is meant by "well-planned"? What is a calculable risk? What are important tasks? What does "prompt and comprehensive feedback about the mistake" mean?)

# Find the Competencies You Need for the Task at Hand

The success of design thinking projects depends entirely on having t̶ competencies for the analysis and solution of your task on your te̶ during your design challenge, systematically identify the skills̶ of the team and adapt them according to the task. The following sections show you how.

## Determining the target competencies

Define the required competencies in terms of the personnel, materials, and finances you'll need for the design challenge. The staff competencies are often in the foreground. Clarify which professional competencies you need for your task. In design thinking, the tasks often have an interdisciplinary character. That's why you should consider which professional disciplines are helpful when it comes to understanding the task and subsequently finding the solution. (For more on team makeup, see Chapter 5.) You have to clarify the following questions with your team:

>> Which competencies are required in order to understand the task and find the solution?

>> Which professional disciplines do you need to have on the team?

**WARNING**

Don't concentrate on just the technical competencies. Pay equal attention to the communicative and social skills of the individual team members. Design thinking is based on the needs of people. For design thinking to work, you must understand your potential customers and be able to communicate with them.

## Taking stock of the actual competencies

When you take stock of your team competencies, identify the presence and distribution of the key staff members who are relevant for the design challenge. When you define the ideal target state, the multitude of potential competencies you could imagine necessarily leads to your having to make a choice. The selection always depends on the specific design challenge. To this end, you have to have the company clarify the following questions:

>> Which personnel-related, material, and financial competencies relevant to the design challenge are present at the company?

>> Which employees or employee groups have which task-relevant competencies, and in which form?

>> Which employees use task-relevant competencies every day?

# Comparing the target and actual competencies and coming up with the next steps

You have to contrast the required (target) and existing (actual) competencies. You can close the gap by way of advanced training of the internal employees or the external cooperative partners. The advanced training activities tend to have a long-term impact for the development of a culture of innovation at the company. (For more on that topic, see Chapter 16.) Examples of external cooperative partners are suppliers, customers, scientific establishments (colleges and other research institutes), consultants, authorities, and associations. By working with these partners, you can be provided with the competencies that are missing in the design thinking project for the short and medium terms.

To make that contrast visible, ask yourself the following questions:

>> Which task-relevant competencies are lacking at the company?

>> Which task-relevant competencies can you develop in the short term with internal advanced training?

>> Which task-relevant competencies can be acquired through external cooperative partners?

>> Which competencies must be developed at the company over the long term?

# Checking the competencies on an ongoing basis

You shouldn't understand the three steps outlined in the preceding sections as a one-time procedure exclusively at the start of the project. Over the course of the design thinking project, you're getting an increasingly in-depth understanding of the design challenge. You receive information about the technical feasibility and the customer benefit and then identify details of your task. The solution may also require additional competencies in other disciplines.

TIP

Regularly review to what extent you need additional competencies. The analysis of a technical procedure, for example, might show you that purely mechanical solutions aren't ideal. That would mean you would also have to look for competencies in the electronics field if you want your process development efforts to succeed.

# Ensuring that the work is appreciated

Part of preparing for design thinking is that you previously define ways to show appreciation for the completed work. At the end of a long haul, one tends to forget to praise the team and show one's appreciation. Keep in mind that you'd be wrong to write off design thinking as a one-time activity. Design thinking is a process that shapes the corporate culture for the long term. You can master this process in a sustainable fashion only with motivated employees. Appreciation and praise are indispensable when it comes to motivating a team.

The form of appreciation ranges from qualified feedback, openly expressed praise, positive written evaluations, articles in a company magazine, recommendations to colleagues — all the way to material prizes (travel, food, theater, dinner with the executive board) and financial rewards as well as promotions. In practice, contributions to innovative ideas are often encouraged with prizes (known as *innovation awards*), either in financial or less pecuniary forms. Shared celebrations after the design thinking processes are completed are also an appreciation (frequently underestimated) for the performance of a team.

IN THIS CHAPTER

» Clarifying and communicating the
  purpose of the project

» Structuring the work

» Organizing the order and duration
  of the work

» Estimating the project materials
  and costs

# Chapter **4**

# Planning a Design Thinking Project

One commonly held opinion states that what we call *planning* is in reality a process whereby you replace the effects of chance with a mistake you've knowingly entered into. There's no way to predict the future with certainty. Plans can never be followed 100 percent. However, with limited resources and deadline pressure for your design thinking project, plans are inevitable. Design thinking without a plan is like a night flight through mountains using just the naked eye — in other words, a blind flight in a dangerous environment with no compass. Plans are the compass you need for the success of your project so that you can clarify your goals, save on project expenses, adhere to deadlines, recognize deviations in the project's progress, and make necessary changes.

In this chapter, you find out how to collect, formulate, and communicate your goals. This becomes the basis for deriving the work packages for your task — the write-ups describing the individual work steps in the project. An agile approach helps in the planning of design thinking projects so that you can intervene quickly and flexibly if the project course changes. Sequence planning gives you and your team an orientation guide on how to complete the project. In this chapter, I give some recommendations on how to plan resources so that you can realistically estimate the number of required employees, machines, and materials. You also find out about budget planning techniques and how to avoid typical errors when estimating costs.

# Defining the Project Goals

Defining your project goals is necessary for a design thinking project to succeed. A project goal describes in detail what you want to end up with at the end of the entire process. The result might be a functional prototype of a product or a concept for a new range of services or a newly designed business model. A clear and realistic definition of the project goal is part of the design brief.

In the *design brief*, you describe your goals, work packages, milestones, required resources, and the budget needed on no more than three pages. The design brief is your guide to the subsequent project work. At the conclusion of the project, you review whether you have reached the goals in the design brief.

The benefit of a clear goal definition is shown by these functions:

>> **Orientation:** You have a basis for your planning and know where you want to end up. This encourages a results-oriented work method in your design thinking team.

>> **Control:** You can control your initiative when the goals are clear and detailed. You have a foundation for a meaningful assessment of the project result.

>> **Motivation:** Having shared goals creates a sense of unity on the team.

When it comes to how things work in the real world, you often encounter a certain fuzziness with regard to goals. This has a negative impact on the implementation. Such fuzziness can be caused by these factors:

>> **Lack of time:** My advice — take enough time to clearly and comprehensibly work through the project goals with everyone involved. Design thinking requires clear goals. The design thinking process starts with the definition of the task (for more on that, see Chapter 6). As you make your way through the project, you'll have to delineate the task *again*. (For more on this process, see Chapter 9.) This gives you multiple occasions during the process where you can analyze the project goals.

>> **Incorrect perception of the nature of your goals:** Goals can be misunderstood so that they impede design freedom and creativity. As a result of this misperception, the formulated goals — if any — are unspecific. In design thinking, you define specific goals — goals that you understand to be changeable. You start with a goal, and as you progress with design thinking, you realize that you have to change this goal.

>> **Going out of your way to avoid conflict in the goal definition process:** Design thinking tasks often include a whole set of goals, which can be a problem if individual team members have different ideas about the goal and

end up competing for limited resources. Multiple goals are possible if you want to develop a new product — a large TV with a roll-up display, for example. The technicians on the team want to optimize the screen resolution, whereas the marketing and sales representatives are aiming for a product that customers can use intuitively. The production department, on the other hand, wants the TV to be manufactured easily and economically. A limited budget and time are available for your project. Confront the differing agendas of competing teams by resolving these conflicting interests upfront. Compile the possible goals and, as a team, order them according to their importance and their urgency, as spelled out in the next section.

## Compiling goals and determining their order

After you have decided on a task (for more on that process, see Chapter 6), you, along with your team, need to compile possible goals for your project. The project can refer to just one phase in the design thinking process, or it can comprise the entire process, from formulating the task to testing your idea. (For a complete overview of the design thinking process, check out Chapter 1.)

**TIP**

If the tasks are extensive and complicated, it helps if you first focus your project on an individual phase in the design thinking process. In the first phase, for example, you have to get a detailed understanding of the task. Together with your team, list your goals for what you must learn about the task by the end of that phase.

Make a selection based on the significance of the goals. A helpful differentiation for the first (rough) determination of the significance of the goals is described in this list:

>> **Mandatory goals:** You must absolutely achieve these in order to successfully complete the project. A mandatory goal for many product development projects is that the product must run flawlessly.

>> **Desired goals:** You may want to implement these later, if you still have the time and the available resources. Desired goals are often geared toward optimization — that the product must have an attractive design, for example.

>> **Non-goals:** Don't target these goals.

**WARNING**

In the real world, people are reluctant to express non-goals. That's why you should take the initiative, clearly designate non-goals, and then communicate them to all project participants. Non-goals can refer to studies or properties and functions that shouldn't be pursued in the project.

**EXAMPLE**

Suppose that your new product idea is an intelligent mirror that uses facial recognition to detect the person in front of the mirror and display personalized information on its surface, depending on the time of day (weather forecast, traffic information, calendar entries, political, and economic news). The goal is to improve facial recognition. You designate other possible improvements for the mirror — such as image resolution, mirror image, new content-specific functions or gesture control — as non-goals in the project.

You determine the order of the goals by having your team weigh them. Use a rating scale from 1 (insignificant) to 6 (extremely significant) to assess the individual goals. (For more on additional rating methods, see Chapter 12.) Make sure that the selected goals don't contradict each other. If you want to lower costs and at the same time increase the quality of service, this can lead to a conflict. Overcoming this contradiction with an innovative solution might also be the express objective of the design thinking project.

## Clearly formulating goals

When you formulate project goals, I recommend that you follow the SMART criteria — *s*pecific, *m*easurable, *a*mbitious (or accepted), *r*ealistic (or relevant), and *t*ime-bound:

>> **Specific:** Goals are formulated with unmistakable, unambiguous, and precise wording. It's clear what the project is intended to achieve. For example, you should define in more detail the goal of developing an athletic shoe made completely of renewable resources. You specify the target users (young, environmentally conscious women between 16 and 25 years old) and the place and conditions for usage (when jogging in a forest or on the street).

>> **Measurable:** Define the degrees of achieving your goal so that the project result becomes measurable. The goal is reached, for example, when "at least" or "at most" a certain number is attained. During the phase of finding ideas, you can set the goal of developing five implementable ideas for the team.

**WARNING**

"In design thinking, the goals aren't measurable; that would stifle design freedom and creativity." This is a common statement in design thinking workshops. The response to this is, "Well, then, how do you know when you have reached your goal?" A goal doesn't always have to be measurable in terms of cold, hard cash. The goal you set might be, for example, the satisfaction of the potential customer with a new service idea or a reduction of operating errors in an innovative product.

>> **Ambitious (or accepted):** Ambitious goals present a challenge and thus have a motivating effect. A slight improvement of an existing product doesn't make the heart race. A material that is simultaneously light, flexible, stable, and

biodegradable presents a (welcome) technical challenge. (*Accepted* is used as an alternative: The goals are recognized by all project participants.)

**EXAMPLE**

>> **Realistic (or relevant):** These goals can be implemented with the resources, competencies, and planned time expenditures under the internal and external framework conditions.

Your goal is the development of an innovative dishwasher. Your company is providing a research budget of over a million dollars; the employees have experience with the development of such a machine; and the development is scheduled within 20 months. You can reach this goal. (Relevant is also used as an alternative: In this case, only significant goals are set.)

>> **Time-bound:** Every goal includes a specific timeline. (You want to gain 10,000 paying customers with your new online shop within one year, for example.)

Don't stick too rigidly to this requirement for clearly defined goals. Your goals can change during the course of the project because you increasingly receive information about not only your task but also any subsequent solutions. The SMART criteria create a good guideline for keeping the required overview of the goals, but they are no more than that.

When you formulate your goal, make sure that you word it in a solution-neutral way. What does that mean in concrete terms? Let's say you want to reduce the time to process customer orders for a service. The goal — an acceleration of customer orders by using instant messaging — already defines the means (instant messaging) to reach the goal. The thing is, you can also accelerate processes with different kinds of changes (overlapping activities, automating processing steps, elimination of waiting times). Separate the goal from possible approaches to the solution.

**TIP**

Summarize your goal in a maximum of three sentences to keep it comprehensible. Describe your goal in a positive way. Instead of saying "We don't want the customer to have to wait for the delivery," say "We want the customer to save 30 minutes during each process."

## Communicating goals

Record the project goals in writing to confirm them. This strategy ensures that everyone involved has the same idea when it comes to the project, that there are no misunderstandings, and that the progress can be measured against the goals at any time.

The formulation of the goal should help make all project participants aware of the existing project goals. The project team performs this goal definition process in coordination with the client or steering committee. You must ensure that the goals are accepted by the customer or client as well as by the project team.

Otherwise, you must complete the steps again so that the project participants accept the goals. The participants' understanding of the goals results in increasing responsibility.

Goals can change in the course of a project. When that happens, you must make goal changes transparent and communicate them to everyone involved in the project. If the goal change is significant, you may have to terminate the project prematurely. If necessary, show the will and the courage to implement the project termination in time.

**WARNING**

In case of projects for new products or services or a business model, you run the risk of becoming entangled in what I call *secondary aspects.* You discover that your project idea is also of interest to other target users. The other target users may demand that you adapt your product idea to fit their needs, under the mistaken belief that you can easily make the adaptations they want on the side. However, the simultaneous pursuit of multiple solutions often can't be handled with just a few tests. Frequently, the time frame and resources are inadequate for working on multiple approaches in a project at the same time. This situation can be prevented by clearly defining the goal at the start. Secondary aspects that emerged from the design thinking project must be executed in a new project with its own time frame, budget, and resources.

## Planning Work Packages

Work packages are derived from the goals. Depending on the project issue and design thinking phase, work packages may include different items, such as the execution of observational studies or surveys, the development and testing of prototypes, or the search for and development of new functions and process steps or new concepts for services or business models.

For a design thinking initiative, the idea is to plan and execute the project according to an agile method. You can implement this by following these steps:

**1.** **Have the project team write down all necessary work packages, in any order.**

**2.** **Ask what has to be done to reach the selected goal.**

   You can use creativity techniques such as brainstorming or mind mapping. (For more on these techniques, see Chapters 10 and 11.)

**3.** **Arrange as few work packages as possible, but as many as necessary.**

**4.** **Assign higher-level terms to the activities, such as**

   • *Phases:* In a design thinking project, such phases would include understanding the task, searching for solutions, creating a prototype, and testing proposed solutions with the customer.

- *Objects:* These can be the components of a product, such as the display, buttons, housing, or battery for a smartphone.

- *Functions:* In online retail, these might be functions such as product comparison, order processing, delivery, and customer service.

When assigning terms, always ask yourself, "What is a part of what?" The object "wheel" consists of tire and rim, whereas the customer service function can include handling warranty matters, processing customer complaints, and dealing with inquiries and orders. Piece by piece, this creates an arrangement that you must always check for completeness. The results of all the work packages must lead to the attainment of your goal.

## Planning work packages for incremental progress at just the right time

When the project starts, the work packages aren't specific yet; rather, they're abstract and associated with a lot of work. Initially, you plan the most important and most pressing work packages in detail. The new information during the project lets you incrementally plan the additional work packages at the appropriate time. This means that the planning is incremental and needs-oriented — "just in time," or when something is impending. When you complete a step, the progress and development outside of the project have improved the information base. Now you can make a better plan for the next step. Delay the planning of the work packages until the last justifiable moment so that you can take the most updated information into account.

With this agile approach, you can quickly and flexibly integrate changes — ideally, in the form of customer feedback — into your planning at an early stage. Changes that are both justified and desired can be advantageous for design thinking projects. In this process, you accept that you don't have all the information right at the start and that, no, you won't do everything correctly, right out of the gate.

This planning method can be illustrated with the pencil-and-pen rule: Your next steps are written permanently with pen, whereas the later steps are outlined in pencil and can easily be changed.

**TIP**

If you can't specifically describe the contents of a work package, you lack the necessary information. Closing this information gap should be the subject of a work package. Consider how you might attain the information. You have several options: You can implement observational studies or surveys, conduct experiments, search for literature, or work your way through the patent databases.

# Formulating and determining the work package order from the user's perspective

With an agile approach, you should formulate the work packages in the form of user stories. User stories help the communication between project participants and describe, in a single sentence, what you need to achieve with a work package. The user stories should be worded so briefly that they fit on an index card or a sticky note. This brevity forces you to precisely describe the necessary information about the work package.

In the description, it can be helpful if you apply the how-might-we technique to answer the following question in a single sentence:

> How might we achieve our goal _____ with the following restrictions _____ so that our target user _____ receives the following benefit _____?

The restrictions can be limited resources (capital, personnel, equipment) or legal or ethical framework conditions. The target user can be a customer or user group. Focusing on the target user's benefit helps you keep your eyes on the goal.

**TIP**

Describe your user stories to someone from outside the industry. This means you have to word your user stories without technical language. Afterward, ask this person to tell you the user stories in their own words. If you spot any discrepancies, you'll also spot the gaps in your stories.

The cards with the user stories are the contact points for discussions within the team. The many possible work packages must be ordered in sequence. One approach is the MoSCoW ranking, which is an acronym for the following evaluation criteria:

>> **Must have:** These user stories are absolutely mandatory for understanding your task or for the functioning of your proposed solution.

>> **Should have:** These user stories are important and should be created.

>> **Could have:** These user stories aren't necessarily relevant, but they can be implemented if the resources are available.

>> **Won't have this time:** There is no time for these user stories.

Two instances of the lowercase letter *o* are added to the term so that it can be remembered more easily in the form of MoSCoW, the Russian capital. As a team, review whether and how the user stories depend on each other. One work package may have to be completed before the next work package can start. You have to clarify the technical and economic requirements for every user story. Technical projects require the availability of equipment or tools. Personnel or resources can meet the economic requirements for a work package.

On the back of the card with the user story, you can define a condition for satisfaction that meets the goal of the work package from the customer's point of view. Here's a possible format for the condition for satisfaction:

When the work package _____ is finished, the following result _____ should take place from the user's perspective.

An acceptance test with the potential customer is carried out for this purpose. You can list the user stories in a table and add (brief) information in columns, such as the number of the user story, a short description (one sentence), a reference to dependencies on other user stories, the conditions for satisfaction, the priority, the estimated effort, and, finally, the potential risks as well as the responsibilities and comments.

## Using a task board

When it comes to work packages, you can illustrate your progress with the help of a task board; it's a useful tool for communicating to everyone involved the extent of the project's progress. You can use this task board to differentiate on a timeline the various development stages of the design thinking project. The task board can show the progress of the entire project with the help of user stories. Sort such stories into just three stages: Ready, In Development, and Done. (You can use table columns to demarcate these stages.) Based on the progress, the individual user stories can be moved into the relevant column on a card or a sticky note. If there you find any problems with a particular work package (deadlines can't be met or the work package requires more personnel, for example), stick a black dot on the card. You can find an example of a task board in Figure 4-1.

Write the name of each individual work package on a card, and sort them on the task board according to each development stage. You can choose different colors for technical and marketing work packages. The left column, labeled To Do, contains all work packages at the start of the project. Sort the cards in the order of their ranking, from top to bottom. (This ranking also lets you know which work packages have the best chances of being carried out.) When work packages are ready to process, the person in charge moves the work package card to the right, into the Ready column. When work has started, it's moved to the In Progress column — under the In Development heading. The In Progress column should always hold a card in for each team member. If the processing has been completed successfully, the project manager can move the card to Developed.

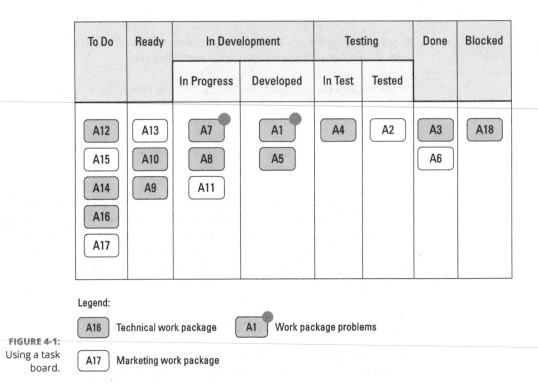

| To Do | Ready | In Development | | Testing | | Done | Blocked |
|---|---|---|---|---|---|---|---|
| | | In Progress | Developed | In Test | Tested | | |
| A12 | A13 | A7 | A1 | A4 | A2 | A3 | A18 |
| A15 | A10 | A8 | A5 | | | A6 | |
| A14 | A9 | A11 | | | | | |
| A16 | | | | | | | |
| A17 | | | | | | | |

Legend:

| A16 | Technical work package |
| A1 | Work package problems |
| A17 | Marketing work package |

**FIGURE 4-1:**
Using a task
board.

The Testing column follows. Each result of a work package should be tested from either a technical perspective or the customer's viewpoint. Here, *testing* can represent a technical feasibility test for technical work packages, for example, or a customer survey if the work package relates to marketing. The Testing column can include the subcolumn In Test with work packages being executed. The person in charge of the work package moves the card into this column. When the test has been successfully completed, the project manager moves the card into the subcolumn Tested. Subsequently, the project manager moves the card to Done or Blocked. *Done* indicates that the contents of the work package have been completed and the conditions for satisfaction have been met. The Blocked column refers to a case where major issues have led you to stop the processing of this particular user story. Issues here might be a lack of resources (the person working on it might be absent due to illness) or technical errors in the processing.

As a team, discuss the significance of the individual development stages before the project starts. Each team member must have the same understanding of what's involved. You should clarify to the team exactly what the stages Ready and Done mean for your task. The Ready status can be understood as follows:

» Everyone understands the contents of the work package.

» The dependencies to other work packages are recognized and pose no barriers to the processing.

>> The team has the required skills and means for the execution.

>> The effort in terms of time was estimated, which revealed that the work package could fit into the planned schedule.

>> The criteria for the successful completion of the work package are clear, known to everyone, and verifiable.

>> The team knows how to process the work package.

You can describe the Done status as follows:

>> All work is complete, or there is no further work.

>> The work package was checked for completion according to the four-eyes principle — approved by at least two people, in other words.

>> The feasibility (for technical work packages) or the conditions for the customer's satisfaction (for marketing-related work packages) has been met or was ensured with tests.

>> No high-importance items remain open.

>> The results are documented.

>> The client or customer has accepted the work package.

You can display the task board on a whiteboard or a metaplan wall and then place it in a work room so that everyone can always see the progress being made. The daily meetings can take place in this room, and the cards can be moved according to the latest status.

In addition to the task board, you can document items that still need to be clarified on an open-items list (a to-do list, in other words) and track them. The open-items list should include the following aspects:

>> **Serial number:** A number that makes it easy to quickly record the work packages

>> **Name:** A short name for the open item; can refer to the structure of the project and can mirror your chosen name for the work packages

>> **Date:** The day on which the open item was reported

>> **Person notifying:** The person who placed this open item on the list

>> **Urgency:** Rated as High, Medium, or Low

>> **Person-in-charge:** The person who has to clarify the open item

>> **Collaboration with:** A list of persons or departments that have to be involved in the clarification process

>> **Resource expenditure:** An estimate of the expenditure for the personnel, equipment, or investment capital needed to clarify the open item

>> **Done:** Describes the condition at which the open item has been clarified

>> **By when:** The deadline by which the open item must be clarified

>> **Status:** The current status of the clarification; can range from Open to In Progress to Done.

By using the task board and open-items list, you're providing a comprehensive overview of the project's progress and encouraging the project team to share information. Each team member is informed about the status of the total project, the state of each work package, and any problems that occur.

# Correctly Planning for the Sequence

Sequence planning involves the scheduling of the work packages. With sequence planning, you determine the logical succession of the work packages. A rough framework to follow here would mirror the phases of the design thinking process — such as understanding the task, searching for solutions, creating a prototype, and testing the proposed solution with the customer. You assign the work packages to the individual phases in the form of a process list, where you determine a rough timeline and logical sequence for the work packages in the course of the project. For the detailed planning, you identify the logical and functional dependencies of each task by evaluating their relationships to preceding tasks. You ask which work packages must be finished, or at least started, with an interim result before you can initiate the work package in question. You start finding ideas only when you have determined the correct target users and have defined the concrete task. You start manufacturing the product when you have successfully tested the prototype with the customer.

In addition to planning the sequence, you should define milestones. A milestone represents a certain moment in time but has no intrinsic set duration. It serves as an interim goal, where the progress of the project can be reviewed and a decision can be made about how to proceed (using Go to continue or Kill to terminate the project). Milestones should be set at the end of each project phase. In design thinking, you can describe the results of each phase by using Task Defined, Target Users Identified, Idea for Solution Developed, Prototype Created, and Test Successfully Completed with the Customer.

Limit the number of milestones in a project and consider these guidelines:

>> One milestone for every two to three months

>> At least four milestones per project

>> At least one milestone at the three-month interval

Laying down milestones has a motivating effect on the employees. When the team reaches an important milestone, be sure to celebrate it with them.

## Estimating the required time

After specifying the sequence of the individual work packages, you have to estimate their duration. You can use the following resources when coming up with an estimate:

>> Values based on experiences from completed projects

>> Time estimates based on expert opinions

>> Analogies (by searching for comparable projects and estimating the duration of the individual work packages)

>> The degree of difficulty and novelty of the task (the more difficult and unique the task, the more time that should be planned for it)

TIP

If only specific time slots are available for bottleneck resources or tasks, be sure to incorporate buffer times as a way to smooth out the process. Durations should always be estimated independently of any concrete ideas regarding the deadline, because such ideas would strongly influence the time estimate itself. Set aside a particular time requirement (5 to 15 percent of the total time needed) for the coordination of your design thinking project. For design thinking projects, you should plan in some detail how long the initial work packages will take and then plan the later phases more roughly.

## Creating a bar graph for a better overview

The best way to illustrate the timeline is a bar graph, which is also referred to as a Gantt chart (after its inventor, Henry Laurence Gantt). Bar graphs are used to create the sequence planning as a basis for status reports and to present the time-related aspects of the project, as shown in Figure 4-2.

The Y axis shows the representation of the project course in the form of the work packages, and the X axis refers to the time units in bar form. The length of the bar is used as a yardstick for the time needed for the work packages. If multiple work packages are occurring simultaneously, the bars are shown on top of each other. Bar graphs can be created and read easily and quickly. In a bar graph, you can record special activities, such as milestones (usually in the form of a rhombus).

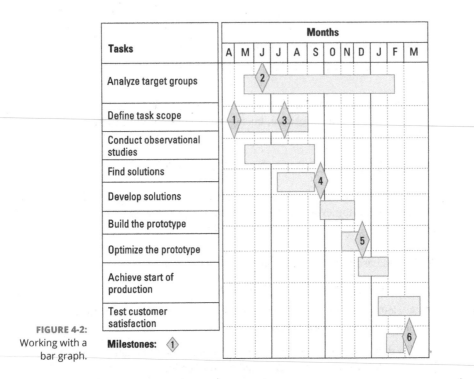

# Correctly Planning for Your Resources

*Resources* are the materials you use to work on a project. Three kinds of resources can be differentiated:

>> **People (personnel):** Internal and external employees

>> **Machines (operating materials):** Machines, tools, software, or rooms

>> **Material (raw materials, auxiliary materials, operating materials, or supplied parts):** The consumables for your project

To keep to your deadlines as well as for cost reasons, it's important that you plan these resources precisely. You have to determine which resources you need and in what amount so that the work packages can be completed. The resources should be available in the right form and quality, in the right amount, at the right time, and in the right place. The personnel must have the required qualifications. (Individuals with special qualifications are always bottleneck resources in design thinking projects.) You also need to ascertain whether all other resources are available or must be obtained (computers, printers, office furniture, and the equipment and tools necessary to make the prototype).

The work packages form the basis of the resource planning. Each work package is considered individually by estimating the amount of work required (presumably) to reach the goal. The shorter and more detailed that the work package is described in the form of user stories, the more easily you can determine the resources.

**WARNING**

Don't assume that the resources are fully available; an availability of 60 to 80 percent seems realistic. Don't forget the effort for the project coordination, which alone may occupy 20 percent of the work time in design thinking projects.

When you estimate the effort for a work package, be sure to integrate the persons responsible. All members should initially estimate their own required effort for each of the individual activities. When that task is complete, compare the results and wait for the group reach an agreement for a shared value. Start the discussion with the central, most important tasks. At the end, have the group check again to see whether the estimated values for the individual work packages make sense in relation to one other. It's advantageous when all team members, as a result of the shared discussion, know the effort involved in the individual work packages and are aware of the assumptions on which the estimates are based. This reduces the risk of misunderstanding. The employees should report if they notice, later in the course of their work, that the effort is higher than the estimate. Keep in mind that effort estimates for new subjects tend to be too low instead of too high.

**TIP**

You can plan your resources by means of a 3-point estimate. Estimate an optimistic value, a realistic midlevel value, and a pessimistic value for the resources. Use the following formula with these three values to determine the total estimated value:

$$Resource\ needs = \frac{OV + 4MV + PV}{6}$$

OV stands for *optimistic value*, MV for *midlevel (realistic) value*, and PV for *pessimistic value*. The midlevel value is included in the result with fourfold weighting.

You need to closely coordinate the resource planning with the other planning tasks. Resources influence the scheduling through their availability, the goals (if tasks can be completed only with certain resources), and the costs.

Keep these suggestions in mind when it comes to resource planning:

>> If possible, use data and information from similar projects in the past.

> » Limit the damaging effects of multitasking, where employees work on multiple work packages at the same time and repeatedly switch back and forth.

> » In design thinking projects, having more resources available for a process doesn't necessarily mean that it goes faster.

**TIP**

Have the resources approved in writing by the persons in charge at the company.

# Correctly Planning for the Project Budget

The purpose of budget planning is for you to determine the project costs you'll use as the basis for determining budget allocations *and* to control costs during the project execution. You should apply an analytical cost method where the costs are determined for each work package and each resource. The foundation of all project calculations lies in resource planning. You have to estimate the various types of costs for each work package. The total project costs correspond to the sum of the costs of all work packages.

Possible types of costs

> » Personnel

> » Materials

> » Capital (interest)

> » External services (legal advice, market research, insurance)

> » Overhead

*Overhead* refers to the electricity costs of the buildings and rooms and other office spaces and the use of the canteen as well as general administrative services (human resource management, bookkeeping, and IT services, for example). You can't assign these costs directly to a project. This is why percentage surcharges are applied to the personnel costs. The amount, which can be based on the company's overhead rate, shouldn't be less than 20 percent of the total personnel costs.

**TIP**

If changes in the project effect the project budget, create an additional budget for each of the changes instead of just modifying the original budget. Changes occur frequently in design thinking projects and can have various causes, such as price increases for materials and external services or additional customer requests.

During the budget planning process, also look at the typical reasons for a poor cost estimate:

>> The project employees overestimate their own performance capacity.

>> Necessary work is forgotten.

>> The client has requirements that can't be implemented.

>> Changes in the design thinking project aren't accompanied by a correction of the cost estimate.

>> There's too much focus on goals and tasks that are nice to have but aren't necessary performance characteristics.

>> Risks are underestimated.

The cost planning ends with the budget allocation for the work packages. The persons in charge of the work packages are also responsible for the costs. If the expected project costs are higher than the project budget, the project management must coordinate this with the client or steering committee.

Chapter **5**

# Supporting Teamwork in the Project

D esign thinking comes alive through communication and collaboration between people — more specifically, between people who have different experiences, opinions, and characters — so that you can utilize the various perspectives, methods, and knowledge of the team members for the project's success. One way to ensure success for your project is to consider how to encourage communication and collaboration in the project team at an early stage.

This chapter starts by giving you an overview of what you should keep in mind when you assemble the team and assign responsibilities. This is followed by recommendations about rules and methods for successful communication within the project team. Since your design thinking teamwork takes place in workshops, you'll find suggestions on how to plan and implement your own. You need spaces and equipment that encourage communication and creativity for your teamwork. Lastly, I provide some ideas about room design and furnishings so that you can implement your teamwork flexibly and efficiently.

# Assembling the Team

In design thinking projects, a team has between five and nine members, gathered together in one place. A smaller group will lack the required amount of experience and the work capacity to master the tasks in a design thinking project. A team that has more than nine team members results in coordination problems that prevent fast and efficient action.

**TIP**

For the number of team members, note the "two-pizza rule:" Never have more team members than you can feed with two large pizzas. Keep in mind, though, that the number of people isn't truly decisive. Pay more attention to the composition of (and the distribution of responsibilities within) the team.

## Relying on variety in team makeup

The variety in the team composition — the team's *diversity,* in other words — is an essential principle in design thinking. Thanks to the various perspectives, levels of knowledge, skills, experiences, attitudes and values a truly diverse team provides, you'll be in a positon to solve the tasks you're facing. My advice to you: Ensure diversity in the team as you assemble it.

**WARNING**

Don't just consider characteristics such as age, gender, or ethnic affiliation in your efforts to make your team more diverse. Also look at the professional and personal experiences and values. These characteristics may not be so obvious, but they are central to effective teamwork.

A requirement profile that can help you select the proper team members involves the search for *T-shaped* individuals, where the *T* stands for the combination of a generalist (the horizontal bar of the *T*) and a specialist (the vertical bar of the *T*). Figure 5-1 shows the skill components and necessary areas of overlap for collaboration in the team. In T-shaped individuals, the breadth of the competence overlaps to make a successful collaboration possible. At the same time, they have a depth of competence that design thinking requires in order to complete a task. Always look for T-shaped persons to handle your design thinking tasks.

The vertical bar in the T describes the special knowledge and skills in a functional area that can be divided into theoretical and application competencies. Individuals who have only a specialized technical competence are described as *I-shaped* persons. In online marketing, this person might be the data analyst who has no other specific skills or experiences in the marketing area.

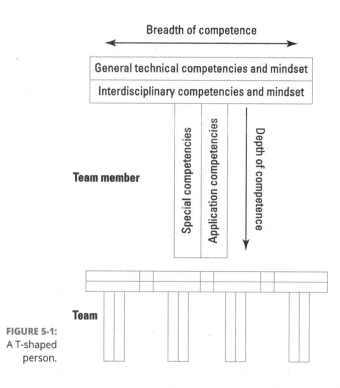

**Team member**

**Team**

Breadth of competence

General technical competencies and mindset

Interdisciplinary competencies and mindset

Special competencies

Application competencies

Depth of competence

FIGURE 5-1:
A T-shaped
person.

# T-SHAPED PEOPLE

In the letter *T*, the horizontal bar stands for the breadth of competence, which can
be divided into general professional competencies or mindsets and interdisciplinary
competencies or mindsets. The horizontal bar represents the generalist, who can collaborate beyond the boundaries of the discipline and function. When it comes to collab-
orative work, that person must have the general professional competencies necessary
in order to understand the technical language, methods, and approaches of other
disciplines. That person also needs to exhibit capacities such as leadership, communication, and cooperation skills, along with a mindset that promotes cooperation. Such a
cooperation-friendly mindset reveals itself through curiosity, openness, and empathy
toward other areas. Empathy — the ability to relate to another person — is a founda-
tional principle for success in design thinking. (You can find out more about empathy in
Chapter 7.)

# Defining roles on the team

The responsibilities for the individual work packages can be distributed according to the technical skills of team members. Each work package includes the work processes that relate to each other, and each has a person in charge. Divide the work packages if they become too complex. One person can work on a maximum of four work packages at a time; otherwise, the scope of the work is too large.

Determine the roles for the following management tasks:

>> A decision-maker for the distribution of resources within the project

>> A person in charge of the overall success of the project

>> A contact person for the steering committee, client, customers, and other external business partners (consultants, authorities, colleges, research institutes, or suppliers)

>> A contact person for reporting conflicts and problems confronting the team

>> An organizer and a moderator of team meetings

The individuals handling these various management tasks should have a good grasp of the company, motivate the team, be empowered to make decisions, and be capable of making said decisions. The individuals taking on these roles are representatives from a customer- or market-oriented area who have basic technical knowledge. Since these individuals work with the project team, steering committee, client, customer, and other business partners, they have to strike a balance between what is economically reasonable and technically feasible. They're responsible for the efficient use of resources.

# Creating a matrix of responsibility

The best way to settle responsibilities within the project team as well as with internal organizational units and external partners is with the aid of a matrix of responsibility, the *RACI matrix*. The word RACI is an acronym:

>> **R:** Responsible

>> **A:** Active (performs the activity)

>> **C:** Consulted (has to be coordinated with)

>> **I:** Informed (must be informed about whatever task is being worked on)

Table 5-1 shows the RACI matrix and offers an overview of the responsibilities associated with the design thinking project:

**TABLE 5-1**     **The RACI Matrix**

| | Responsible Steering Committee | Research | Marketing | Sales | Production |
|---|---|---|---|---|---|
| Define design challenge | C | A | R | I | I |
| Determine target users | R | C | A | C | I |
| Find ideas | C | A | R | I | C |
| Create prototype | C | R | I | I | A |
| Ask customers | C | I | A | R | I |

TIP

It wouldn't hurt to create a team directory with contact details, such as first and last name, email address, phone number, and information about availability and responsibilities in the team. Make the team directory available to everyone involved in the project.

## Applying the principle of self-organization

You want to distribute the individual work packages for fulfilling the design thinking task in the team according to the members' skills and competencies. Rather than have a project manager assign the work packages to the individual team members, they are discussed and distributed independently within the team. The team members themselves select their tasks — as many as they can work on.

TIP

If any work packages remain open after the distribution, you and the team have to discuss who can handle the work package and whether you need additional team members or external cooperative partners, such as consultants, colleges, or research institutes. Make sure that individual team members don't take on too much.

The principle of self-organization motivates the team. That is how the team members can successfully achieve their results.

# Clarifying Communication within the Team

Communication within the team must work according to the principles of the obligation to provide and the obligation to obtain. Convey to the team that the employees initially have an obligation to provide. Each team member must immediately communicate important and new information about the progress of the project as well as any changes in the costs and deadlines. Paired with this obligation to provide, you also have the obligation to obtain. On a daily basis, each team member must determine whether information required for their work is missing. And they must obtain the missing information, either from sources from within the company or with the help of external cooperative partners — and this has to happen as soon as possible and as comprehensively as possible. The self-disclosure principle also applies: The project members must immediately report problems and any unexpected changes without being asked. Such principles become part of the fabric of project work if you have a culture of trust in the team and establish an effective reporting system. (For more on establishing a culture of innovation, see Chapter 16.)

## Determining the project reporting format

Early planning of a reporting system (also called *project reporting*) is an important task. Project reports are created to share information in presentations and for meetings.

**TIP**

Each report should contain information about the contents, creator, recipient, and date of creation of the report, as well as the nature of any requested response. Responses can include the release of resources, approval of a content-specific suggestion, acceptance of a prototype, or agreeing to the implementation of a customer survey.

You have to take care of the following when it comes to project reporting:

>> Defining the information requirement for the project members

>> Clarifying the information requirement for the steering committee or client for the project

>> Inquiring about the information requirement for internal service departments (Legal and Patents departments, controlling, quality assurance) or external partners

>> Determining the frequency, due date, and form (in writing or electronically as a report or verbally as a presentation) of the reporting

>> Dividing the responsibilities for the reports among team members

The length of the report should range from one to three pages. Reports don't replace the verbal communication that is more important for the success of the project.

# Communicating is more important than documenting

When you're working as a team, prioritize communication over documentation. Reduce to a minimum the documentation in the form of reports. Design thinking relies on speed and the early acquisition of informal customer feedback, and extensive and formalized documentation gets in the way of that. If any documentation is carried out, it's only so that you can visualize the future course of the project. The preferred communication method involves spontaneous face-to-face talks and project discussions.

TIP

The team should work in the same place and, if possible, near the customer or user. When it comes to software solutions that facilitate joint work in separate locations, use video chats, instant messaging, or collaboration programs sparingly and stay away from email.

Show results in the form of a prototype. Follow the principle "Demonstrating is better than presenting." (For more on creating prototypes, see Chapter 13.)

## Setting up communication rules

Before starting the project, jointly set up rules on how to communicate within the team. Plan for regular and daily communications regarding the progress of the project. That way, the project participants can gain insight into the work of the other team members, review team successes, and inspire changes with their feedback. One approach based on agile project management is a daily status meeting, in the form of a daily *scrum* — daily team meetings according to uniform rules. Their purpose is for you to review, coordinate, and potentially fine-tune the progress of the joint work. You should implement the daily scrum according to the following guidelines:

>> **Meet every day and always in the same place.** *Daily* means daily and can't be postponed. The meeting should take place in a workspace furnished with a *task board* — a graphical depiction of the project's progress that shows the current status of the individual work packages. (For more about task boards, see Chapter 4.)

>> **Always hold meetings punctually and at the same time of day.** Don't start at the beginning of the workday; begin at 10 a.m. or later. Then you can still finish tasks from the previous day or check important emails.

>> **Limit scrums to 15 minutes — never longer.** A strict time limit forces the meeting to stay focused. If you have to deal with any major problems, discuss them separately with the relevant persons in a follow-up meeting. Enter the problems that need to be discussed into an open-items list, which you display

on a board so that everyone can see it. (For more on the open-items list, see Chapter 4.)

>> **No sitting!** Consider conducting the daily scrum as a stand-up meeting — one where everyone stands for the duration. Having participants stand during the meeting keeps talk to a minimum and keeps participants engaged. (People who sit get easily distracted by other activities.) If you're serious about limiting discussions, have whoever is talking hold a heavy weight, like a dumbbell, while they talk.

>> **Insist that all team members be present.** Accept no excuses — aside from illness or vacation — for being absent from the daily scrum.

>> **Always answer the same three questions about work packages.** Briefly discuss all ongoing work packages. The persons in charge of the work packages have to describe

- *What was achieved since the last daily scrum*

- *What should be achieved that day*

- *What is now holding back progress on the work package*

Obstacles to progress might include a lack of equipment and tools or missing information that still has to be provided by others (suppliers or internal service departments).

>> **Make sure all participants are always prepared.** Because the questions about the work packages are known beforehand, every team member should be able to answer them immediately. Each team member must prepare for them before the meeting.

>> **Document only the final decisions and any problems that still need to be addressed.** In the hope of maintaining a bureaucracy-free communication style, document only final decisions. Use the framework of the daily scrum to communicate to the team by updating the task board and the open-items list. (For more on the task board and the open-items list, see Chapter 4.)

In the daily scrum, all participants acquire brief, concise, and updated information about what's happening in the project, the status of the project, and the next steps and current or anticipated problems.

**TIP**

You can keep things interesting during the daily scrum by adding a new fourth question each day. (Refer to the sixth bullet in the preceding list.) You can ask participants what they have learned so far, for example, or what was surprising or who else would be able to help with the work package. This fourth question can also be directed less toward day-to-day developments and more to long-term concerns — why the work package should be discontinued immediately, for example, or why the work package can't be resolved.

# Arranging Workshops

In design thinking, group work and focused individual work take center stage. One way of combining both is the workshop format — a format that promotes an in-depth exchange between team members. In each phase of a design thinking project, you should arrange for workshops so that you can complete tasks together. Workshops encourage a sense of community and the development of a uniform language, approach, and culture in the team. For design thinking teams made up of members with different characters, different experiences, and different attitudes, workshops can serve to strengthen team cohesion.

## Preparing a workshop

In order to succeed, workshops demand careful preparation. In preparing for a workshop, you have to carry out the following tasks:

>> **Determine the workshop's objective:** First you have to clarify what you want the workshop to achieve. The goal of the workshop might be that you develop a shared understanding of the task, characterize the target users more precisely, conduct a customer observation, find ideas, or create prototypes.

>> **Determine the composition of the participants and roles for the workshop:** Consider whom you'll invite to join your team in the workshop. This might be employees at the company's service departments (the Legal and Patents department, for example, or Controlling, Quality Assurance, or Customer Service) or representatives of external business partners, such as suppliers, existing customers, or research institutes and colleges.

TIP

Before starting the workshop, choose a moderator and arrange for someone to keep minutes. In the case of a more demanding workshop or a workshop that includes customers and suppliers, an external moderator is appropriate.

>> **Plan the process in detail, but design the content flexibly:** Consider the time span and plan the workshop process down to the minute. After setting the time limits for the various stages of the workshop sessions, avoid planning the content for each stage in too much detail, and be sure to leave plenty of room for creative freedom. After the greeting and introductory stage, structure the various workshop tasks. Don't forget to plan for longer breaks during the workshop to accommodate informal exchanges between the participants.

>> **Get the technology and room accommodations necessary for success:** Depending on the workshop activities planned, you can probably squeak by with just a wireless Internet connection, a projector, a projection screen, and a conference room with a few simple chairs. Rooms that allow for a flexible

division of group and individual work well because they tend to promote workshop tasks. If you plan to create prototypes, you have to have the right materials available, including technical devices like 3D printers and scanners. (For more on creating prototypes, see Chapter 13.)

>> **Compile and copy documents:** Distribute the workshop agenda, presentations, research reports (literature, patents), scientific studies, results of market research, customer surveys, and customer observations before or during the workshop.

>> **Organize a recreational program after the event:** By offering a shared recreational activity or dinner with entertainment after a particularly important workshop, you can reinforce the sense of community while enabling informal exchanges in the project team. (This is especially appropriate if the workshop includes external participants such as customers and suppliers.)

TIP

Send the information about the workshop's agenda and goals to the participants in advance, and ask the participants to do some homework by thinking about a topic or reading or preparing a report having to do with the workshop topic.

EXAMPLE

If you're arranging a workshop in which your team should work out innovative digitization options for customer service, ask the participants to conduct advance literature and Internet research on topics such as chatbots, social networks, artificial intelligence, and virtual reality technology. If you're holding a workshop to find ideas, you can give the participants advance information about the creativity techniques you plan to use. (For more on creativity techniques, see Chapters 10 and 11.)

## Holding workshops correctly

You are sure to hold multiple workshops during the design thinking process. The thing is, when you have several workshops intended to promote creativity and communication, nothing is worse than organizing them all according to the same pattern. So be sure to change the composition of your groups as well as the kind of group work and individual work you assign so that you can keep things interesting. This can be as easy as varying the length of the work and break times, switching rooms and furnishings, recruiting external moderators, and applying different methods.

TIP

In workshops for the design thinking process, you can apply a number of different methods when it comes to defining tasks and searching for, evaluating, and presenting ideas. Inform yourself about the individual methods, and expand the pool of methods you use. (You can start your research by reading Chapters 7, 8, 10, 11, 12, and 13 in this book.)

**TIP**

The participants will barely know each other at the first workshop, so use warm-up methods for groups with participants who don't know each other, groups with an interdisciplinary structures, and groups with members from different departments or various cultural circles.

The following rules help in the execution of workshops:

>> **Leave the supervisory roles at the door:** A design thinking workshop has no hierarchy. Roles and titles should be left at the door. Each participant is equally important, merits the same talking time, and deserves equal input when votes are held.

>> **Permit wild ideas:** Give your imagination free reign. Each offbeat idea counts, and each idea is treated equally.

>> **Quantity tops quality:** You need to generate a lot of ideas so that, later on, you can pick a good one. Collect lots of suggestions — the analysis, evaluation, and selection can come later.

>> **Build on the ideas of others:** No one is being guided by copyright law in a workshop. The result is a collaborative product. Ideas from others should be picked up, supplemented, or modified.

>> **Focus on people:** Design thinking requires thinking about people. In design thinking, the aim of a workshop is neither to develop a technology nor achieve economic goals such as market shares, an improved company image, or profits. The idea is to figure out how you can put yourself into the position and situation of other people. (For more on stepping into someone else's shoes this way, see Chapter 7.)

>> **Make it graphic and tangible:** For your workshop tasks, use drawings, reproductions, photos, videos. and prototypes. (Chapter 13 has more on adding visual elements.)

>> **Do not criticize:** You have to separate the task of finding ideas from the task of evaluating those ideas. If you're continually evaluating ideas the instant they're presented, not only are you certain to stifle creativity but you'll also promote an atmosphere where self-censorship rules — definitely a sad state of affairs.

>> **Fail early and often:** Failing means learning. Failing a lot means that you learn a lot. Communicate to the workshop participants that you don't just allow mistakes — you consider them opportunities to learn. (For more on tolerating mistakes, see Chapters 3 and 16.)

>> **Stay focused:** Set boundaries for yourself. Keep to the specific tasks in the design thinking process. Although this rule seems to contradict the one that permits wild ideas (refer to the second bullet in this list), experiences with creative processes have shown that success is more likely if you first define clear boundaries by setting the limits within which the imagination can be given free reign. These boundaries might include a general directive based on

specific time-and-cost goals ("the product or service offer should be launched on the market within ten months"), a regional focus, or a consideration of the legal limitations involved.

>> **Have fun:** The development of new ideas should be fun for everyone in the team. Creativity requires fun. Fun overcomes mental blocks, makes you curious, promotes openness, and encourages new perspectives.

**TIP**

Write down all the workshop rules on a flip chart in large letters and display them in common spaces or hallway areas. Continue to remind the participants of the rules during meetings and workshops.

## Providing equipment and materials

Depending on the product area or industry, the technical equipment for the workshop rooms can vary. In addition to the standard office and telecommunication equipment, you can have 3D printers, scanners, crayons, smartboards, or virtual reality devices. These devices simplify the communication and visualization of work results. No permanently installed projector is needed, because it would limit the flexible use of the room. If you have white walls, you don't need an additional projection surface. For image projections, use a laser pointer or your computer's presenter remote. The rooms should have multiple electrical outlets. Use cables and power strips only in exceptional cases, because they're distracting and can become tripping hazards. A good Wi-Fi connection is mandatory, unless you deliberately want to avoid using digital media during the workshop.

The materials for design thinking workshops vary according to the task. The basic supplies include paper and transparencies in various sizes and colors; presentation cards and sticky notes in a range of sizes, colors and shapes; different kinds of pens (a variety of colors and widths, lead, felt-tip and colored pencils, markers); and pins, magnets, and adhesives.

Additional materials and aids can help, especially in that part of the workshop where you want to create illustrative and tangible prototypes for your idea. Here are some suggestions for materials that you can use to form stuff, design stuff, label stuff, stick stuff together, and cut stuff apart:

>> **Form-and-design materials and tools:** Fabrics, crepe paper, cardboard, plasticine, modeling clay, Styrofoam, cardboard boxes, toilet paper and rolls, aluminum foil, wood, measuring tape, sandpaper, artwork, magazines, newspapers, bags, stickers, and colored dots

>> **Construction materials:** Hot glue, adhesive tapes, glue, paste for papier mache, string, ribbons, insulating tapes, cable ties, wires, pliers, nails, screws, screwdrivers, clamps, hammers, scissors, box cutters, and saw

These materials make it possible to shape the design, usability, and functionality of products and devices. You can also use these materials to illustrate how service ideas would impact people in certain situations. You might, for example, create figures out of modeling clay to represent customers and customer advisors and then place them in different room situations you've created with cardboard. (Think diorama.) As a team, ask yourselves how the rooms should look and how the customer advisors should position themselves in them so that the customer feels comfortable as they're being attended to.

**TIP**

If modeling clay isn't your thing, you can use Legos, model cars and figures, and other children's toys to act out the individual steps of a certain service process. Use role-playing games so that you can put yourself into situations where you act out first the role of the customer advisor and then the role as customer. Select the right costumes for your puppet figures and the right toys. The playful elements liven up the workshop atmosphere and encourage the participants to look at situations from a different perspective.

A clock, gong, whistle, or ship's bell is a good tool for the moderator to use when calling for a pause or for starting things off. A soccer referee's yellow card is a great way to indicate to somebody that the workshop has gotten off track. The materials should be readily available, well sorted, and easily stowed away — otherwise, a design thinking workshop might quickly descend into chaos. Modular cabinet systems or stools as storage boxes ensure flexibility.

# Designing Common Spaces

Design thinking involves group work as well as individual work in different constellations, where groups with the same number of people work alongside groups with a quite different makeup. As a result, the spaces must meet certain requirements. You have to make group workspaces and separate individual spaces available. These are referred to as "we spaces" for group work or for meetings where everyone is expected to communicate openly, as opposed to "me spaces," which are for quiet individual work and deep focus.

## The right rooms promote communication and creativity

Because you want to be able to divide workshop participants into small groups, use room dividers to create distinct spaces, work collaboratively on prototypes, and freely move participants around, you need more space for a design thinking workshop. It's probably best to choose different spaces, rooms, or furnishing arrangements for the different design thinking phases — understanding the task, redefining the problem, developing and evaluating solutions, and creating and testing prototypes. Make the effort to create new environments that are appropriate for the work and that can provide new stimuli. You can also rent co-working spaces from external providers. Such rooms are usually already set up with equipment and furnishings and can be used jointly by multiple companies. This can support communication and the development of networks with external partners.

The spaces, including outside areas in case of good weather, can be unusual locations you've rented out. The developing-solutions phase can benefit from rooms and locations that encourage creative work. You can choose an offbeat place. (The redefining-the-problem phase, on the other hand, calls for more focused work — here, stick with a conventional office building location with good technical equipment.)

TIP

Your design thinking work doesn't always require unusual offsite spaces. Take the rooms you have, and rearrange the furnishings for a new look. Transform that conventional conference room into a faux reception counter, shop floor, or train station lobby to encourage new impressions and stimuli for creative work. Also ask your team members to bring furnishings or their favorite items from home and set them up in the "we spaces." A new look fosters new ideas.

## A flexible environment promotes flexible work

During design thinking, you switch between group and individual work in the space of a few minutes. The rooms and furnishings have to support this flexibility. It should be possible to spontaneously divide large work areas according to the requirements (type of work, group size) with the help of sliding doors or easily movable partitions. You can create a space for various small groups that don't want their work to be disturbed by using sliding whiteboards or pin or metaplan walls as room dividers. Working on different floors is a quick solution. Work areas can be divided with the help of several small storage elements, such as chests or stackable stools with storage space. This enables fast access to materials.

TIP

Use the walls in a room thematically. For example, the first wall might contain information about the customer, whereas the second wall offers information about the customers' problems and needs. The third wall might provide contextual information about the situation under consideration or its parameters. And finally, the fourth wall might illustrate the first approaches to solving the problem at hand. Space for working together on developing the prototype is provided in the center of the room.

Avoid normal meeting rooms with typical table constellations. Meeting rooms often lack white walls for projections and partitions. Furnish group work areas with standing tables and bar stools so that people form new groups. Be sure to encourage the participants to move — movement promotes creativity.

**TIP**

Set up rooms so that they have a number of different horizontal and vertical surfaces in the form of large desks, writing areas, or walls. Don't hesitate to post sticky notes on windows, doors, and white walls. An electrostatic whiteboard transparency that you can attach to almost any surface is a flexible, inexpensive alternative.

The room climate promotes the work atmosphere. A room with daylight is conducive to good work habits. You can use the surfaces of large windows to attach sticky notes. Make sure that the work and presentation areas have good lighting. Echo-free acoustics are needed in the rooms set aside for small group work. Warm, natural wall colors, as well as high ceilings and fresh air, create a pleasant room climate. The temperature should be between 18 and 22 degrees Centigrade (65 to 72 Fahrenheit). (You want a workshop room to be a little cooler than rooms for regular work done while sitting, because the workshop participants often move around.) When you choose the colors of walls and furnishings, keep in mind that blue tones have been shown to promote creativity, whereas orange and yellow encourage communication. You can select some furnishings in red, which stimulates creativity and communication.

Break areas encourage exchanges and rest. Set up comfortable chairs, armchairs, or sofas in the work rooms or in a separate room. Set out beverages and pastries as light refreshments. All this ensures that the participants can relax and chat informally during breaks

**TIP**

As a small reward during workshop breaks, bring out a treasure chest filled with candy and other treats. For those special moments, you can even set up one of those chocolate fountains where you get to make your own chocolate-covered cherries or strawberries.

For rooms intended for rest and breaks, choose green as the color for all wall decorations, room accessories, and seating. Add some plants to improve the overall atmosphere of the room. The burbling sound of an indoor fountain creates a calming atmosphere that can balance out a lively workshop. You can even go a step further and offer athletic equipment or games of skill in the break areas. A trampoline or treadmill can set your thoughts in motion. A yoga mat can help you create the necessary distance from a problem.

# 2

# The Problem Phases

Start searching for your target users' problem and identify which information you still need.

Examine needs and problems by applying various methods to put yourself into the role of your target users.

Conduct systematic observations and get to know your target users better.

Define a clear question for the problem that your target users have and that you want to solve.

# Chapter **6**

# Understanding the Task

I n the first phase of the design thinking process, you have to define the search field and understand the task that you want to solve. To accomplish this, you have to analyze the task and examine the determining factors and causes and then reformulate the task so that you can identify new facets. You should take the time to gain this basic understanding of your task because this is the only way to carry out the next steps in your search for ideas in a meaningful way. Only when you have compiled this information can you decide which technical perspective you must integrate in the steps ahead and which expertise is relevant.

## Finding the Right Search Area

You've decided you want to develop something new. To do that, you first have to define what it is that you're actually looking for. Is it in response to a specific customer problem, a customer wish, or the application of a particular technology — or are you looking for a possible application of your skills? The *search field* describes the scope of your search. Defining the search field can help you orient yourself so that you can analyze more purposefully and find ideas more effectively. Just keep in mind that the search field shouldn't be too narrow; otherwise, you'll unnecessarily limit yourself when it comes to finding creative solutions. Nor should your search field be too broad; otherwise, the focus will be too vague, which makes the next step in analyzing the problem more difficult.

A search field that's too narrow is how someone can use 3D printing technology to manufacture keychains. A focus that's too broad is a search for ways to apply artificial intelligence in general. A search field with the appropriate level of specificity asks how you can use artificial intelligence in the field of brand communication.

In principle, you can categorize your search field using three different variants. In the market segment, you can search for new social changes that lead to new needs. For new technologies, you can systematically search for applications that previously didn't exist — or at least not yet in this form. Ultimately, your own competencies and resources provide the starting point that form the basis for you to design new products, services, processes, or business models.

## Searching in the market segment

Social changes that can show up in modified buying habits and new customer wishes or new customer problems is a promising area for generating creative ideas. This is why you should track down developments and trends in society as a whole as well as in corporate life.

Globalization, for example, has a major impact on society. In addition to *economic* globalization — the increase in worldwide trade — there is also *cultural* globalization, driven by an assimilation of diverse cultures, the worldwide dissemination of lifestyles and values, and the fusion of different cultural traditions. The worldwide presence of fast-food chains, the global success of western music and fashions, and the use of social networks around the world are examples of this cultural globalization.

Another trend is the demographic shift in industrial countries represented by an increase in the aging population. The relative increase of people age 55 or older results in new entrepreneurial opportunities for this target group, which can be characterized as sophisticated, quality-conscious, active, and consumer-friendly connoisseurs with above-average purchasing power.

If you want to develop products or services for an older population, don't develop and promote them as offers for seniors. That's exactly what this target group doesn't want. The characteristics and features of whatever you're offering must correspond to the desires of — and problems faced by — this target group and as such should appeal to older people. A vacuum-cleaning robot with large, illuminated buttons, self-explanatory menus, simple operation, and robust construction will appeal primarily to this target group without your having to refer to this robot as a product for people age 55 and over. Also keep in mind that older people can have different interests. Here you can find sophisticated opera aficionados as well as rock music lovers, folks who hike across Thailand with a backpack, and group travelers on a Caribbean cruise.

What distinguishes trends like globalization and the demographic shift is that they aren't short-term fads but rather represent customer wishes or problems that are here for the long term.

In addition to the demographic shift, you can look at many other trends, including the ones described in this list:

>> **Health:** Increasing health awareness and medical progress are developments that have been evident for years and will play an even greater role in the future.

>> **Ecology and sustainability:** This refers to a new and intensified trend toward practicing an environmentally conscious and sustainable lifestyle. It's no longer a niche for "eco-freaks;" instead, it's a sign of an increasingly broad and new environmental awareness that can be observed in a broad spectrum of society.

>> **Urbanization:** This trend involves an increase in the urban population or the rural exodus. Both of these are responsible for many resulting developments, such as the aging of small towns, price increases in real estate and properties near large cities, an increase in commuters, and rising environmental and waste problems in high-density metropolitan areas.

>> **Female shift in society:** The term *female shift* refers to a number of factors, including an increase in the number of women with higher educational attainments, the growing number of working women, and the increasing proportion of female managers.

**EXAMPLE**

The female shift trend also describes the growing significance of more "feminine" competencies in professional life, such as team working and communication skills. There's also a development of men handling previously "typical" women's roles in the household and child care.

>> **Individualization:** This term summarizes the increase in single households, the trend toward fewer strong interpersonal relationships and many loose ones, and a rise in highly individualized wishes when it comes to products and services. This tendency will also arise in developing countries as a result of pent-up demand.

>> **New work:** The term *new work* references the structural change from an industrial society to a service society, the increase in part-time employment along with multiple simultaneous jobs per employer, and the growing prevalence of telecommuting jobs.

>> **Education and knowledge:** In the education and knowledge trend, you see an increase in the significance of higher educational qualifications, particularly in the highly developed industries. You also see the growing relevance of a lifelong learning model and knowledge in general.

>> **Security:** The dynamic nature of the political/legal, economic, and technological transformations currently occurring reinforces the desire for stability and security. Threats caused by natural environmental events, new forms of terror, violence, and crime (cybercrime) turn the basic need for security into a trend.

It's worth your while to focus on the trends in this list and ask which tasks will arise from them in the form of solutions for new needs or problems. These trends are long-term, ongoing developments that will generate a strong demand for new ideas. When summarizing this demand, people talk of *market pull.* In contrast to this concept, the *technology push* approach, outlined in the next section, looks for applications of new technologies.

## Searching in the area of technology

In addition to searching for social changes that affect the market segment, you can look for applications of new technologies. With the technology push approach, technical progress is the basis for many new products, services, processes, and business models. For many industries, technology can get a strong boost from digitization, which summarizes the increasing spread of modern information and communication technologies in all social areas.

**EXAMPLE**

Digitization involves several technologies that are used on a long-term basis in many application areas and thus constitute a technological trend. These technologies include artificial intelligence, virtual and augmented reality technologies, cloud computing, the 5G wireless standard, and blockchain technology.

Many originally separate technologies spur each other on in the course of development and will merge into a new, shared technology. This technology convergence will give rise to new application areas. The combination of Internet technologies with TVs, for example, opens up new possibilities to users in terms of how and when they can watch TV programs. In general, you need to clarify which relevant technological developments exist and which interesting applications might emerge from them.

## Searching in your own area of competence

You can also find a task for design thinking by looking at your own competencies and resources. Ask yourself which tasks might benefit from your contributions. The best way to picture this approach, which is both competence- and resource-oriented, is to imagine that it's all like taking a creative approach to preparing dinner. If you used the traditional approach, you would pick up a cookbook, select a recipe, create a shopping list, buy the food, and prepare the dinner according to the recipe. With a competence- and resource-oriented approach, you consider which meals you can make well and which foods you already have in your refrigerator. You compose a dinner on this basis. The available resources thus determine the task. In a number of studies, Saras Sarasvathy, from the University of Virginia, showed that this entrepreneurial method — she refers to it as the *effectuation approach* — is the secret to the success of numerous start-up companies.

**EXAMPLE**

Jason Goldberg and Bradford Shellhammer asked themselves which business model they could develop, based on their passion for design and their professional experience in e-commerce. They outlined their idea on a paper napkin in a Manhattan restaurant. In February 2011, these considerations led to the creation of the company Fab.com, which introduces new design ideas daily on an Internet portal and offers exclusive designer products for a limited time to its users.

On a company level, first analyze its strengths and identify its unique competencies and special resources. These can be tangible (materials, special devices and tools, equipment, infrastructure, location), intangible (patents, brands, image, databases, customer data, knowledge, corporate culture), personnel-related (number of employees, particularly qualified personnel, and know-how), or financial (cash reserves, financial strength, owner). You can also use the effectuation approach on a personal level. Answer the following questions for yourself:

» What do you know? What can you do? What do you have in terms of resources and experience? What in particular do you like to do and do well?

» Whom do you know? (The answers might be companies or individuals, such as scientists or experts.) Which resources do they have?

» What might you do and achieve by using these resources and contacts?

The advantage of this approach is that you'll find a task you can work on with your own competencies and resources. The available resources point you in the direction of an attainable task that you can complete with design thinking. Because you're starting with your strengths, this frequently leads to greater motivation.

# A Well-Defined Task Is a Task Half-Solved

An essential element in the design thinking approach is that you develop a thorough understanding of the task and situation before you look for creative ideas for products, services, procedures, or business models. Don't rush into things and immediately search for solutions for something that you haven't really worked through yet. Give this analysis of the tasks all the time it needs. Separating the analysis of the task from the search for solutions to the task is a success factor. When you know and understand the details and reasons for the problems or desires of a particular target group, it will be much easier for you to find ideas designed to solve those problems or fulfill those wishes. In many cases, you already find the initial approaches to innovative ideas during the fundamental analysis.

When analyzing your task, systematically work through the six W questions: What? Whereby? Who? Where? When? Why? On this basis, you'll develop assumptions about the cause of the problem or desire and test these assumptions with your target users. (For more on testing assumptions, see Chapter 15.) In addition to getting a detailed task description, this gives you initial insights about possible solutions.

TIP

When you work through the individual W questions, you can compare the task with a case in which the problem or desire (surprisingly) doesn't occur. This case can be similar or come from a different area (different target users, another scientific field, or an external industry, for example). Afterward, perform a systematic check of what is different and what is the same in your task and the comparison case.

## Clarifying what the task is and how it manifests itself

For the first step, you have to clarify exactly what the task consists of. The task can be a desire of (or problem faced by) a particular target group. Problems reveal themselves when something occurs differently than expected or desired. Describe these expectations or wishes and compare them with the actual situation. The expectations can also relate to an ideal condition that hasn't been achieved yet. Also scrutinize the expectations and wishes to see to what extent they might just be subjective or shared by only a few people. When you compare the ideal condition with the current situation, you can systematically find gaps that you'd be able to close with new products, services, processes, or business models. *Ideal* means that something creates high usefulness (high quality and reliability, good design, user-friendliness, convenience) or reduces a disadvantage (cost and risk reduction, lower consumption of resources, time savings) for the target users. A fully automated, intelligent, and solar-powered lawnmower can describe an ideal condition.

TIP

Compile all the information and describe what you know about the problem. From this you can detect what in turn you don't know or understand. Write down the gaps in your knowledge in one sentence: for example, "We must clarify how often an error appears while operating a device" or "We must clarify how to increase customer loyalty for our service."

With an eye toward the solution, you should check which efforts were already made in the past to solve the problem. If it's a technical problem, you can get information in literature databases or with a patent search. The persons affected by the problem can give you information about the solutions that have been used so far. Ask the persons involved why these solutions failed or why they're unsatisfactory. As part of this process, you'll also clarify which elements are absolutely mandatory for a satisfactory solution.

Follow this stage by asking yourself what is not necessary, or at least not important, about the solution. The search for what *doesn't* constitute the problem goes in a similar direction. Ask older people about their behavior when they use smartphones. It is shown that, on average, only three or four features are actually being used. A smartphone with even more features, therefore, can't be the objective.

Find out whether there's anything related to the task that you may not change or that is absolutely required. A technical product must have certain material characteristics, or a children's toy may consist only of elements that don't pose a health risk. A financial consultation requires a signed privacy policy, even if this seems unnecessary and time-intensive to the customer. However, note that these requirements can change over time. The security conditions related to self-driving cars will certainly change in the future along with the technical progress.

After clarifying what the problem or wish is, describe in detail how, exactly, these requirements are shown. A problem or wish can refer to quality issues, service, design, image, user-friendliness, convenience, security, usage period, price, or environmental or social compatibility. You can develop an electric scooter that is reliable, robust, comfortable, compact, easy to use, stylish, and cheap and has a long usage period.

**TIP**

Focus on a few significant characteristics of the problem or wish. Some requirements can also contradict each other. In many cases, it's difficult to manufacture a high-quality product consisting of high-grade materials in an inexpensive way. However, your tasks could lie precisely in resolving this contradiction.

## Clarifying who has the problem or wish

Who has the problem or the wish is important information about the task. Some tasks are theoretically relevant to many people. Smart-home solutions that improve the home quality through networked and remote-controlled devices and systems are certainly interesting to many people. It has proven to be expedient to make a selection at this early stage of the design thinking process. Older people or those with physical disabilities can particularly benefit from smart-home systems, for example. However, this group will have special requirements regarding the operability and functionality that you have to focus on.

You can initially limit the group of persons by describing who isn't affected by the problem or doesn't have a desire for a solution to the present task. From the remaining group, I recommend that you focus on the target users for whom the solution to the task has a certain relevance and urgency. The following questions will help you decide:

>> Who is most annoyed by the problem?

>> Who might benefit most from a solution?

>> Who can save money or time with a solution?

>> Who needs a solution as soon as possible?

>> Who is most dissatisfied with the alternatives available on the market?

>> Who would pay the most for the solution?

At this early stage, you shouldn't view the relevance of (and urgency for) the task too narrowly. You already achieve a lot when you can roughly distinguish the groups of people according to the relevance and urgency related to the task. In the subsequent design thinking phases, you'll increasingly get information about the target users you selected at the beginning. You'll also continue to narrow your selection. (For more on making selections, see Chapter 7.)

**TIP**

Ask yourself for whom the solution might be useful outside of your selected target group. This group of persons isn't initially in focus, but as you develop the solution, it may be revealed that this group in particular has a special interest in the found solution and will quickly adopt the new product or new service after the market launch.

In addition to looking at the groups of persons interested in the result of your search for a solution, you should use this phase to look for people who can contribute to this search. You can query these people in the later phases of the design thinking process or integrate them into joint workshops.

Some people may not be interested in the solution or will deliberately or unintentionally stand in the way of the solution. For your further analysis, and particularly for the subsequent implementation of your proposed solution, it's helpful for you to also become aware of and characterize these people.

You can characterize the individual relevant groups with the Persona method. A *persona* represents a fictitious person with individual characteristics that stand for the target users (or some of them) for whatever innovation you have in mind. In a study profile, describe the characteristics of this person (age, gender, education level, values, opinions, lifestyles, hobbies, modes of behavior, consumption habits) with keywords or in short sentences. (You can find out more about the Persona method in Chapter 7.)

## Clarifying where and when the problem or wish occurs

You shouldn't neglect the where-and-when aspects of your task. The situation can be an everyday event (for example, a shopping spree, household activities, surfing online, travel, leisure, or cultural activities), personal circumstances (the person is pregnant, in a financial predicament, or under time pressure or stress), or a special place where your target users' problem or wish occurs. The requirements for a meal can differ on the road, at home, at work, or during recreational activities (hiking, sailing, bowling, at the movies). The task may also depend on the time, duration, and frequency of occurrence. The need for information about snow skiing opportunities is much higher in the winter than in the summer. You always have to consider your task in connection with the specific situation and the special aspects of the location or time.

You can discover the significance of certain situations and times when you compare various situations and times. Clarify when and where the problem or wish of your target users doesn't occur. On this basis, contrast differences and commonalities in terms of the situation and time.

**EXAMPLE**

When buying flowers, for example, you can see differences depending on when the purchase occurs. Study when and where your target users buy flowers, by observing people at garden centers and flower shops at various times. You'll certainly find differences among the customers in terms of the length of the shop visit, the type and number of purchased flowers, and the use of customer service in the morning as opposed to the late afternoon.

## Clarifying why the problem or wish occurs

Only if you know and understand what caused of the problem or what drove the wish can you find a satisfactory and permanent solution. You can use the fishbone diagram by the Japanese chemist Kaoru Ishikawa (also called the Ishikawa diagram) to systematically structure the causes of the problem. The fishbone diagram is a simple diagram that lets you provide an illustrative identification of causal relationships. (See Figure 6-1.)

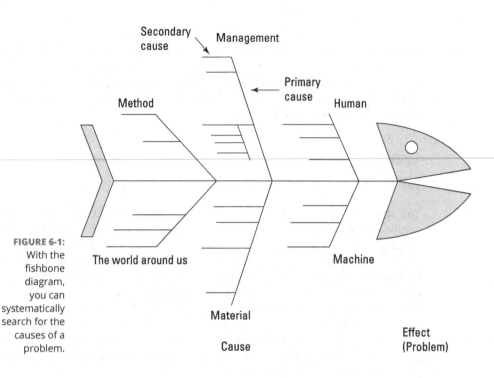

**FIGURE 6-1:**
With the fishbone diagram, you can systematically search for the causes of a problem.

For a better overview of the relationships between cause and effect, the various causes are written along the individual lines (bones) — as either the main cause or a secondary cause, depicted in the form of a branch. As a system, the main causes are divided into the areas of man, machine, material, method, management, and Mother Nature, where the latter stands for the environment of the problem. Because these areas share the initial letter, this is also referred to as the 4M (man, material, machine, method), 7M (with the addition of management, Mother Nature, and measurement), or even 8M (expanded to include money). Individually, the following causes of the problem or wishes are considered in these categories:

>> **Man:** Special weaknesses (or strengths) of humans. These can be in the areas of skills (technical, methodological, and social), performed activities, or modes of behavior. A lack of customer orientation and employee motivation in customer service can result in low customer satisfaction.

>> **Machine:** Special weaknesses (or strengths) of the machine or tools used for the task. Using an outdated machine in production can be a cause of the low productivity.

>> **Material:** Special weaknesses (or strengths) in the material used or information required for the task. Increases in the prices of raw materials result in higher costs in the manufacturing of a product.

» **Method:** Special weaknesses (or strengths) in the technical or organizational approach. The delivery times for customer orders take too long because the merchandise is unnecessarily checked for completeness by two departments at a time.

» **Management:** Special weaknesses (or strengths) in the organization, planning, management, and control of a task. A scheduling error can be the cause of delays in business processes. The communication deficits between two departments can explain the slow processing of customer inquiries.

» **Mother Nature:** Special weaknesses (or strengths) in the external environment of the task. "The environment" can refer to environmental influences as well as the activities of external business partners and competitors. High temperature fluctuations in the supply chain cause a high amount of rejects in food transports. The declining market shares of a product can be explained with the successful market launch of a better product by the competition.

» **Measurement:** Special weaknesses (or strengths) in the measurement of technical or economic processes. A defective measuring system intended to recognize deviations in the paint can be a cause for subsequent paint damages in a new product. Exclusively using the number of processed customer inquiries as the key indicator in an employee evaluation can be the cause of low-quality consultations during customer inquiries.

» **Money:** Special weaknesses (or strengths) in the available financial resources (money) for the task. Insufficient financial means can cause a lag in the development of a sales team in Asia.

In this early phase of the design thinking process, the fishbone diagram gives you an initial overview of the cause-and-effect relationships. In the following phases, you'll use surveys, observations, and experiments to collect additional information that you can adopt into your fishbone diagram.

**TIP**

After compiling the causes, you need to evaluate them. One simple approach is to perform the evaluation with your team by applying red adhesive dots on the causes in the fishbone diagram. Each evaluator gets five adhesive dots that can be applied freely. If a cause is especially significant, a participant can give it multiple dots. The sum of the adhesive dots provides the order of the causes, from least to most significant. You should discuss the most important causes in more detail among the team.

Lastly, make sure that you've listed every possible cause. Ask yourself whether the causes you came up with are sufficient for explaining the problem or wish of your target users. When doing this check for completeness, you might come up with additional causes.

As a supplement to the fishbone diagram, I recommend that you use the 5 Whys technique for each identified main cause. Behind every problem or wish is a chain of causes that you must identify. Like a small child, ask at least five times in a row why something is the way it is. In cases where the cause of failure is initially felt to be technical in nature, the 5 Whys technique often reveals that human error or mismanagement is often the root cause.

**EXAMPLE**

Let's say you have a quality problem with a new product, where a plastic part keeps breaking after constant use and customers are complaining about it. You ask: "Why is that?" Answer: "The manufacturing process is defective." You ask a second time: "Why is that?" Answer: "The process couldn't be tested adequately." You ask a third time: "Why is that?" Answer: "There wasn't enough time to develop the process before the market launch." You ask a fourth time: "Why is that?" Answer: "The research unit told the production department about the technical specifications for the new product too late before the market launch". You ask a fifth time: "Why is that?" Answer: "There's no organized coordination process between the research and production units at the company." Ultimately, the cause of a technical problem lies in a communication deficit between two departments.

# Identifying Knowledge Gaps

After clarifying the first task you've set for yourself, reflect again on everything you know and don't know about the task. This way, you can find the *blind spot* in what you know — that knowledge gap you hadn't considered before. Use the following strategies in order to close that gap:

>> **Compile current knowledge.** Ask yourself what you know in total about the task. Compile the current knowledge that you've become aware of as a result of your systematically working through the *6W questions:* what, whereby, who, where, when, and why. Write down the facts about the task.

>> **Identify the knowledge you lack.** Ask yourself what there is about the task that you have no knowledge of. These are the gaps in your knowledge that you want to close with additional analyses. Formulate questions about the gaps in your knowledge that you want to answer with additional information.

>> **Explore what you have no knowledge of.** The knowledge you're not aware of is, so to speak, the blank page in the book of knowledge — the blind spot, in other words. The Austrian philosopher Karl R. Popper summarizes it this way: "We might know all kinds of things about the future. In principle, there's just one thing we can't know, namely, what we will know in the future. Otherwise

we would already know it now." You can only discover the knowledge you're not aware of by means of exploratory research. Ask questions or make assumptions about your task and use surveys, observations, or experiments to get more information — information that previously you didn't know existed.

# Systematically Closing Knowledge Gaps

You need convincing and up-to-date information to close your knowledge gaps. You can get this information from various sources, depending on your task. Take advantage of the following sources of information:

>> Publication and patent databases

>> Newspapers and trade magazines

>> Technology, market, and industry studies by associations, consulting companies, scientific establishments (colleges, research institutes), or national and international governmental institutions (ministries, authorities, the European Union (EU), Organization for Economic Co-operation and Development (OECD), the United Nations (UN)

>> Statistics [the US Bureau of Labor Statistics (www.bls.gov), for example]

>> Analyst reports, trend and market research reports

>> Business reports, sustainability reports, presentations, press releases, and websites of other companies (competitors, suppliers, start-ups)

>> General Internet research, forums, blogs, social networks

>> Conferences or trade shows

>> Customer surveys and observations, supplier surveys, joint workshops with customers or suppliers

>> Personal networks of own employees

>> Expert talks or surveys, association work, organizations

>> Cooperative work with scientific institutes or companies

>> Employee surveys

# Estimating Influences on the Task

With the information from the sources listed in the earlier section "Systematically Closing Knowledge Gaps," you will quickly realize that numerous factors have an influence on your task. The risk is that you will drown in an overwhelming amount of information and become too paralyzed to analyze further. You must analyze your task without paralysis. You can prevent paralysis based on too much irrelevant information by following these two steps:

1. **Identify the environmental influences.**

   The initial priority is for you to gain a better understanding of the search field and identify important environmental influences on your task. The information about the most important influencing factors can be structured and prepared with the PESTEL method. (PESTEL stands for the political, economic, social, technological, environmental, and legal spheres of influence.) This gives you an overview of the basic conditions for your task.

2. **Identify the stakeholders and analyze the influences on the task.**

   In the second step, identify the persons or groups who are directly or indirectly related to the task at hand — the stakeholders, in other words. The influencing factors identified in the first steps have an effect on your selected stakeholders. This is why you have to assess these effects in relation to your task.

## Evaluating environmental influences

The PESTEL method is an analytic compilation grid for identifying influencing factors in the environment of your search field. You can use it to analyze numerous factors in the political, economic, social, technological, environmental, and legal spheres of influence. However, always ask yourself whether a particular factor is at all relevant or has any real influence on your search field. You will find a compilation of some of these influencing factors here:

>> **Political:** Political climate and the stability of the political system, an understanding of democracy, results and participation in elections, party engagement and reputation, government expenditures in various areas (labor market measures, health, infrastructure, construction, education, research, environmental protection, consumer protection, development aid), financial and tax policy, health policy, retirement policy, merging of economy and politics, lobbying and bureaucracy

>> **Economic:** Economic and industry growth, liberalization of markets versus protectionism and trade barriers, privatization, government debt, inflation rates, interest rates, unemployment versus employee shortages in certain

areas, labor costs and productivity, purchasing power of the population, wealth growth, income distribution, poverty/wealth gap, influence of trade unions, tariff conflicts, propensity to invest, stock indices, company valuations, subsidies, nationalization, exchange rates, fragmentation and specialization of the markets, market saturation, competitive activities, order volumes, costs of living, housing costs, private health expenditures, private versus state provisions, health promotion, customer satisfaction, customer loyalty, churn rate, propensity to consume, propensity to save, consumer behavior (quality awareness, price sensitivity, individual wishes, brand awareness), status awareness, need for consultations and information, growth of e-commerce and digital money

>> **Social:** Values and norms, social justice, social cohesion, attitudes toward tolerance and justice, social engagement, social contacts (number, intensity), population growth, changes in family structure, fragmentation of society, smaller households, geographical population shifts, regional differences, ethnic changes in the population structure, migrations, religious and ethnic conflicts, spiritualization, change in age distribution, school/university/ education quality, work mentality, career awareness, attitude toward (lifelong) education, attitude toward technology, prestige of science, technological competence, ownership structures (sharing economy), reputation of economy, attitude toward foreign investments and profits, leisure behavior, environmental and sustainability awareness, consumer behavior, health awareness, acceleration of social change, media influence and reputation, transport and mobility volumes, mobility behavior, security needs, corruption, petty crime, violent crime, and terrorism

>> **Technological:** Scientific progress, dynamics of technological change, innovation rate, significant product and process innovations, development times, expenditures for research and development, number of patents, interdisciplinarization, technology convergence, digitization of education, automation, miniaturization, cyberattacks, and the spread of computer viruses

>> **Environmental:** Natural events (flooding, volcanic eruption, tornado, drought, cold), environmental pollution, climate change, species extinction, desertification, raw material shortages (crude oil, rare metals), water scarcity, energy and raw material prices, recycling, waste-related behavior and systems, disposal costs, epidemics and resistance formations

>> **Legal:** Change in rights to freedom (travel, individual, media), changes in the national and multinational legal situation (taxes, competition, antitrust and patent laws), product liability, regulation, enforceability of contracts, and the influence of interest groups on legislation (associations, environmental protection and consumer protection movements, nongovernmental organizations)

From this multitude of potential influencing factors, you must select the factors relevant to your tasks from the environment today as well as 5, 10, or 15 years in the future.

**EXAMPLE**

If you want to develop ideas for an online shop in the Indian market, you should consider economic factors such as trade barriers or legal influences, like competition and patent law. If your task is to look for a method to process aluminum with resource efficiency, look at technological factors such as scientific progress and patents in selected technology areas or environmental influences like the prices of energy and raw materials.

It's important that you understand the cause and origin of this change and can trace the previous development from the past until today. Evaluate the influencing factor on the basis of this information from the past. First describe the influencing factor in keywords and the effects a change in this influencing factor will have in the future. Then estimate how relevant the influencing factor is and what the probability is that this change will occur at two different times in the future. You can also add an estimate of the long-term development to your evaluation, showing an ongoing trend of at least five years. Also examine possible reciprocal effects of these influences and whether there will be conflicting developments. See the evaluation diagram in Table 6-1.

**TABLE 6-1**   **Evaluation Diagram for Influencing Factors Outside the Company**

| Influencing factor | Signal/ Key indicator | Relevance: 0 = irrelevant up to 5 = very significant | Occurrence probabilities 2025 2035 | Long-term development | Reciprocal effects with other trends |
|---|---|---|---|---|---|
| | | | | | |

Some of the influencing factors you select won't directly affect the task. Changing the factors will influence people or groups, which in turn will be relevant to your task. Social changes regarding values, norms, social justice, or communal solidarity influence the behavior of people who are interested in the solution of your task as customers, for example. A change in the social factor of environmental awareness is evident in that potential customers increasingly demand ecofriendly products. That's why it's important for you to identify the relevant persons or groups and explore the effects of changed environmental influencing factors on these people.

## Identifying stakeholder influences

Persons or groups who have or will have an interest in your task in the broadest sense are the task's stakeholders. You'll have external as well as company-internal stakeholders who are both relevant for the project. The stakeholder relationship to your question or task can be expressed in different ways, as in desire for information about the task or interest in the solution you develop. Stakeholders can support but also block your design thinking project. These persons are affected in some way (positively or negatively, directly or indirectly).

TIP

Dealing with the relevant stakeholders and their goals, worries, needs, and influences at an early stage will help your project succeed. The goals of this type of stakeholder analysis would include an initial compilation of all stakeholder influences on your design thinking task, the early detection of potentials and problem areas while working on the tasks, and any evaluation of any barriers that arise in the later implementation of your ideas.

First you have to identify the relevant stakeholders. *External* stakeholders are persons or groups that you would find outside of your company or organization. External stakeholders can be

>> **Customers or users:** Differentiate between existing, new, and noncustomers or individual customer group segments.

>> **Suppliers:** Where appropriate, differentiate between existing and new suppliers.

>> **Competitors:** Where appropriate, differentiate between existing, new, and potential competitors.

>> **Cooperative partners:** Differentiate according to the area of cooperation (research and development, production, marketing, sales) or according to institutions (company, consultant, state-run authorities).

>> **Science:** Differentiate according to the research area or institution (university, non-university research institution).

- **》 Owners or investors — the shareholders, in other words:** Differentiate between equity providers and outside creditors, sponsors, financial advisors, analysts, rating agencies.

- **》 Interest groups:** Differentiate between local, regional, national, or international or according to area of interest, as in environmental protection, consumer protection, unions, associations, chambers, citizens' initiatives, and residents.

- **》 Media:** Differentiate between television, newspaper, online, and radio, or in the trade press, business press, and general press.

- **》 Politics:** Where appropriate, differentiate between municipal, state, federal, and international policies or by policy areas: financial, tax, economic, trade, labor market, health, infrastructure, consumer protection, environmental protection, and development aid policies, or differentiate according to institutions in ministries, authorities, parliament, or political parties.

*Internal* stakeholders are people or groups who work at your company or organization and directly or indirectly influence your task. Internal stakeholders can be

- 》 Employees (possibly also former, potentially new employees)
- 》 Other business units or departments
- 》 Internal clients
- 》 A shop committee
- 》 Top management

Not all external and internal stakeholders are relevant for every task. You can identify the most important stakeholders for your task by asking these questions:

- 》 Who can block work on the task?
- 》 Who can provide support for finding the solution (also intangibly)?
- 》 Who can benefit from finding the solution to this task?
- 》 Who might be affected adversely by a potential solution?
- 》 Who might have an interest in the results?
- 》 Who can draw attention to the results?
- 》 Who is performing activities in connection with the task?
- 》 Who wants to participate in finding the solution?

Subsequently, you should collect necessary information about the relevant groups for the analysis and evaluation. It's enough if you limit yourself to three or four stakeholders.

**TIP**

The Persona method can help you more easily put yourself in the position of individual stakeholders. Compile, in a short profile, information about the characteristics, preferences, and behavior of the stakeholders. (For more about applying the Persona method, see Chapter 7.)

After identifying and selecting your stakeholders, examine what effects any change in the external influences you've identified would have on the stakeholders. This lets you systematically identify patterns of change at an early stage. Focus on developments in the political, economic, social, technological, environmental, and legal areas that have consequences for your stakeholders' behavior, attitude, or needs.

From the effects you see on individual stakeholders, extrapolate the consequences for the task of your design thinking process. Your task can become more significant in the future if an increasing number of people are affected by the problem. Let's say you want to develop new assistance systems for older people who want to live at home without outside help. The number of these people will grow in the future and thus increase the need for new assistance systems. Your task can become more complex if the effects on your stakeholders continue to multiply and if these influences change dynamically over time. The legal and safety-related requirements for assistance systems are increasing and changing over time. Additionally, it's possible to use different technologies for assistance systems that will continue to advance in the course of technical progress.

You can summarize the results of your stakeholder analysis with an analysis grid, like the one shown in Table 6-2. This gives you an overview of the groups of people affected by your task or which groups influence this task. With this knowledge, you can reformulate the task more specifically.

**TABLE 6-2**    **Analysis Grid for a Stakeholder Analysis**

| Influencing Factor | Change for Stakeholder Customer | Change for Stakeholder Supplier | Effects of the Stakeholder Changes On the Task |
|---|---|---|---|
|  |  |  |  |

# Reformulating the Task

After you analyze the task, you should reformulate the task to gain another insight into the problem or question to be solved. An initial approach can consist of considering the problem or wish from the perspectives of the affected or participating persons. Ask yourself what the problem is from the point of view of individual groups and how serious it is. You can also think about what the ideal solution might look like from the perspective of individual affected persons.

Another possibility is to formulate the task from the viewpoint of an external person or company and consider how these persons or this company would see and solve the task. The persons could be famous athletes, politicians, artists, preachers, judges, journalists, psychologists, craftsmen, doctors, or even children. For companies, you could consider Apple, McDonald's, Microsoft, Walmart, Google, Facebook, or BMW, with each one standing for a particular strategy or business model. The idea is, as always, to provide you with new stimuli for your task.

**TIP**

Describe your task by using the formula "What if . . ." — as in "What would happen if Apple or another company had to solve this task?"

You can also formulate your task on different abstract levels. The more abstractly you formulate your task, the more you can distance yourself from it so that you form a more holistic view of the task. You could, for example, start out by addressing the task of how to make truck transport between your production site and the distribution center more environmentally friendly, but you could also expand the scope of this task by looking at your entire logistics system, from the supply of materials from China to the delivery to customers in the USA. This lets you identify the overall correlations and interdependencies of the individual steps in the process. In contrast, you can define your task more specifically so that you examine the details and various nuances of a problem or question. In the example of the truck transport, you could focus exclusively on the route planning. You realize that you have to consider in your task the amount and type of freight, the availability of trucks and drivers, the trucks' loading restrictions (volume, weight), the transport routes, the time of day, and the loading and unloading options at the sites.

**TIP**

To reformulate the task, divide the main problem into different individual problems: You can first see it as a whole and then in its individual parts. This is a proven technique to reduce the complexity of a question. If your task is to bring to market an electric vehicle made of renewable raw materials, you should first focus on the individual components, such as materials for the car's interior. Then you can look at the crash-resistant components, such as the car chassis.

You often develop new ideas about a task by simply describing the problem in different words. There are various approaches to this strategy. Sometimes, it's enough to merely reformulate the problem with synonyms. Look at the existing task and use only synonyms for the keywords. If a product or service should work quickly, use terms such as "in a jiffy," "rapidly," or "immediately." If a product should be easy to use, reword it so that it can be used simply, intelligibly, conveniently, or without exertion.

You can also look up, in dictionaries or on Wikipedia, the definitions of words used in your task description. Consider whether this opens up a new perspective of the task for you. You want to give your Internet platform a more user-friendly design. In your research, you find a definition of *user-friendliness* in which the term is explained with the goals of "faster" (more efficient), "in the right way" (more effective) and "in an illustrative and convenient way" (more satisfied). Accordingly, you reformulate your task with the desire to make your Internet platform more quickly accessible to users, with the right information, and a more illustrative design.

**TIP**

Tasks in a technical area are often described with specialist terms that are difficult to understand. Use colloquial language or describe the problem to a layperson in simple words without technical terms. Also ask yourself how you would explain the problem to a 6-year-old.

You can also disassociate your task or your way of looking at it by trying one of the following techniques:

>> **Enlarge or shrink the problem:** Use the power-of-ten technique for a tenfold reduction or tenfold increase of the task in your mind. You want to increase the productivity of a technical process. Describe this task with the goal of boosting the productivity tenfold.

>> **Illustrate your task:** Create an image of your task, or perform your task as a role-playing game. You want to simplify travel planning for families. Outline how parents discuss their plans with their children in front of the computer screen at home. Assume the roles of the individual persons and play out different situations.

>> **Change or reverse your task to its opposite:** For example, if something should be improved, consider how you could make the starting situation for your task even worse. You want to improve the consultation quality in customer service. Think about how the task would be presented if the consultation quality would be even worse than now.

By reformulating your task, you can get a better understanding of the specific issue. On this basis, it will be easier for you to find the right solution.

IN THIS CHAPTER

» **Learning the meaning of empathy**

» **Gaining empathy for people**

» **Characterizing the target person comprehensively**

» **Methodically empathizing with a variety of situations**

» **Exploring the customer's steps**

# Chapter **7**

# Putting Yourself in the Roles of Others

This chapter is all about figuring out how you can put yourself in the role of your target person, a concept known as *empathy*, which is a significant success factor in design thinking. First, you'll find out about the potential of an empathetic approach and then come to understand the basic tenets of developing empathy. Finally, I'll explain how you can systematically collect information about the people and situations you're interested in and methodically evaluate that information.

## Recognizing Empathy as a Key to Success

A key principle of design thinking is empathy. When you empathize, you put yourself in the role of another person. When you adopt the feelings of another person by "feeling along with" someone else, you show emotional empathy. With design thinking, you even go a step further: You identify and understand the emotions, characteristics, needs, wishes, goals, motives, and attitudes of another person and anticipate their future behavior on this basis — a process known as *cognitive empathy*. The idea here is that you don't need direct personal contact with this person —although this would, of course, be helpful! — but instead mentally put yourself in their shoes so that you can come up with solutions for the needs, wishes, and problems of this other person. That's why people also refer to *empathic design*, which means that you create concepts, work methods, products, services, procedures, or entire business models from the user's perspective.

An empathetic approach offers numerous advantages. You understand

>> How this person feels, thinks, and acts

>> Which problems, needs, goals, and wishes this person has

>> How serious the problem or needs and wishes are

>> What is particularly important to this person

>> What satisfies this person

Empathy also helps you in the next step, when you develop innovative solutions and focus on what's essential. Ultimately, empathy is the foundation of your ability to develop sustainable solutions that will subsequently be accepted and used. To summarize it in a single sentence: Show me what you do, hear, see, smell, and feel and I'll tell you what you need.

In the next few sections, I tell you which success factors you have to keep in mind and which methods you can apply to find an empathic design.

# Proceeding with Empathy

Proceeding with empathy means that you have to penetrate the thoughts of the user and try to identify unstated needs and wishes. You create an emotional bond with the person and look at the world from their perspective. In the following sections, I use five success factors to show you how to achieve this bond.

## Create openness

Approaching people and having a serious interest in them and curiosity about the problems of others distinguishes an open attitude. Openness toward other people doesn't appear out of nowhere. Try not to evaluate people and situations immediately. Ask yourself what kinds of actions are taking place and which situations are being created. Describe what you see without evaluating anything. Here are the questions you need to answer: Who is acting in this situation, what is happening, and when and where exactly is it happening?

The result of an open stance is that you see things that others tune out. In everyday situations, pay attention to the small details that you hadn't seen before. When you look at something, deliberately avoid searching for the obvious answers.

TIP

Here's an exercise for developing an open attitude: Take three minutes to think about what you might use an object for, such as a brick. Find original ways to use it. Did you also come up with applications as a paperweight, a piece of furniture, an art object, a door stop, a free weight for workouts, or a weapon?

Doing something completely new creates more openness. Do activities you haven't engaged in before. Try a new recipe, read a different newspaper, attend a rock concert if you love classical music, or take the subway instead of the car.

## Discount your own ideas/Tamp down your own biases

A basic impartiality toward people and new situations is closely aligned with openness. Try not to make snap judgments or immediately categorize things. It's often a mistaken assumption that you, as a solution designer, already know the problems and wishes of your potential customers.

You should act without biases during an observation or survey as well as during the subsequent evaluation. Dissolve your entrenched thought patterns. This isn't about your own experiences and skills. Distance yourself from your own competencies and attitudes. Gain clarity about your own ideas by verbalizing them, writing them down, or visualizing them. You can reveal your own ideas and biases by answering these questions:

>> In your opinion, where do you imagine that your customer is, and what action do you think that customer is contemplating?

>> How do you think the customer will act in this situation?

>> When will your customer do this, in your opinion?

>> How often do you think the customer acts like this?

>> Why do you believe this?

You should accept as is the results from observations and surveys. Even if you consider them wrong, you have to document and interpret them.

## Share results

Share your insights with others. These might be colleagues as well as friends, acquaintances, or family members who come from an entirely different professional context. Confront uninvolved people with descriptions from your observations or surveys. Ask them how they would interpret and evaluate this information. Also ask which information is still lacking or would be useful to have. Analyze and reflect on your results from different perspectives.

## Proceed methodically

Proceeding with empathy means researching people. When you adopt the attitude and approach of a researcher, you find indications of previously never-formulated problems and unexpressed wishes of a potential customer. Act like an ethnologist who wants to explore a foreign, exotic tribe on an expedition. First collect and structure information, and then evaluate it systematically. I explain the specifics of how to do this in a methodical fashion in the next section.

# Collecting Information

You can select different approaches to obtain direct or indirect information from the target person about themselves or their behavior and feelings. You have five possible survey methods to choose from:

>> **Analysis of secondary material**: Already existing information about the customer is referred to as *secondary* material. It can be varied: Search online and offline for studies, articles, and newspaper reports about your target users. Collect statements, contact details, or other relevant information in social networks (Facebook, Twitter, Instagram). Search for blogs by or about your target users. Use internal sources of knowledge from marketing and sales. Customer complaints are a good source. Use this secondary material as a basis for considering which information you already have, which information you still need, and how you can best compile both kinds of information through surveys, observations, and own experiences.

>> **Surveys**: Survey those individuals who most interest you. Be sure you are willing and able to really listen. Anyone can *ask* customers what they want; listening intently is the hard part. Let customers freely tell stories about what they did, where and when they did it, how they did it, and how they felt when they did it. (See Chapter 14 for more on how to conduct a survey.)

>> **Observations**: Observe individuals either as they live and breathe or in an artificial environment, such as a lab. This approach — observing flubs when

using a product, seeing customers come up with workarounds when faced with a problem, recognizing unspoken customer needs — can spark lots of great ideas for innovations. Observation studies are applied much too infrequently in practice. Too often they are used only within the context of usability tests, which are about the usability of a product from the perspective of potential customers and tend to take place at too late a stage in the innovation process. I am here to tell you that you can find valuable customer-relevant information for solutions and new ideas far earlier in the process if you follow a design thinking model. (For more on carrying out systematic observations, see Chapter 8.)

>> **Experiments**: Like any scientific researcher, you can also use experiments with your target persons to gain information about their needs, problems, wishes, and attitudes. Such an experiment is a mix between observation and survey. The basic approach goes like this: First, you prepare an assumption stating the what and how of a problem or wish of a potential customer. Through the survey responses or the reactions noted in an observation, you can test whether your assumptions are correct or have to be discarded. This allows you to get to know your target person better, step-by-step. (Chapter 14 has more on conducting experiments.)

>> **Your own experiences**: You gain an in-depth sense of another person's problem if you physically step into the other person's role. If you want to get a feeling for the everyday problems of an older person or someone with a disability, use glasses that affect your vision adversely, attach weights to your wrists and ankles, or move with a walker or wheelchair. Ask yourself how you feel, what you perceive, and which problems you have to master. This experience is sure to sharpen your eye for details and problem areas that you previously may have overlooked or were unaware of. This kind of "acting as if" adds a playful component to the discovery phase, which increases your curiosity and openness toward the unknown.

# Evaluating Information

When it comes to data collection methods such as secondary analyses, surveys, observations, experiments, or your own experiences, you can choose between a number of methods to evaluate what you've collected. These evaluation methods can be applied in three ways:

>> You can use these methods to not only structure the results of your secondary analyses, surveys, observations, or experiments, or your own experiences, but also describe the status quo.

>> You can identify which information is still missing and where there are gaps in your findings.

>> You can use these evaluation methods to find new ideas and solutions and formulate a projected condition of how things should be in the future from a user's perspective.

You have a number of options when it comes to tapping the potential offered by secondary analyses, surveys, observations, experiments, or your own experiences. The following methods focus on persons, situations, and processes:

>> Use the Persona method, described in the following section, to describe and analyze your target person.

>> Use the empathy map to examine these target persons in a specific situation to see what they're doing, how they're feeling, what they're hearing, and what they're seeing.

>> Use the customer journey to track every step of your target person and to discover weak areas along the journey or ideas you can use to redesign this journey.

## Characterizing a customer using the Persona method

With the Persona method, you fictitiously assume the role of a customer or user who represents members of a real customer or user group. You can apply this method in the development of ideas or business models as well as in the configuration of marketing activities.

The Persona technique can be used to establish distance to yourself while also creating proximity to the customer. In other words, this approach orients you to the customer. Direct your next steps toward this person and, according to this persona, choose the individual needs that you want to focus on. The Persona method also makes it possible to increase awareness of customer needs among employees — in the areas of research, development, and production, for example — without frequent customer contact. Everyone is in the know when it comes to what the persona is supposed to be like, so each and every employee can put themselves in the situation of that individual person. The customer is no longer seen as an anonymous object in an undefined mass, but gets a real character and is thus "brought to life." Furthermore, you can apply this method inexpensively and combine it with other approaches.

The selected person for the persona represents a fictitious person with individual characteristics that stand for the target users — or at least for some of them.

**WARNING**

Rather than configure an average persona, concentrate on coming up with various personas with distinct, unique specifications. The informational yield for an average persona lacks distinctiveness, offering little in the area of fresh ideas for actual innovations.

Represent the different personas carrying out different functions in the buying process. For example, you could include

>> A persona representing a certain target segment

>> A first-time buyer

>> Extreme users (ones who use products often or under special conditions)

>> Nonbuyers (negative persona)

>> Customer and user personae

The Persona method can also be used in the business-to-business (B2B) area by differentiating decision makers, influencers, or possible saboteurs as the persona.

To get the Persona process started, take a sheet of paper and write up a description of the person in the form of a short profile that makes heavy use of keywords. (Another option is to write short sentences on larger sticky notes and arrange them in an order that works for you. Whatever method you choose, it helps if you assign this persona a specific name.) You shouldn't reduce the persona to a single characteristic, which is often done in traditional market research, as part of the customer segmentation. You should describe the person holistically in their entire personal environment. A (fictitious) quote or slogan by this persona can start off the description. Figure 7-1 shows a fully fleshed-out persona.

The following biographical information can describe this person:

>> Gender, age, origin, family status (married or single; children? How many? How old? What parenting style?)

>> Profession (job, position), educational background, special knowledge, expert on a specific topic

>> Friends and social environment, pets

>> Living conditions (own house versus condominium versus rented apartment or shared apartment, as well as type, design, quality, and furnishings of the home)

**Motto: "Don't make me google"**

Christian (Age :-)

Male, born in the middle of Germany, who eventually moved via Boston, Hamburg and Berlin to near Cologne, married, two sons, a family man, Professor with a business administration and technical background, enthusiastic about innovation, a technophile and online enthusiast, was an active handball player at one time, wants to do more sports in the future, prefers Japanese and Indian food, is a chocoholic

**Wishes?**

- An electric car with a range of 1000 kilometers
- Markers that can paint in every color
- Being able to eat chocolate without a guilty conscience
- Self-tying shoes

**Annoyed by?**

- Science Fiction
- Having to look up everything on the Internet
- Products that are not pretty much self-explanatory
- Products whose batteries run down quickly

**FIGURE 7-1:** Example of the description of a persona.

>> Asset status

>> Attitudes (values, interests, preferences), frustration tolerance, awareness of health, life goals

>> Hobbies and leisure activities (Athletic? Which sport? How often?)

>> How much time does the persona have for particular topics or activities?

>> Which media and information sources does it use for which topics?

>> Attitude toward digital media (User of social networks or more of a loner? Likes to share information with others openly?)

>> Consumption habits or factors that influence buying decisions: How fast is the buying decision made? Is this a spontaneous buyer, or is there a tendency to plan? Which information channels does it use? Price-, quality-, or service-oriented? Brand awareness?

It's also a good idea to analyze the problems (pains) and wishes (gains) of this persona — for example, with the following questions:

>> What annoys or frustrates the persona? What problems does it have? What are the persona's challenges in life? What does the persona consider too expensive, too inconvenient, too time-consuming, too inferior, not user-friendly enough, or too complex? What makes it angry? What risks does it fear? What would the persona be embarrassed about in front of friends? What are its frequent mistakes? What can't the persona do? What kinds of opposition does it face?

>> What are the persona's needs? What does it desire? What does it dream about? What are its goals in life? What are its (buying) motives? What kinds of sale offers does this persona need? What would it expect from such an offer? What would make the persona's life easier? What would make it happy? What would inspire it? What would make it admired by others?

These questions can be adapted specifically for the problem under investigation and expanded as well. You should outline the answers in keywords on a sheet of paper. It also helps if you describe the persona and its problems or wishes in a personal way and in a personal form. The persona should be updated continuously because problems and desires tend to change over the course of a design thinking project.

TIP

Bring the persona to life. Give the persona a catchy name that suits the character. Use small drawings to visualize the persona and its environment. Outline what it looks like with its family, when it's indulging in its favorite hobby, or when it performs certain actions and uses particular objects.

## Understanding the situation with the help of an empathy map

With an empathy map, you can holistically put yourself into the role of a person or a group faced by certain situations. Imagine a specific person in their natural environment. This situation can be an everyday activity (a shopping spree, for example, or using a certain electronic device, taking part in household activities, surfing the Internet, or engaging in travel, leisure, or cultural activities), which the person should look at from different perspectives. Using the example of a specific person in this situation, ask the following questions and answer them in keywords on sticky notes. You can stick your answers on the notes onto a poster with a diagram similar to the one you see in Figure 7-2.

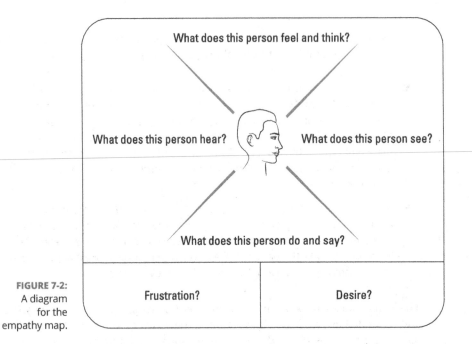

FIGURE 7-2:
A diagram
for the
empathy map.

First, find out what the person you're observing is feeling or thinking. The key question is what does the person think and feel in this situation? This gives you a good impression about what drives and motivates the person. Other questions can be helpful, too:

>> What does this person want or desire?

>> What does this person not want?

>> What does this person think of while doing the activity?

>> Which emotions often play a role in how they act?

EXAMPLE

Imagine that your target person is a pregnant woman strolling through a shopping center with her 4-year-old daughter. Let's call her Sabine, and her daughter, Charlotte. Sabine made a long shopping list beforehand. She feels stressed (quite natural, given her condition), and shopping with Charlotte is always a challenge. As a pregnant woman, she is of the opinion that she shouldn't have to walk a lot in the shopping center and that a restroom should always also be nearby. Sabine wants the shopping to be as relaxed as possible. Charlotte feels bored and wants to visit the playground.

Every person is always actively dealing with the outside world. Now you have to analyze what that individual says and does in this environment. You can characterize her behavior and actions more precisely with the following questions:

>> What does this person say to others, and what is she doing?

>> What can be observed about this person?

>> What behavior is she displaying?

>> What are some of the quotes, key terms, or statements often used by this person?

>> Which modes of behavior and activities does this person often engage in?

**EXAMPLE**

Sabine often calls out to her daughter, who is running around the shopping center like crazy. In each individual store she visits, she always quickly looks for a salesperson and addresses her directly. The consultations with the salespersons are repeatedly interrupted by Charlotte.

The next question you have to answer is what does the person hear in this situation and environment. Here you analyze what the target person hears (noise, advertising messages, information) as well as how and by whom this person is influenced — talks with relatives, friends, and colleagues at work, for example, or information on the radio, TV, or Internet. Here are some other questions:

>> What do the family members, friends, or colleagues say to the person?

>> What should she do or not do?

>> Which communication channels are relevant here?

**EXAMPLE**

Sabine still remembers the many pieces of advice from her girlfriends and her twin sister about all the things she has to buy before the second child arrives — a second high chair, a new stroller, baby clothes in sky blue, and pillows in various sizes. Charlotte is growing increasingly whiney. It doesn't help that it's also very loud at the shopping center. In addition to music, each store plays promotions, which she hardly registers.

Next, describe the person's specific environment in the examined situation (during the course of the day, at work, at home, while shopping, during a recreational activity). In other words, what does the person see in the specific situation? You can describe the situation or surroundings more specifically by asking the following questions:

>> What do the surroundings look like?

>> Which visual impressions is she getting in this situation?

>> Which offers is she seeing or not seeing?

>> What does she see others doing?

Sabine permanently sees advertising in various forms. Today, she has an eye only for baby clothes. She purposefully looks for special offers. She watches other mothers take care of their children while shopping. Sabine keeps looking at the clock while shopping, and this distracts her so that Charlotte always manages to break free.

A decisive question is what kinds of problems or what frustrations this person has or will develop in the particular situation. Here the person's frustration is in the spotlight. At this point, write down which problems, worries, fears, obstacles, and urgent needs are confronted by this person. The following questions supplement your analysis:

>> What are the risks that the person feels confronted by?

>> What does the person try to avoid?

Sabine permanently has an eye on where the nearest restroom is. She hopes that Charlotte isn't too bored and won't disturb her while shopping. She worries that she is forgetting something. She is increasingly under time pressure because she has to be home no later than noon. She is annoyed that she can't quickly find her way around the individual stores.

In conclusion, look at the positive aspects. Think about what makes an individual happy in this situation. Here the focus is on pleasure. The answers here will give you starting points for finding ideas later. This can be approached with the help of the following questions:

>> Which goals is Sabine pursuing?

>> What is she striving for?

>> What does she want to achieve?

>> How does she measure her success?

>> How does she try to be successful?

Sabine would be happy if she could occasionally sit down as she makes her way through the stores. Play areas in the individual stores for her daughter Charlotte would also be a relief. She would be especially pleased if she could count on a calm and relaxed atmosphere.

Write down the answers in key words and group them into the diagram for an empathy map. (Refer to Figure 7-2.) Keep the target person at the center — the one you describe using the Persona method.

# Exploring the process with the customer journey

For the customer journey, imagine which steps a potential customer (preferably, in the form of a concrete persona) experiences before, during, and after using a product or service. You can execute this customer journey as described next:

Create a description of the target person using the Persona method, and supplement it with an empathy map. You can also use different personae in order to work out differences and special aspects of the customer journey. Potential target persons might include

>> Personae in a certain target segment

>> First-time buyers

>> Extreme users (who use products often or under special conditions)

>> Nonbuyers

>> Customers or users

>> Decision makers in the buying process

>> Influencers of the purchasing behavior

>> Potential saboteurs during the sales process

With the help of information from surveys, observations, or records of sales, or from your own experiences, customer satisfaction analyses, or a brainstorming session, summarize the phases of a customer journey with keywords on sticky notes. First provide a rough description of the phases. (You can describe the phases — especially that of consumption – in more detail later.) Figure 7-3 shows you the steps involved in acquiring hotel accommodations as an example of a customer journey.

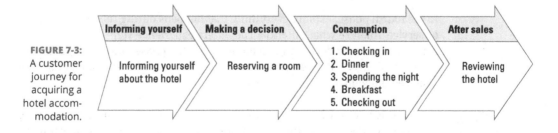

**FIGURE 7-3:** A customer journey for acquiring a hotel accommodation.

| Informing yourself | Making a decision | Consumption | After sales |
| --- | --- | --- | --- |
| Informing yourself about the hotel | Reserving a room | 1. Checking in<br>2. Dinner<br>3. Spending the night<br>4. Breakfast<br>5. Checking out | Reviewing the hotel |

TIP

Keep in mind that there can be different customer journeys, depending on the target person, or that different target persons can have individually distinct customer journeys. Create separate customer journeys for different people and compare them afterward. In many cases, it was only this step — creating separate customer journeys — that led me to find interesting differences.

## Describing the phases of the customer journey

In the first phase, give a detailed description of how a customer becomes aware of a need, a problem, or an offer. Summarize how the customer gathers information about wishes, about a solution to a problem, or about an offer. Address how the customer compares one offer with another.

EXAMPLE

Imagine that you were looking at the customer journey for a hotel accommodation. A person — let's call him Fred from Hamburg — becomes aware of a Rolling Stones concert in Munich. He gets this information from an online ad on an information portal about rock music. Online, Fred gets information about the Stones appearance, about Munich, and about the possibilities of traveling to Munich and spending a night there. Excited about the prospect, he views hotel offers on a hotel comparison portal and initially compares them only superficially.

In the second phase of the customer journey, a decision is made. Examine how and by whom or through what the customer is positively or negatively influenced during his buying decision. You should also ask the basic question of *why* the customers make a selection.

EXAMPLE

Based on recommendations from friends, Fred is seriously considering only a few hotels in downtown Munich. He compares them in terms of the location and the price-performance ratio. A quiet location, good and inexpensive transport access, and a well-equipped fitness area in the hotel are important factors in Fred's decision. He ultimately decides on a hotel based on the recommendation of a friend.

In the fourth phase, explore everything that happens during the use of the product or service. Analyze what potential customers experience step-by-step when they use a service or product. You should describe this phase quite specifically and in some detail. Every step, every activity, every move, and every thought should be analyzed individually.

EXAMPLE

Fred travels to Munich and takes the subway to his hotel. Because he doesn't find any signs for the hotel at the subway station, he wants to use his smartphone for navigation. The battery on his smartphone is dead, which means he has to ask pedestrians for directions. Mildly annoyed, Fred finally finds the hotel. No one is at the reception desk. A half-hour later, an unfriendly receptionist receives him.

Fred wants to get dinner at the hotel before the concert. Because Fred is a vegetarian, his only choice is between potato salad and potato soup. The next morning, Fred goes to have breakfast at the hotel: pork fat with cracklings, beer cheese dip, and mashed potato spread with a fresh pretzel and a peasant loaf — not quite a "selection" to Fred's taste. After being unable to pay with a credit card, Fred hastily leaves the hotel.

The last phase, the after-sales phase, focuses on the customer's activities after he has had some experiences with the product or service. Describe the customer's needs, tasks, or expectations in the after-sales phase. The question of how and by whom or what means the customer can be motivated to make another purchase is of particular interest to you. You shouldn't underestimate the fact that the customer will use word-of-mouth communication to share these experiences with the product or services. Check how and by whom or by what means the customer is persuaded to report a positive buying experience. Look at where (on the Internet, at home, or in the office) and on which occasions the customer will report about the experiences.

**EXAMPLE**

Fred has returned to Hamburg. First he tells his friend who recommended the hotel in Munich to him all about his experiences in Munich. Although he has never reviewed products or services on the Internet, he talks extensively about his bad experiences with the hotel on the hotel comparison portal, which he also used to book the hotel. On the same day after submitting his review online, the hotel contacts him directly by email via the comparison portal. The hotel owner apologizes sincerely to Fred and invites him to a weekend in Munich, including a first-class trip by train.

In each phase of the customer journey, ask yourself the following questions:

>> What does the persona want here? What does it want to achieve?

>> What does it do, or (surprisingly) what doesn't it do? How does it try to achieve its goals or wishes?

>> What does it use for this purpose, and in what order? With whom is the persona in contact? Where are the contact points — the touchpoints, in other words — with the company? How long does each of the contacts with the company last? How long are the individual customer journey phases in total?

## Discovering the problems (and improvements) in the customer journey

The *touchpoints* are particularly important in the customer journey — these are places, occasions, or moments during which people come in contact with the product, brand, or company in the broadest sense. Touchpoints could be something in control of the company, such as advertisements, television or radio commercials, brochures, catalogs, flyers, trade fairs and events, customer hotlines, call centers, mailed items, personal advice, points of sale, store furnishings, an Internet presence, or online advertising (emails, newsletters, banners, e-shops, landing pages, and company/product blogs). Additionally, you have to take into account the touchpoints that can't be influenced yet, or only indirectly, such as family members, acquaintances, friends of the target person, social media networks, reports in newspapers, magazines, forums, blogs, comparison websites, or rating portals.

You should analyze each touchpoint with the following questions:

>> Which touchpoints are particularly effective from the customer's perspective — and which aren't?

>> To what degree does each touchpoint positively influence the customer experience?

>> Are the possible touchpoints coordinated with each other throughout the customer journey?

>> How do your own employees rate the individual touchpoints in terms of effort compared to benefit? Are there touchpoints that offer few customer benefits but are complex? Are there too many touchpoints that confuse the customer?

>> Which touchpoints do your competitors have? Which ones do they not have? Why or why not?

>> Are there enough touchpoints throughout the customer journey? Where are the gaps? Which additional contact points could be created for the customer?

>> What can be automated, and how?

In addition to analyzing the touchpoints, you should look at all steps in the customer journey and uncover potential problems for the customer. The customer might recognize these problems or not be aware of them yet. Pay particular attention to negative emotions. Here are examples of problems or negative emotions:

>> The customer is annoyed.

>> The customer is unpleasantly surprised by the price or costs.

>> The customer doesn't know what to do in a certain situation.

>> The customer performs the activity incorrectly.

>> The customer tries to solve the problem on their own.

>> The customer has to wait and thus loses time.

>> The customer performs unnecessary activities (waste).

>> The customer is disappointed by the quality.

>> The customer considers the situation or activity too complicated.

>> The customer considers the situation or activity not user-friendly enough.

>> The customer worries about risks or feels uncertain about the outcome.

>> The customer is embarrassed in front of others.

These problems or negative emotions can be evaluated and selected in terms of their significance (extent, frequency of occurrence) and analyzed according to their cause.

Customer satisfaction is assessed for each phase and each step in a phase — a process that can be summarized in what is referred to as a customer experience map. How does the persona feel? (In working out the map, feel free to use simple symbols, such as various emojis.)

In addition, you can identify the key *moments of truth* for each phase or step. These are moments or situations that are particularly important for the customer. Different moments of truth are located along the customer journey:

>> **The first moment of truth:** When the customer first becomes aware of the product or service

>> **The second moment of truth:** When the customer is actually using the product or service and is evaluating the product or service based on the customer's quality standards of the moment

>> **The third moment of truth:** When the customer has a positive, neutral, or negative feeling or experience after using the product or service

You can also add these:

>> **The zero moment of truth (the moment of truth before starting):** When the customer first perceives a problem or need through a suggestion or an impulse (such as advertising) and searches for or compares information about possible solutions

>> **The ultimate moment of truth:** When the customer tells others about their experiences and feelings about the product or service (through social networks, review portals, or virtual communities, for example)

# ANALYZING WEAK AREAS IN THE CUSTOMER JOURNEY

Weak areas in the customer journey can be analyzed using what is referred to as the *critical incident technique*. With this technique, the customer survey focuses on particularly memorable events in connection with the advice devoted to, and use of, a particular product or, even more so, a particular service. These critical events often live on as stories passed on by word-of-mouth communication and thus also become significant for the company.

Through personal interviews with standardized, open-ended questions, customers should recall and report about critical incidents that they experienced at touchpoints with the company and its employees. These incidents often result in a nonpurchase or the return of the product.

The following basic questions are suitable when it comes to analyzing critical incidents:

- Do you remember any particularly unsatisfactory contact with an employee?
- When did this happen?
- Which specific circumstances led to this situation?
- What exactly did the employee say and do? What did you say, and what did you do?
- What exactly happened for you to consider the contact unsatisfactory?
- How did you feel before, immediately after, or a week after the incident?
- Did you change your behavior after the incident?

In principle, a query about incidents that were considered particularly positive is also possible. Negative events in particular often stay in the customers' memories for a long time. This survey about critical incidents must refer to a specific situation, which must have caused severe dissatisfaction, be sufficiently detailed, and have happened within a clearly delineated timeframe.

The evaluation of the mostly qualitative statements offers the opportunity to identify the customer's minimum expectations, an inability to meet a standard, and the behavior of the personnel or process that is perceived to be extreme. Then you can classify the results into problem categories according to their cause. Specifying the frequencies of the individual problem categories enables an initial quantitative assessment of the importance of certain problems with the service (or product consultation and use).

You can combine the customer journey with the customer-benefits matrix method in order to develop possibilities of improving each phase or step. The following questions will give you suggestions for answers:

>> Where can you simplify something for customers?

>> How can you provide more benefits to your customers?

>> Where can you reduce or minimize risks for your customers?

>> Is it possible to integrate more fun and entertainment?

>> What would inspire your customers?

Figure 7-4 shows the entire analysis grid for a customer journey.

You can use a variant of the customer journey when you outline a day in the life of a customer.

By dividing the journey into 15- or 30-minute blocks of time, for example, you can ask the following questions using the sample of a specific person:

>> Where and how does the persona spend the day?

>> Which products or services does it use?

>> How much time does it spend using the product?

>> How would the life of the persona change after it receives its product?

>> How often is the persona online? Does it use a PC, laptop, tablet, or smartphone?

>> Which devices does the customer use, when, and how often?

In addition to activities in the household and leisure time, you can focus on a typical workday.

**TIP**

The customer journey, particularly the variant "a day in the life of the customer," can be supplemented by not only a keyword description but also images, cartoons, and videos to visualize the information and make it more illustrative.

| What steps does the customer take? → | Attentiveness | Informing yourself | Making a decision | Consuming | After Sales |
|---|---|---|---|---|---|
| What do they want? | | | | | |
| What do they do? | | | | | |
| What do they use? Which touchpoints are present? | | | | | |
| What Problems arise? | | ☺ | ☺ | ☺ | ☺ |
| Satisfied | | ☺ | | ☹ ☹ | |
| Dissatisfied | ✪ | | ✪ | ✪ | ✪ |
| Moment of truth | | | | | |
| Ideas for improving the process | How could one simplify things for the customer? | | | | |
| Additional benefits? | How could one bring about additional benefits? | | | | |
| Reduce risk? | How could one minimize/reduce risk? | | | | |
| Fun factor? | Is it possible to build in more fun and entertainment? | | | | |
| What would excite? | What would excite the customer? | | | | |

**FIGURE 7-4:** Analysis grid for the customer journey.

# Chapter **8**

# Observing People in Action

I n this chapter, I explain the potential gains you can achieve from observational studies. Careful preparation is a significant success factor, so in this chapter, go out of my way to fill you in on all the necessary prerequisites. You'll find out how to observe the right thing and how to observe correctly. Along the way, I point out a few errors that are typical for analyses — errors you must avoid — and, to round things off, you'll find out about a few particularly useful methods for executing and evaluating your observations.

## Putting Observations to Proper Use

Although observations can be elaborate in terms of time and costs, a study that closely looks at how real people act in real situations promises interesting ideas for truly new products and services. At an early innovation stage, you should definitely use observations to compile initial impressions and information about the problems and needs of people in real environments. Only by way of observations can you capture the actual authentic and spontaneous behavior of people as they live and breathe. Sometimes human behavior is hard to put into words and is therefore inaccessible if you rely on written questionnaires.

**TIP**

Focus on the unconscious actions of people — actions that you can be trace back to problems or that indicate an unsatisfactory situation. The gestures and facial expression evident when following a person's eye movements as they use a tool or device, for example, will reveal difficulties in the object's usage and provide starting points for new solutions.

If you just observe the behavior of people in certain situations, you don't have to depend on the observed person's active cooperation and willingness to provide information. People often don't want to talk about their problems, inadequacies, or negative feelings, or their statements are subjective, if not actually dishonest. You can only identify such user dissatisfactions or product deficiencies objectively through observations.

Neither do you have to depend on the verbal abilities of the people whose needs you want to analyze. Imagine that you want to develop a new product for small children. By observing the behavior of children in certain situations, you can gain valuable new ideas.

If you want to analyze services, you'll often find yourself confronted by complex situations where many people interact with each other. Only observations make it possible for you to register multiple activities or entire sequences simultaneously while noting expressions of feelings. Based on your evaluations, you can then optimize or completely redesign the service from the customers' point of view.

When you observe situations over a longer period, neither do you have to depend on the recall of individual persons — that means you can gain a representative sample of impressions. Ultimately, observations give you the opportunity to capture situations on a daily basis, thus getting an immediate and realistic account of the wishes, needs, and problems of your potential customers.

Before you start with your observations, I want to recommend the three most important success factors for this phase:

>> Prepare thoroughly.

>> Conduct your observation systematically.

>> Apply the right methods for the observation and evaluation of the information.

# Thoroughly Preparing Your Observations

I start off this section by explaining how you can observe correctly, and then I present you with a number of methods to help you systematically carry out observations or evaluate the results of the observations.

**TIP**

Prepare thoroughly. Often, you get only a single chance to observe a person or situation undisturbed. Use these chances. In your preparation, clarify

>> Whom and what you're observing

>> How you're observing

>> How you will methodically and systematically evaluate your results

## Determine who should be observed

During the observation phase of design thinking, the focus is on the potential customer or user. To get a comprehensive understanding of the person, you should select a real target group. I recommend that you focus on customers or users who share the same needs or problems and are looking for the corresponding solutions.

**WARNING**

Don't describe your target group just with superficial facts such as age and gender. There are in fact older, active Internet users, and the buyers of sports cars are increasingly women. Many demographic twins can be totally different target groups: Do you know an Englishman who lives in London, was born in 1948, is very wealthy, has children and dogs, was divorced and got remarried, and likes sports cars and good wine as well as traveling to the Alps? Yes, Prince Charles does fit the bill, but so does Ozzy Osbourne, lead singer of the heavy metal band Black Sabbath. Same target group? Hardly.

If you have a completely new idea, it helps if you look for lead users — those users whose needs precede that of all other customers in the market and who have a strong incentive to resolve these needs — rather than focus on the "average customer." Lead users are aware of specific problems and are actively or urgently searching for a solution. They may even have already developed a solution. They'll probably be quite willing to provide qualified customer feedback. In addition, look for extreme users who use products in specific (extreme) situations (in case of coldness or heat, constantly, or in certain regions, for example). You can research online and in trade communities to find such people.

Write down the names and relevant information about the observed people.

>> Who are they? (Customers, employees?)

>> What kind of behavior can you observe? In other words, which wishes and needs do they show?

>> Which roles and relationships do they have with one other?

>> Who influences them?

# Determine what you should observe, whom you should observe, and when you should observe

When it comes to specific actions and procedures, you should clarify two sets of questions:

>> What is the target person doing in their interactions with others? What aren't they doing?

>> What does the target person say, see, hear, and feel? What don't they say, see, hear, and feel?

The examined activities can include not just the use of a product or service or the use of a prototype for a new product; they can also incorporate all possible day-to-day activities as well as all one-time occurrences in a private as well as a professional context. You can look at the daily routine of a potential customer along with their recreational activities, actions at home, or whatever steps they take before, during, and after work.

The observation isn't just about the specific superficial activities — the persons and the situations they're dealing with must be viewed as a whole. You capture the environment in detail, including all relevant objects, the situation itself, and all activities or interactions of the people as well as their emotions. I recommend that you follow these steps for this observation:

1. **Describe the surroundings.**

   Give a detailed description of the rooms or outside areas where the target person is spending time. Answer the following questions:

   What do the surroundings look like, and how is the atmosphere in which the persons are active?

   What is the character and function of the room?

## 2. Analyze the objects.

Make a note of the objects and items that the persons use or find in this situation (furniture, computer, or special devices, for example).

Which objects or devices are consciously or unconsciously used or not used, changed, or moved?

Who uses these items and in what environment?

What is the relationship of these objects to each other?

What meaning do the customers or users give the objects or materials with which they interact?

## 3. Identify the situation.

Describe the events or situations the customers find themselves in.

What type of event or situation is it (meeting, small talk, discussion with a customer, recreational activity, housework)?

How can the atmosphere of the event or situation be described (formal, serious, informal, or exuberant)?

## 4. Understand the actions and interactions.

Summarize the activities carried out by the people. Highlight the individual actions of the target persons. Make a note of the sequence in which the individual actions and interactions occur:

What is happening?

What activities are the people carrying out in order to achieve something?

Which tasks do the people perform?

What do the people touch, open, close, press, pull, move, and carry in certain situations?

What happens before a particular situation or activity, and what happens afterward?

Which interactions are happening between which people?

Are these interactions routine processes, or does each interaction happen differently?

What are the actions of the individual persons?

What do the people read, what do they look at intensively, what do they decide to do, and what do they carry out?

What do their interactions with their environment look like?

How are the people interacting with each other? Are they acting more formally or informally, playfully or seriously, distant or familiar?

What are the points of contact between people?

How do they talk, decide, negotiate, or work together?

5. **Detect the emotions.**

Write down the customers' emotions in different situations. This also includes the nonverbal expressions of the target person through gestures, facial expressions, and movement:

What feelings and thoughts are the people showing?

How are these feelings and thoughts expressed?

Which special form of gestures and facial expressions can you observe?

6. **Consider the time.**

You should record at which time the observations take place and how long they last:

When are you carrying out the observation?

How do the time and/or duration influence the persons or situations you're observing?

## Determine how you want to observe

After clarifying who and what should be observed comes the question of how to observe. Observations are not all the same; there are different forms. You can carry out the observation openly or covertly. In the open variant, the target person basically recognizes you as the observer; they know that they are being watched, in other words. In contrast, with the covert method, the person is unaware of the observation. Although the covert method allows you to capture much more natural behavior and minimize observation errors, such a monitoring of individuals gives rise to legal and ethical concerns. For that reason, when it comes to observing individuals, I recommend that you choose the open variant.

**TIP**

Keep the legal and ethical dimensions of observations in mind. Without their explicit agreement, investigations into the private sphere of individuals is neither legally nor ethically justifiable. Choose an open observation, and ask for the consent of the people you want to observe.

When observing larger groups, a covert observation may be justifiable or may be the only option possible. You should proceed with sensitivity and, if in doubt, gain the consent of the individuals. An open observation can lead to your getting closer to the action so that you're better able to capture situations, gestures, and facial expressions. However, you should be aware of the potential observation errors that might arise from this open type of implementation.

**WARNING**

Consider the numerous possible observation errors related to open observation. Above all, the Interviewer effect must be taken into account (also known as the Observer effect or the Hawthorne effect). This effect refers to the fact that, by your observation alone, you can bring about a change in the behavior of the target person.

Observations can be carried out in either a natural or artificial context. Field observations represent the behavior of people in a natural (normal) environment. This type of environment is preferable to an artificial environment, such as a laboratory or another external place. In a natural environment, you can mostly avoid the observation effects that can lead to errors in the collection and evaluation of information. Lab tests are comparatively elaborate and expensive. However, they might be necessary. Often, the observed person is unwilling to participate in an analysis of situations in a private setting. One example is the behavior of older people when they use their home computers.

Using a lab, you're better able to simulate similar conditions so that the situations for the observations are comparable. You can compare how different people behave under otherwise similar conditions. In a lab, you can also avoid interferences that would falsify the behavior or make it unrecognizable. An environment that's too loud or plagued by poor air quality and lighting, unpleasant temperatures, or other stimuli provided by the surroundings might interfere with the actions while using a product or service.

It may also be possible that you either want to use or have to use special equipment for the recordings that is difficult or impossible to use in field observations. One example would involve the use of eye-tracking systems to investigate eye movements while shopping or using online applications. Eye-tracking systems make it possible to evaluate what people are looking at in succession when they see a product, an environment, or a website. Heat maps can be used to analyze the gazing behavior of users; the more saturated the color is, the more often the eyes are focused on individual regions. Other examples of such behaviors requiring an intensive use of equipment include galvanic skin response (GSR) measurements, voice frequency analyses, and recordings of the pupil reactions, brain activity, or breathing.

**TIP**

Perform field observations whenever possible. This lets you analyze normal behavior, detect influences from the natural environment, and minimize observation effects. This kind of observation is more reality-based and shows people acting naturally.

# Determine who should do the observing

Don't underestimate how important it is to make the right decision when it comes to determining who should take on the role of observer and whether that person should participate in the observed situation.

In most cases, you want to carry out an external observation, where you observe another person (who might be a stranger to you). In theory, you can also observe your own behavior — you might observe your own behavior when you shop at the supermarket, for example. Yet I recommend against this kind of self-observation, simply because you probably lack the necessary mental distance to the analyzed situation and this won't give you an objective view. You can also overwhelm yourself if you analyze your own behavior at the same time as you act. During preparation, self-observation can be useful to reflect on your own role as an observer. Before the (external) observation, you should generally reflect on the influence you will have as an observer on the individuals involved or the situation.

TIP

Clarify the expectations you have for the situation and the people who are involved. This gives you clarity about your biases or prejudices. In connection with the self-reflection about your role as an observer, you should clarify the answers to these questions:

>> How do you picture the target person in terms of appearance, age, gender, or special modes of behavior?

>> What would be your own wishes and needs if you were the target person?

>> As the target person, how would you imagine the situation and its surroundings?

>> What would you, as the target person, expect of other people with whom you interact in this situation?

>> How would you act in this situation as the target person?

>> Which problems, difficulties, or conflicts would you expect as the target person?

After you have reflected on your ideas about the planned observation, you should determine a few methodological aspects:

>> Where and how you will sit and/or move as an observer

>> What gestures and facial expressions you will have as an observer

>> Whether, what, and how you would say something as an observer

>> How you want to register the actions

**TIP**

Have different people with a range of skills perform the observations or evaluate the recordings. Psychologists, engineers, computer scientists, or design experts might pay attention to different aspects of the customer's actions. If you're able to find just a few others to support you and whose different observations you can compile and compare, that would probably be sufficient.

With external observations, you have to decide whether you want to participate — or have to participate — in the interaction as an observer. With the participating observation (also referred to as *action* research), you're closely participating in the action, which means that you can gain more in-depth insights face-to-face. For example, imagine that you're an expert in autotuning who is participating in an event on this topic. In a direct interaction with other tuning experts, you can evaluate the body language and statements of other people much better than if you were off standing by yourself.

An external observation of how customers deal with certain situations, as well as their interactions, lets you capture the sometimes complex actions and behaviors in their entirety. If you participate, you're sure to influence the situation to some degree. The target persons feel watched and might change their behavior, which can falsify the results. One variant of the nonparticipating observation, which can also involve participation at certain times, is called *shadowing,* where you closely trail a person for several hours or even days. In general, you should try to behave inconspicuously and discreetly in your role as the observer. However, it's possible to direct questions to the observed person if something is unclear.

# Your Observations in a Systematic Fashion

You can carry out an observation systematically, or you can intentionally choose to be unsystematic, where you devise only rough categories, if any, about what you want to observe. This can make sense during an early innovation phase, if you know nothing or very little about the problem at that time. When the observer has this level of freedom and flexibility to operate, it may lead to completely new insights. However, there's a risk of getting "lost in the weeds" of dealing with minor aspects — following only the observer's personal interests and not focusing on the objective details. Additionally, an unsystematic process makes the subsequent evaluation much more difficult. Because you haven't defined what you want to focus on, you'll capture a vast amount of useful information as well as a lot of irrelevant data. You're stuck trying to develop categories based on this mountain of information and then trying to come up with a useful analysis. This can lead to analysis paralysis — the biggest trap for any observer, especially when it comes to complex actions. If you use multiple observers, an unsystematic process can also make it more difficult to compile information in a uniform manner.

Based on these drawbacks, I recommend that you perform observations systematically while remaining flexible when it comes to dealing with unforeseen events. Clarify who will carry out the observation, what will be observed, and how the observation is to be carried out and by which methods the data should be evaluated. The main characteristics of this approach are that it's planned, targeted, and verifiable. It lets you carry out observations effectively (observing the right thing) and also proceed efficiently (observing correctly).

## Observing the right thing

During your preparations, you have to decide whether you want to, and are able to, observe persons and situations directly or indirectly. You can observe the user behavior for online applications directly when you "look over the shoulders" of Internet surfers and thus record their activities. If you create a user profile only from the clicking behavior, that's an indirect form. Similarly, you can indirectly observe buying behavior by way of a loyalty card system in retail.

With indirect observation, the relationship between the cause (the action and behaviors) and effect (result of the action) isn't always easy to identify, or there may be misinterpretations.

TIP

Even if you're interested only in the results of an action, try — if possible — to observe the action directly. This is the only way to clearly identify the various cause-and-effect relationships.

If you want to carry out your observations systematically and record all aspects in detail, complex actions may cause you to reach the limits of your ability to grasp everything. To master the overwhelming amount of information coming your way, you have to focus on the essential mode of behavior and actions. In other words, you have to observe the right thing. The question is, what exactly is the right thing?

TIP

Focus on the following clues to behavior as part of your observation:

>> Uncertainty, a hectic pace, or a misunderstanding on the part of the target person

>> The need for additional effort on the part of the person being observed or signs that the person is overwhelmed by an activity

>> The "problem areas" of the target person — where the process made the target feel uncomfortable, where it progressed too slowly or was too difficult or too boring

>> Any disturbances that might occur (either with or without the person's influence)

>> The target person's unexpected use of something differently or incorrectly

>> The target person's decision to skip a step or decline to do something

>> Any observable emotions felt by either the target person or their discussion partner, such as anger, annoyance, despair, curiosity, interest, enthusiasm, or dedication

To focus on your research, become aware of the limits of observational studies. Observations undoubtedly have the high potential to reveal previously undiscovered problems, wishes, and needs. However, they can only detect modes of behavior that can be perceived with the senses. If you're interested in the underlying motives and attitudes, observations will provide you with only indirect information at most.

**WARNING**

Put your overall focus only on the respondent's actions instead of on their mindset, values, and norms; the observation method can shed light on these matters only indirectly — if at all. You're better off using interviews as a means of gathering that kind of information. You might, for example, link the observation with a survey by additionally asking the target users about their motivation behind performing specific actions. You can perform such a survey before, during, or after the observed situation. This can clarify which emotions the target person felt while performing the actions, for example. This is of particular interest when you detect contradictions and discrepancies between their answers and the actions you observed. For example, the person asserts that he is happy with the product, but you could observe problems of the customer while using the product.

You can further narrow the focus by concentrating on particular actions and events that occur more frequently. If you repeatedly see the same phenomenon while observing different people in various situations, pay attention to the details of this phenomenon. Watch for recurring patterns between the different observed situations.

An observation always has a time limit. If you want to research buying behavior at an electronics store, you're sure to gain good insights by way of an observation of relatively short duration. However, if you want to learn about the decision-making behavior when purchasing real estate, it would definitely exceed the scope of a single observation. In practice, this decision-making process undergoes many stages, in different places and at very different times.

**TIP**

Modes of behavior partially depend on the time of day of the observation. Select the specific time or time span of the observation carefully so that you observe the right thing and achieve representative results.

## Observing correctly

Though it's true that there's an art to conducting an observation correctly, you can train yourself to master this art. Here's a simple exercise: Take a focused look at an everyday situation for 15 minutes, such as the behavior of people at a heavily used subway station. After the observation, ask yourself the following questions and write down your observations using keywords:

>> How many trains entered and exited the station during the specified period?

>> How many people (approximately) entered and exited the trains?

>> How would you characterize the people — age, gender, attire (casual or business)?

>> Were the people relaxed or rushed?

>> Did the people move as groups or on their own? Did spontaneous interactions occur between individuals, and if so, what kind?

>> What did people do while waiting?

>> What sounds and smells were there at the subway station?

By asking yourself these and other questions, you can sharpen your sensibilities for future situations and continue to increase your awareness of details in observational studies.

Take enough time for your observation. You'll see that you have invested enough time if there's an increasing frequency of interesting patterns in the observations. If additional observations only confirm these patterns, you can skip further studies.

You have to clarify in advance how you plan to document and/or record the wealth of information you're sure to gain. Numerous schemata can help capture the observations in a structured way and not neglect any essential aspects. I recommend the use of a data sheet like the one laid out in Table 8-1, which you can adapt for your own studies. When you have a data sheet like this one on a clipboard and are equipped with a camera or an audio recording device, you're optimally prepared for field observations. Of course, you can also use a tablet, but keep in mind that a simple pen and notebook can sometimes be more convenient.

TABLE 8-1 **Data Sheet for Observations**

| Name of observation | Date and time: |
|---|---|
| Name of observer | Place: |
| Dimensions of observation | Notes (keywords, symbols): |
| Surroundings and objects | Your observations: |
| | Information (appearance, character, and function) about the room or outside area |
| | A listing of the objects and items that are present, such as furniture, computer, or special devices |
| Situation | Your observations: |
| | Type of situation: meeting, small talk, discussion with customer, recreational activity, housework |
| | Atmosphere of the situation: formal, serious, relaxed, exuberant |
| Persons | Your observations: |
| | Number of persons involved |
| | Age, gender, recognizable characteristics, appearance |
| | Roles and relationships of the persons to each other |
| | Identifiable behavior, wishes, and needs |
| Actions and interactions | Your observations: |
| | Types of actions in chronological order (with each step described in detail) |
| | Persons and/or objects that interact with each other |
| | Type of interaction: formal/informal, fun/serious, distant/close |
| Emotions and unique occurrences | Your observations: |
| | Special verbal and nonverbal expressions of the persons through gestures, facial expressions, and movement |
| | Special expressions of feelings by the acting persons |

TIP

Don't bother taking notes for all areas of the observation. Write down as much as necessary, but as little as possible. Focus on the essential aspects, such as individuals, certain actions, or certain interactions with another person.

You should also quote particularly important (especially emotional) statements word-for-word. Create symbols to quickly and easily capture facial expressions, gestures, body language, and expressions of feelings. You can use emojis, for example, so that you can capture the type of emotions (annoyance, worry, frustration, curiosity, excitement). In your notes, describe what you have seen, heard, and experienced as neutrally as possible without immediately interpreting it.

TIP

Record which problems the customer has with the specific product and in which situation these problems occur. If you simply write down that the customer doesn't like the product, it's only your interpretation or even just an assumption. This strategy increases your observation's objectivity.

Given the time constraints, it's certainly expedient for you to write down keywords during the observation. However, I recommend that you elaborate on the essential observations later. For one, you can then reflect more deeply about your own impressions. For another, this type of summary makes it possible for you to share your observations with other people who aren't involved. It's precisely this sharing that can result in the creation of valuable ideas, especially if individuals who weren't involved interpret the results of the observation with fresh eyes. Together, you can decide whether any further observations are needed and, if so, in which areas.

Don't let too much time pass between the observation and the evaluation of your results; otherwise, your memory will fade and you'll lose important details. I recommend that you also document the process in the form of photos, videos, or audio recordings. If this strategy is technically and spatially possible and acceptable to those being observed, you can then later process the sizable amounts of information and impressions more easily. Sometimes, your own smartphone is all it takes. During the observation, you can focus on those aspects that you may have difficulty reconstructing later using your records. Keep in mind that people sometimes behave differently in front of a video camera.

WARNING

Recordings in the form of videos, photos, or audio require the prior consent of the observed persons. I recommend that you give each individual a full explanation of why and for what purpose you want to use the observations. I strongly recommend getting their consent in writing. Explain how important your studies are. I am continually pleasantly surprised by how many people are happy to support my observational studies.

Direct observation can be supplemented by the *think-aloud* technique, where, during the observation, you ask the target person to explain their activities or state what they're feeling or perceiving. This technique can be applied while the activity is performed (*concurrent* think-aloud), or you can take a video when the person is acting without speaking. Afterward, this person comments on the activities while watching the video (*retrospective* think-aloud). This variant has a couple of advantages: The person can focus on the activities, and is subsequently better able to explain their intentions, thoughts, and feelings in a relaxed atmosphere. When you ask the person to explain their activities or feelings, always ask whether something is unclear. Don't assume anything — address it directly instead.

# Avoiding observation errors

To document observed situations objectively, internalize the following list of potential observation errors so that you can avoid them in the field:

>> **Hawthorne effect (or Interviewer effect):** When observed, a person almost always changes their natural behavior. We're all familiar with this effect: Whenever you're in front of a camera, you change your behavior, your mode of expression, or your actions. As an observer, however, you don't want to interfere — you want to find a natural situation instead. Refrain from using audio or video formats to document the proceedings if you suspect that this effect may occur.

>> **Rosenthal effect:** The observer's expectations, attitudes, convictions, and stereotypes influence the result by means of a self-fulfilling prophecy. You expect older people to have numerous problems while using an online application. You focus on incorrect activities particularly by older people, and some of your observations meet your expectations — you see this as a confirmation. But many older people have no problems using the online application. To avoid the Rosenthal effect, clarify your attitudes and possible prejudices about the people and situations you want to observe. This is necessary for you to start an observational study unencumbered.

>> **Halo effect:** Individual characteristics or activities outshine everything else. If the observed person makes a particularly ingenious remark, don't assume that they will respond competently in all situations.

>> **Cognitive dissonance:** This happens when observers are looking only for confirmation of their expectations because they would find an incompatibility with their expectations unpleasant. As an observer, you expect people to always have problems when they use a specific device. If those problems don't occur, this is a result that you shouldn't ignore.

>> **Primary effect or recency effect:** The first (primary) or last (recency) impression outshines everything else. Right off the bat, your target person makes a negative statement about the allegedly poor user-friendliness of a product. However, the subsequent process makes it clear that this lack of user-friendliness consisted only of initial problems. When you observe, don't just focus your attention at the start or the end; instead, document every mode of behavior over the course of the entire observation.

>> **Role effect:** A certain expectation accompanies a person due to their role. A scientist is usually an expert in their specific area. Don't assume that every scientist knows how to operate certain devices, for example.

>> **Contact effect:** The more often a person is observed, the more you see them in a positive light. As an observer, the frequent observation of the same person results in your forming a relationship with them because the person will seem familiar to you over time.

>> **Similarity effect or contrast effect:** The observer's own characteristics (age, education, origin) and modes of behavior (hobbies) are transferred to the observed person. Any similarities that are revealed generate sympathy. Any differences that are revealed generate antipathy. Suppose that in your observations, you discover that a person likes the same recreational activities as you. As the study progresses, you perceive this person in a particularly positive light and give only a passing glance to other people.

>> **Attribution error:** The characteristics, behaviors, and attitudes of the observed person are systematically overestimated and outside factors are underestimated. You might observe how numerous people at a high-traffic train station have problems with the ticket machine. In your evaluations, you ignore the fact that these problems might be caused by the noisy environment and poor lighting. People should never be seen as detached from the environment and the situation in which they act. Always view the events comprehensively, by recording not just the people but also influences from the environment, the special aspects of the situation, and the significance of certain objects.

>> **Logical fallacies:** What you accept as the logical conclusion of an observation is based on a mistaken assumption or condition. A cause-and-effect relationship is assumed on the basis of events happening together at a certain time. The classic logical fallacy is this one: A return of storks in the spring causes an increase in the number of births in the spring. A similar variant is one where you conclude that a spatial correlation of events means that the content of these events is related. After all, statistics can play a trick on you: It is assumed that the content of certain events is related because these events occur frequently.

>> **Show effect:** Depictions that draw attention create greater significance. You overrate the angry tirade of one person while using a smartphone app but don't attach much significance to the many other users who have no problems. Analyze these kinds of effects carefully and avoid overrating them.

>> **Sticky effect:** An observed behavior from the past is projected into the future. On a few occasions, you observe someone who previously always complained that a technical device was too complicated to use. You expect exactly the same behavior from this person when using a new device. Based on your experiences, you ignore the fact that this device has a completely different functionality and that the situation is also different. You stick falsely to the past. Especially when you observe a person multiple times in various situations, you should always evaluate each situation on its own. You should derive patterns only during the evaluation.

>> **Periphery effect:** The focus isn't on the observed person; instead, the observation is influenced by the aura of the periphery (environment, atmosphere, setting, adjacent objects, existing objects, other persons, or additional aspects).

When you observe a service, differentiate between impressions from the environment and the quality of the action.

» **Selective perception:** Because of your observation, you're focused on only a few properties, characteristics, or behaviors. Sometimes, the value of an observation for you can be that you document something as supposedly irrelevant. In your observations, you focus exclusively on your target person's verbal statements. Because of your selective perception, you don't notice that these statements contradict the facial expressions and gestures of your target person.

» **The Golden Mean effect:** You probably know this from your own experience: People tend to favor neutrality when evaluating people and situations, looking for not too hot and not too cold, but just right. In other words, you're likely to strive toward the golden mean in your evaluation — even when, seen objectively, this golden mean isn't always the case.

» **Mildness effect or Strictness effect:** If you know in advance that a person has suffered a misfortune, is still very young, or has a disability, you will probably evaluate this person with more mildness. In contrast, you would probably evaluate them particularly strictly if you became aware of negative aspects of this person's past.

# Applying Consistent Observational Methodologies

You can apply helpful methods for systematically observing and then evaluating different situations in practice. This list presents the four methods I discuss in more detail in the following sections and describes what they are designed to do:

» **Artifacts analysis:** Analyze the customer's objects.

» **Behavioral mapping and tracking:** Document movements and activities of the customer.

» **Mental models:** Describe the real behavior of the customer.

» **Mystery shopping:** Identify the shopping behavior.

You can also use methods to help prepare yourself thoroughly so that you can focus on essential tasks. You can learn more about these methods in Chapter 7. Other methods make it possible for you to structure and, ultimately, analyze the most important results of your observations. I tell you more about this topic in Chapter 9.

# Artifacts analysis: Analyzing the customer's objects

*Artifacts analysis* refers to the systematic examination of objects, items, and other items owned, used, or desired by the customer or user (a personal inventory, in other words). First, look at the objects, and then touch or feel them. In addition to this visual and tactile analysis of the objects onsite, you can take videos or photos or make drawings for the subsequent analysis. The examination of the object can involve these characteristics:

>> Value

>> Functionality

>> Complexity

>> Physical properties

>> User-friendliness

>> Aesthetics and color design

>> Frequency of use

>> Location of object

>> Description of the brand character

You can then gain information about the customer and draw important conclusions, such as

>> The customer's characteristics (age, gender, special preferences)

>> The customer's habits and needs

>> The problems that occur while using the object

>> The extent to which the customer can be culturally or socially characterized on the basis of the object

The objects can come from the customer's professional or personal environment. The potential customer can be asked, for example, to name the objects that have a great intrinsic value in and of themselves. This also allows for informative analyses about the use of competing products.

You can also ask the customer or user about these objects. For example, you can ask

>> How and how often does the customer use it or store it?

>> What does the customer associate with it?

>> Why does the customer acquire it?

>> How would the customer feel if they would no longer own it or if it were damaged?

# Behavioral mapping and tracking: Documenting the customer's movements and activities

With behavioral mapping and tracking, the customer's movements and activities are systematically recorded and examined. There's a distinction between place-centered mapping and individual-centered mapping, which can also be combined:

>> In **place-centered** mapping, people are observed at particular previously determined places within a certain timeframe. Here, you can document these characteristics:

- How these people can be characterized (age, gender, habits)

- Whether the person is at the place alone or in a group

- How people interact with each other in the place

- How long people spend in the place overall

- How long certain activities can be observed

You can enter your notes into a plan, floor plan, or sketch of the observed location (aisles and stands at a supermarket, for example). In the analysis, you can compare different time periods to see whether the observations change depending on the time. Photos taken at different times in the same place can support the analysis.

>> In **individual-centered** mapping, a particular person is watched to see how they move or how they perform which kinds of activities in a place and during a certain timeframe. You must have the person's consent for this kind of intensive observation.

**WARNING**

The Hawthorne effect (Interviewer effect), where observed persons change their behavior when they know that they're being observed, is particularly pronounced in behavioral mapping and tracking cases. You should therefore give individuals some time to get used to the situation. With the consent of the observed persons and in compliance with data protection and personality rights, you can also record the situations on video.

# Mental models: Describing the real behavior of the customer

Describing the real behavior of the customer is possible with *mental models*, which describe a person's assumptions about how something should function or proceed. These assumptions may deviate from the actual processes or from how the provider of a product or service thinks it should proceed. From the user's perspective, this deviation can lead to operating errors, frustrations, annoyance, inefficiencies, superfluous actions, or misunderstandings. For that reason, such an analysis offers numerous starting points for improvements or for developing innovations.

# Mystery shopping: Detecting shopping behavior

For mystery shopping (also called *silent shopping*), systematic observations are used to assess the service quality with all its defects and potentials for improvement. In this process, an observer participates in a real-life consultation or buying action as a test customer. This market research method can also be performed as a test call *(mystery call)*.

## HOW TO USE MENTAL MODEL DIAGRAMS

A person's assumptions are always based on prior experiences, on prior knowledge, and on wishes, expectations, and free interpretations. The actual action steps and behaviors of people can be analyzed on the basis of observations and surveys of particular user groups, where *action steps* and *behaviors* can refer to physical activities or mental and emotional processes that are broken down into individual actions or thoughts or feelings. Here, it's important to deal with actual specific actions, not with abstract wishes or expectations for the future.

The sidebar figure shows a mental model diagram, in which the example is about searching for, finding, buying, financing, and inhabiting a new property. The mental model diagram shows all action steps with the individual activities, thoughts, or emotions related to how a person or group wants to reach a goal (such as finding a property, in this example) or handle a task. Similar or closely associated activities, thoughts, or emotions are grouped and given headings. They represent individual "towers" in the diagram. The tower labeled "Viewing properties," for example, would consist of all activities before, during, and after seeing an apartment, such as "Making an appointment with the Realtor," "Planning the drive there," "Driving to the property," "Asking questions," and "Following up on the visit." The abstraction level depends on the goal of the study.

Below the line, concrete offers of your own or outside products or services are visually contrasted with the towers. In this example, this would be an online comparison portal for the real estate search. Based on the comparison at the top of the line (activities or thoughts or feelings) and at the bottom (offers), it's possible to identify weak areas and gaps (the mental spaces). You can then use this information to derive action needs or approaches for new ideas.

In this example, the online real estate portal doesn't offer a comparison of different cities. There are also gaps in supporting offers of "Searching for next tenants," "Renovating," and "Furnishing," for which there are competing offers. It's also possible to identify individual service contact points *(touchpoints),* which support individual customer activities. In this example, one might imagine an automated search function for handymen for renovation jobs or the offer of a personal onsite consultation about the apartment's interior design.

Mental model diagrams also enable you to compare different user groups with each other to see whether they vary in terms of the individual activities or thoughts.

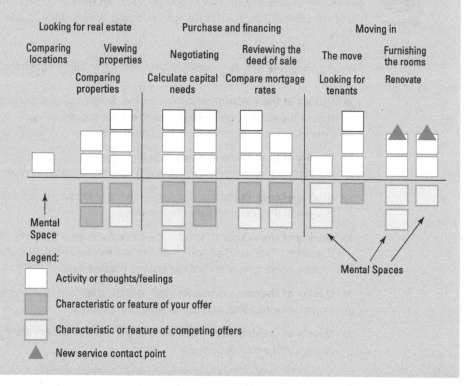

Test persons have to be trained for the mystery shopping so that they behave like real customers, register the environment, and, above all, note the behavior of the salesperson or consultant in detail. If possible, the test persons should have no corporate affiliation and should appear like a true potential customer. Outside experts or in-house employees (also known as *checkers*) can also be used. Exercises, in the form of role-playing games or realistic rehearsals, can prepare the test persons for various situations and thus train a knowledgeable eye to detect areas where there's potential for improvement.

**TIP**

Create a standardized catalog of criteria and a set of guidelines in advance to specify how, what, and when you will observe. The type of observation should be as representative as possible in terms of place and time and should (preferably) be performed multiple times with various test persons. You should also focus on critical process steps in the consultations or sales transaction.

**WARNING**

In theory, mystery shopping also enables concealed benchmarking with the competition, which will provide information about improvement potentials or the strengths and weaknesses of competitors. All the same, this concealed analysis of the competition is ethically questionable, which is why I don't elaborate on it here.

Mystery shopping makes it possible to observe the following characteristics:

>> **Quality of the environment:** Includes the design and cleanliness of the spaces, the room atmosphere, the discreet consulting atmosphere, seating, facilities, and the appearance of the employees

>> **Quality of time management:** Including adherence to schedules, availability, waiting times, delivery times, business hours, or consultation times

>> **Quality of consultations:** Especially in terms of the scope and depth of the analysis of the customer's problem or need

>> **Quality of the solution:** Includes the correctness and objectivity of the statements, individual advice, credibility and motivation of the customer advisor, presentation, and intelligibility of the benefits

>> **Quality of the communication:** Includes the friendliness, politeness, empathy, helpfulness, and conversation atmosphere

>> **Quality of the delivery or flexibility:** Concerns the delivery itself, return options, and available payment methods

In addition to specific suggestions for product, and especially service, innovations, this process sensitizes employees to flaws in their consultations and thus improves the service quality. This also makes it possible to objectively determine the customer's level of satisfaction.

IN THIS CHAPTER

» Precisely characterizing your
target users

» Describing the question being
asked and problem to be solved

» Understanding the problems faced
by target users and the wishes
they express

» Summarizing the task to continue
finding a solution

Chapter **9**

# Redefining the Problem

The phases of design thinking that I spell out in earlier chapters are about collecting meaningful information about the selected problem. In this chapter, I provide a few guidelines on how to use this information to formulate the specific task at hand. Gaining clarity about your target user is an important step. With the help of this definition, I'll show you how to closely examine the needs of your target users. For one, you have to take a detailed look at their problems in the relevant situation. For another, you have to describe their wishes precisely.

Because you're sure to discover a variety of problems and wishes, you must make a choice. Based on the selected problems or wishes and the specification of your target person, I'll show you how to ultimately find a concrete task for your design thinking project.

## Finding the Task

After you have come to an understanding of the problem and have observed how this problem manifests itself in the real world, you have to pull this information together — *synthesize* it, in other words — in a more compact form. The question or problem is the design challenge that you and your team must master. A well-formulated question or problem is of key importance for the subsequent phase of generating ideas. You need this in order to know which task to focus on and what needs a solution.

The information you collect must answer these two basic questions, which are crucial for solving the problem:

>> Who are the target users that matter here?

>> What's the specific need that you want to satisfy?

These two questions comprise a new definition of the original question, which you should have asked yourself already when starting the design thinking project. Usually, the term *redefinition* is used to describe this process, but I personally don't much like the *definition* part of the term. It sounds too academic and dry and doesn't express the key idea behind a well-formulated task. Such a task always has a visionary character as well and should be motivating. If I, despite all this, still use the term *definition*, because it's the one that's commonly used and I somehow manage not to talk about a vision, please take it upon yourself to view your task nevertheless as an inspiring one with a long-term relevance for the future. On the whole, you should note the guidelines outlined in the following sections whenever you redefine the question.

## Preventing a search field that's too broad or too narrow

Your question or problem should be neither too broad nor too narrow. The search field for finding the solution is based on the question. If the question is too narrow, you run the risk that you'll be unable to explore ideas outside of the search field when you generate ideas. Doing so stifles creativity when it comes to finding ideas for a solution. A specific search field can result in niche solutions, especially in the case of technical questions. With a specific task, however, you make it easier to find the solution. You prevent a detour into details and secondary matters that are outside of your focus. However, these details and secondary matters can reveal a high potential for innovation. Aim for a balance between a question that's too abstract and one that's too specific.

You can start with a broader question that you make more specific, step-by-step, in the design thinking process. With a complex topic, you can alternatively formulate multiple questions that focus on different facets of the topic. If you have a wide-ranging task, such as determining how to benefit from the opportunities and challenges of digitalization developments in a certain industry, you can focus on individual technical, economic, ethical, or legal aspects of this topic. The question "How can we answer customer inquiries about XY product by email within ten minutes?" is certainly already specific, but still broad enough for multiple possible solutions. You have found a well-formulated task when this task still offers you numerous approaches to such a solution.

**WARNING**

If your question is too broad or unclear, you're sure to get lost during the processes of finding ideas and developing prototypes. You might be overwhelmed by the breadth of a question without knowing where to start when finding ideas. My personal experience with design thinking projects is that a slightly more specific question is more helpful than a broad and comprehensive task. You can focus it further in the course of the design thinking process.

## Avoiding the temptation to prescribe solutions

In this phase, avoid offering any indication of what a possible solution might look like. Always separate the wording of the challenge from finding the solution. Avoid the temptation to provide answers on how something should be achieved, or even to map out the approach. The focus of the task is more on the Why and What and less on the How. For the task "How can we use 3D printing technology to quickly and easily manufacture bicycle accessories?," the approach by way of 3D printing is already predefined. "How can we help our customers get bicycle accessories within a few hours without spending a lot of money and time?" is worded more openly.

**WARNING**

Avoid describing the task with negative words: "How can we prevent our customers from suffering financial damages when using XY?" Assume a positive attitude instead: "How can we make it possible for our customers to gain profits by using XY?"

## Formulating a meaningful and challenging question

The problem and question should be relevant and challenging. The greater the significance, the more attractive your solution becomes. This in turn increases the motivation of the participants to actively contribute to this challenge. A task creates pressure for resolution and pushes toward implementation.

A problem that's seen as meaningful and challenging draws attention. Keep this information in mind later on, when you need resources to implement the solution.

**WARNING**

Avoid comparisons when you word the task. Here are a couple of examples: "We want to develop a better product than the product of competitor XY" and "Our solution should offer customers more functions than the current standard solution." Your task should be unique, not just better than something else. Your idea should be everything except ordinary — extraordinary, in other words.

## Writing clearly from a user's perspective

The person for whom you want to develop the solution or whose wish you want to fulfill must be at the center of your task. Writing up tasks from a user's perspective means that you use wording that's appealing on a personal, human level, with an emphasis on feelings. Your task is not a business goal that has to be worked through to completion. Nor is your task a purely technical problem that you should solve. Technology must benefit people, and when it benefits people, you also reach your business goals. Focus on people, and push aside the technological or business matters. To see what I mean, look at the following formulations:

>> **Too technical:** "How can we make a battery with a high storage capacity that's still light enough to use in electric cars?"

>> **Too business-like:** "How can we renew our battery products in ways that make them so attractive that we increase our market share by 10 percent?"

>> **Puts the user in the spotlight:** "How can we support our customers in the car industry so that a family of four can conveniently and comfortably travel from Boston to Chicago in their electric vehicle without stopping to refuel?"

**WARNING**

Don't use the task as a way to address your personal goals or the goals of the company. You might end up achieving those goals anyway, but don't use them as your only guide. Design thinking can in fact help you achieve your personal and business goals, but keep in mind that it isn't the priority. The only perspective you should assume is the user's perspective.

## Formulating tasks clearly and comprehensibly

The question or problem should be worded clearly for all participants of the design thinking process — that's the only way to find a goal-oriented solution. Simple and pictorial language helps it become intelligible. "How can we develop an electric bike for our customers that makes it possible for them to ascend the steepest road in the world without having to pedal?" This wording is clear and, with a slope of 35 percent, also a challenge. Discuss your task with your team as well as with uninvolved outsiders. A complicated question won't work; I recommend a task that can be easily communicated.

TIP

Make sure that everyone involved in the design thinking process actually understands the question. Ask the participants to formulate the question in their own words. That way, you can see to what extent everyone has the same understanding of the task. Talk about what each project participant expects in terms of results.

The next three main sections show you how you can precisely formulate the task on the basis of these guidelines in three simple steps, a process that prepares you best for the next phase to come — finding ideas:

1. Select and describe your target person.

2. Identify, analyze, and select the needs of the target person (their problems and wishes).

3. Summarize the task and determine the right point of view.

# Focusing On the Right People

Together with your design thinking team, you should agree on a target person whom you will analyze in detail and for whom you will develop a solution. The Persona method is the best way to summarize the relevant information when it comes to describing target users. (For more on the Persona method, see Chapter 7.) You can come up with different people if you want to work out different angles or special aspects of the problems or wishes.

WARNING

Be careful if you notice differences, or even incompatibilities, in the stated problems and wishes of your target users during your observations and surveys. Differences and incompatibilities can indicate that your target group consists of different persons, and different persons may need a variety of solutions for their problems and wishes. In such a case, I recommend that you take another look at your target group and form different subgroups. You can only be positive that your target group has a uniform composition when you detect a similar pattern among all members.

In theory, the target user can not only be a single, unique, living, breathing individual but also comprise an organization, such as a company. In the business-to-business (B2B) area, different persons in various roles often contribute to the decision-making process at a company. Mention is often made of a buying center, or decision-making unit (DMU), which can house the following roles:

>> **Initiator:** This person actively searches for innovative solutions to entrepreneurial problems.

>> **Influencer:** This person influences the buying decision because it poses special requirements for the offered solution. The IT department of a company can set forth requirements so that the software solution you offer must be compatible with the software infrastructure in use.

>> **Recommender:** This person is an opinion leader at the company and is asked for advice in case of inquiries.

>> **Buyer:** This person is responsible for selecting suppliers and for sales transactions up to a certain volume.

>> **Decision-maker:** Starting with a certain purchasing volume, this person is the authority for the final decision.

>> **User:** This person applies your solution and thus has a lot of knowledge about the applications and products.

>> **Saboteur:** For whatever reason, this person is against your solution, on principle. Think about who might experience any disadvantages at the customer's business as a result of your solution.

Become aware of these different roles, and separate people based on the various roles in a buying center. This task becomes easier with a stakeholder analysis (I tell you more on that in Chapter 6), which can be supplemented with the following questions from a buying center analysis:

>> Who belongs to a buying center at a particular company?

>> How do these persons influence the decision?

>> Which goal do the individual persons pursue in the buying center?

>> How do these persons get information about new products?

>> How is the decision made?

You can characterize the individuals by using the Persona method, where you describe in keywords the key characteristics, wishes, and problems of a hypothetical customer or user. (For more on the Persona method, see Chapter 7.)

TIP

Include current noncustomers, and analyze them in the next step. Then you can generate interesting and new search fields for innovations. Instead of customers, each stakeholder can be picked out and analyzed in the broadest sense.

# Recognizing the Needs of Your Target Users

When you describe customer needs, you must first ignore the fact that your target users want to obtain a certain product or specific service. This phase is not about specific products or services. Theodore Levitt, professor at Harvard Business School, already hit the nail on the head, in 1986: "People don't want to buy a quarter-inch drill. They want a quarter-inch hole!" The customer's need is expressed as a task that should be solved, no matter by which means.

So that you can formulate the need as a task, I recommend that you apply the jobs-to-be-done concept. This concept, popularized by Professor Clayton Christensen at Harvard Business School, focuses on the tasks or activities — the jobs, in other words — initiated by or for the customers. These tasks satisfy a specific customer need, where a problem is solved or a wish is realized.

## CONSIDERING JOBS IN DIFFERENTIATED WAYS

You can further subdivide the individual jobs of your target person into these types of jobs:

- **Functional:** Certain functions, characteristics, activities, or process steps must be, or should be, present, executed, or completed (from the customer's perspective).

- **Social:** By completing the task, the customer gains prestige, power, influence, status, or a particular (desirable) image. In other words, the question of how the customer wants to be perceived by others (family members, friends, acquaintances, other organizations) is answered.

- **Personal (or emotional):** This type is enjoyed by the customer, who considers it interesting, exciting, stimulating, entertaining, cool, aesthetically or beautiful — or who afterward feels secure or experiences pride and a personal satisfaction that the job is finished. In other words, the question of how the customer wants to feel when the job is done is answered.

The social and personal (emotional) jobs represent a psychological benefit for the customer. With this differentiation, you can analyze why customers want to have certain tasks (jobs) completed. You can collect this information by way of secondary analyses, surveys, observations, or experiments, or you can use your own experiences. (For more on this kind of analysis, see Chapter 7.)

In general, you can picture a job as a task that's completed in a certain situation or a specific context in order to make progress from the customers' point of view. Consider the task less as a result and more as a process. This job must always take into account the specific situation and specific context, meaning that jobs always depend on a certain situation that has limitations or special aspects. That can be a certain stage in the customer's life, their family status, their financial or personal situation, the local environment, or other situational factors. Customers don't buy products and services just like that; instead, they hire them so that they in turn can do certain jobs (tasks or activities). Levitt's quote also expresses this focus on the task and less on the product. Customers don't want products — they want *solutions* for their tasks (needs, problems, wishes) that will result in progress.

# Analyzing Needs as Tasks

This section focuses on how to systematically identify the essential jobs for which you can later find a solution to solve these tasks. Analyzing the jobs has nothing to do with understanding how a customer interacts with a product or service. Instead, you should ask yourself what and why your target user wants to achieve something in a particular situation. This strategy takes you a step deeper into your analysis. That's the main difference from the customer journey concept, which focuses on the actually performed activities in connection with a specific product or service. (For more on the customer journey, see Chapter 7.) The jobs should be separate from certain products and services. They are in no way, shape, or form characteristics, functions, or process steps of products and services.

For this deeper job analysis, look at the actions of your target person before, during, and after the task is completed:

>> **Before the task is performed**

Which goals are the target person pursuing with the task? Why does this person want to complete (or have someone else complete) these tasks or activities? What outcomes does the person want to achieve with these tasks? What kind of progress does the person want to make in a particular situation?

Is the task important to the target person?

Which aspects must the person plan and clarify? How does the person plan the completion of these tasks? How does the person assess which resources are needed to complete the tasks, and how do they select these resources?

Which steps must the target person take before wanting to complete the task or activity?

Which necessary resources must the person look for in order to complete the tasks? These resources can be material (tools, materials, other persons) and immaterial (information, knowledge, licenses). How difficult is it for this person to find these resources?

How must the target person prepare and organize these resources as well as the situation in order for the task to be completed? What does the person have to check, before the task begins, in order to start the task? Does the person have to confirm (or get a confirmation of) the functionality of these resources?

In which situation does the target person want the tasks to be completed? Where is the person when they want to complete the task or activities? When should the task be solved?

While doing the job, what are the framework conditions faced by the target person? Which limitations need to be considered when it comes to completing the job? Does the person have the capabilities for solving the tasks on their own?

**» While performing the task**

How, by whom, and with what means are the tasks currently completed?

What does the target person have to do to finish the task successfully?

Do particular characteristics and past experiences of the target person influence the completion of the job?

Does the target person use particular devices or tools to complete the task in an unusual way?

What else can the person use to accomplish the task? What are the current alternatives? Some alternatives are doing nothing, doing something else, delaying, and accepting partial solutions.

Which social, cultural, or political influences affect the completion of the tasks?

Are there differences between the target person and noncustomers, in terms of completing the tasks?

Which tasks or activities prove to be problematic for the target person? Which tasks or activities cause the target person to feel frustrated, bothered, or annoyed? What are the target person's greatest difficulties?

What are the tasks that the target person would be happy to complete? What does the person desire?

**» After completing the task**

What must the customer do to finish the task completely? Which steps come after this task or have to be worked out afterward?

What does the target person have to adjust later on in order to finish the task successfully?

How does the target person review the success of the task after completing it?

What will the customers do after completing the job?

You must analyze these steps in the context of a specific situation. The jobs have to be identified at the right level of abstraction. It shouldn't be too abstract, or else important detailed information might get lost. Nor should it be too specific, to avoid restricting the scope for finding ideas later.

When you complete the tasks, you need, above all, to analyze the problems and wishes that have come to light. The next few subsections show the best way to do this.

## Determining the problems of the target person

The problems, frustrations, and pains of your target person when handling a task are often the starting points for the subsequent solution. It's worthwhile for you to identify the problems and analyze the nature and causes of these problems. In the following list, you'll find several questions that can help you in your analysis:

» Which tasks or activities will be (physically, intellectually, or emotionally) strenuous for the target person? Which activities or tasks are uncomfortable for the person?

» Which tasks or activities will generate costs for the target person?

» Which tasks or activities will require the target person to wait? Which tasks or activities take too long?

» Which tasks or activities does the target person consider too complicated?

» Which tasks or activities does the target person (using current solutions) perform inefficiently or not ideally? What are the person's typical mistakes when they perform (or have others perform) these tasks or activities?

» Which tasks lead to results where the target person isn't 100 percent satisfied?

» Does the person understand what would constitute fulfilling the task?

>> Is the target person hesitant to perform the activities, either on their own or undertaken by others? Which barriers prevent the target person from receiving external help for the tasks and activities? Does the expenditure (in the form of time or money) prevent the person from using external help for the tasks or activities?

>> From the target person's perspective, what risks lie in the completion of these tasks?

>> Does the target person expect negative social or emotional disadvantages if the task isn't completed?

>> What are the barriers that prevent the target person from solving the task in a different way than before?

>> Which tasks or activities are barriers for noncustomers? Are there differences between noncustomers and the target person?

# Identifying the target person's wishes

Along with their problems, consider the (unstated) wishes of the target user. These wishes offer you the possibility of finding new offers for the target person. They might be new products, services, procedures, or business models. Ask the following questions to help you in your analysis:

>> Does the target person hope for a personal advantage with this task?

>> Does the completion of the task trigger positive emotional feelings in the person? If yes, which ones?

>> Does the target person hope for social recognition by completing the task?

>> Which cost savings in the execution of the tasks would please the target person?

>> Which time savings in the execution of the tasks would please the target person?

>> What level of quality does the target person expect in the execution of the tasks and activities?

>> What makes the tasks easier for the target person? Which service does the target person want for the tasks?

>> How does the target person assess high quality in the execution of the tasks?

>> What does the target person want if problems occur in the completion of the task?

>> What additional completed tasks would please the target person?

**TIP**

When you analyze the wishes of your target person, also consider the current (competing) solutions. A comparison of the current alternatives can provide not only information about unfulfilled results (underserved outcomes) but also over-fulfilled results (overserved outcomes) produced by these alternatives. *Overfilled* in this context means that the current alternative completes the task with the desired result but has too many functions and features — also referred to as *overengineering* or *gold-plating*. It may indicate that this particular alternative is wasteful — that it's too expensive or too complicated, in other words. This situation might benefit from what's known as a *disruptive innovation*, where you're able to seize the competitive advantage by offering the customer simplicity, convenience, user-friendliness, accessibility, and an economical price.

## Comprehending the reasons for particular problems and wishes

In your analysis, you should not only identify the problems and wishes but also understand the individual motivations behind these needs. This makes it possible for you to find approaches for new ideas. With the means-ends analysis (MEA), you can determine the functional, social, and personal jobs (tasks and activities) and analyze them with an appropriate survey technique (the laddering technique, for example, as described a little later). Means-ends analysis offers approaches to explain why customers prefer particular product features and what they (subconsciously) hope to gain from these features. This means that the focus here is on the basic motives of buying behavior.

Means-ends analysis is based on the approach that customers understand the product or service innovation as a means to fulfill their personal wish or goal (end). As shown in Figure 9-1, the connection between product features and values can be depicted as steps on a ladder.

Product features (the *means,* as in the technical product characteristics) initially offer the customer a functional benefit that can also create an additional psychological benefit. This psychological benefit can be emotional (the customer perceives the product as aesthetically appealing) and/or social (the customer can share the benefit of the innovation with friends).

In turn, these functional and psychological components of the benefit can influence the short- and long-term values. The short-term values (also known as *instrumental* values) represent desirable modes of behavior for the customer. Examples of instrumental values are that customers want to be helpful, performance-oriented, or imaginative. The long-term values (also known as *terminal* values) are ultimately desirable life goals, such as having fun, enjoying life, possessing wisdom, experiencing freedom, benefiting from equal rights, feeling secure, being recognized socially, or creating self-realization. On the whole, you have to consider the possibility that multiple values might determine multiple user components, which in turn would influence multiple product features.

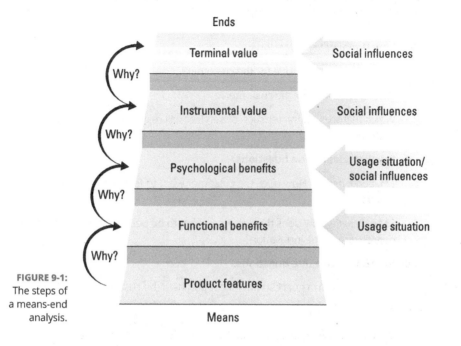

FIGURE 9-1:
The steps of
a means-end
analysis.

You can't consider the components of the benefits and values independently of external influences. The benefit components depend on the customer's current situation while using the innovation (the influence of the usage situation) or on which social influences the customer is exposed to (any expectations regarding the social environment). These social influences also determine the created values.

With the means-ends concept, you can apply the laddering technique to analyze these steps incrementally — like the steps on a ladder — from the specific product features to the more abstract values. With what is known as *vertical* laddering, you can proceed step-by-step from the product features to the benefit components with this recurring question: "Why is this important to you?" Additionally, you can use *horizontal* laddering to query why the identified features correspond to the real product characteristics from the customer's point of view. In that case, the recurring question is, "Why does the product characteristic XY correspond to the feature you desire, or why not?"

Another variant is the laddering-down technique. Using the values as a starting point, ask How questions. Ask the customer how they want to reach a certain goal or achieve a value by means of which particular benefit or feature of the product, such as "How do you want to achieve XXX?" You can give the customer an example of specific product features as possible selections in the survey.

By using the laddering technique, you can find answers to questions that are crucial when it comes to developing ideas in the design thinking process, such as

>> **Functional value questions:**

What is actually valuable for the customer?

What is a benefit for the customer?

Which features, characteristics, or services will result in a value for the customer?

>> **Psychological value questions:**

*Emotional benefit:* How does the customer want to feel after using the innovation?

*Social benefit:* How does the customer want to be perceived by others to some degree due to the innovation?

>> **Instrumental value questions:**

Which short-term goal can the innovation help the customer reach?

>> **Terminal value questions:**

Which long-term goal can the innovation help the customer reach?

# Selecting the Most Important Wishes and Problems

Following your analysis of the target person's problems and wishes, you're faced with quite a large selection of potential needs. Select and prioritize the identified problems. Ideally, the target person should be the one to evaluate the jobs (tasks and activities) and thus the associated problems and wishes. Here are the two basic questions you can ask your target person, using a simple rating of 1 = Not Important to 5 = Very Important:

>> "What significance do you attribute to the task (jobs) XY?"

>> "How do you rate the current alternative solution for completing this job?"

For one, this gives you information about the relevance of the task, which also represents the task's attractiveness. For another, you identify tasks that are currently least satisfied by existing solutions. The most interesting case is a significant task that has no satisfactory solution at the moment. (For more on the specific implementation of surveys — surveys where you can also ask these two questions — see Chapter 14.)

## DIFFERENTIATING CUSTOMER REQUIREMENTS WITH THE KANO MODEL

The Kano model, proposed by Dr. Noriaki Kano, is a way to divide customer satisfaction along the lines of different types of requirements. The following kinds of customer requirements are distinguished here:

- **Basic (must-have criteria):** These are requirements that customers take for granted or consider obvious, which means that they often aren't even mentioned explicitly. They must definitely be present; otherwise, the customer is dissatisfied and will switch to the competition.

- **Performance (linear satisfier; target criteria):** The customer's satisfaction is proportionate to the fulfillment of this requirement. The higher the quality, the greater the satisfaction, and vice versa. In other words, if the requirement is satisfied, the customer is satisfied, and if the requirement isn't satisfied, the customer is correspondingly dissatisfied.

- **Enthusiasm (delighter; potential criteria):** The customer doesn't expect these requirements or may be unaware of such an expectation. If they're present, they will make the customer happy. If they aren't present, however, this won't lead to dissatisfaction.

Added to these requirements are product features that are rated neutrally from the customer's perspective ("It doesn't matter to me") and features whose presence might even result in the rejection of the product.

On the whole, the Kano method leads to a better understanding of the customer requirements and helps with setting priorities in the product development. Keep in mind that the Kano method takes a great deal of effort on your part — especially when it comes to executing the survey — and that the evaluation by the customer can be quite subjective. Furthermore, customers can often only evaluate features that are comprehensible, clear, and tangible to them. Here, the prototype phase of design thinking can be of help. (For more on prototypes, see Chapter 13).

If user feedback tells you that a task is unimportant, take this message seriously and include the task in only a secondary position in your considerations. Then take a critical look at the user ratings about their satisfaction with the current solution. In my experience, users aren't always in a position to realize that the current alternatives have shortcomings. Don't become discouraged if your target persons are satisfied with the current status. Your goal must be to develop something that the prospective customer didn't even realize was possible. Your goal shouldn't be the mere satisfaction of the users; instead, you want to generate enthusiasm among your target users.

You can also expand your evaluation by suing the Kano model. (See the nearby sidebar, "Differentiating customer requirements with the Kano model.") It lets you differentiate the jobs from the customer's perspective into basic, performance, and enthusiasm requirements.

To supplement this evaluation from the user's perspective, you can also add an evaluation from the company's point of view ("Is the task economically significant?") as well as from the competitor's perspective ("Is it possible to reach a competitive advantage with a [perhaps better] fulfillment of the task?").

Please don't overrate the evaluation from the perspective of the company and the competitor. This phase is about the perspective from the user's point of view. You will ignore many interesting tasks if you place the focus too narrowly on the economic viability and competitive attractiveness of a task.

Follow this list of do's and don'ts when applying the jobs-to-be-done concept:

>> Don't analyze only functional jobs — also take emotional jobs (personal) and social jobs into account.

>> Don't ever consider jobs separately from their specific situation.

>> Don't combine different customers with different tasks or customers in different situations.

>> Don't make the description of the tasks too vague.

>> Do express jobs with verbs that describe a process, and less in the form of adjectives or adverbs that describe a condition.

>> Because the jobs of customers change dynamically and are exposed to numerous external influences, do use this concept regularly.

The jobs-to-be-done concept helps you develop solutions or offers in the form of product, process, service, or business model innovations that can complete these jobs better than the alternatives.

# Determining the Right Point of View

After analyzing and selecting the target person as well as their problems and wishes, you should formulate a concrete task — it defines your point of view. This point of view is the basis from which you will develop ideas or concepts for solutions for your target person in the next step of the design thinking process. Your goal in determining the point of view is to summarize the task in a short message format consisting of a single sentence of approximately 280 characters.

TIP

Create a *user story* to focus the information about target users and their problems or wishes into a single sentence. This format is also referred to as the *how-might-we* technique:

How might we

help or support or convince [name of target person]

so that

[their problem] is solved or [their wish] is fulfilled

with [the following result] _____

in [the following situation] _____ and

with [the following limitations] _____?

When it comes to the limitations, focus exclusively on framework conditions that cannot be changed, such as legal provisions, environmental regulations, or ethical principles. Otherwise, you'll feel much too restricted when it comes to generating new ideas as part of the next step of the design thinking process. In addition to this user-story sentence, you can add a reason that explains the target person's problem or wish.

This key sentence should be posted clearly in a central location in the common rooms for all employees in the design thinking process to see. All other information about the target person, their problems and wishes, and the situation they're facing should also be made visible (photos, graphics, interviews). A mood board, which is a good option for this purpose, can be created to clearly capture the mood of certain situations with the help of a collage of texts and images and the use of relevant objects. You can also narrate the task in the form of a story that vividly explains the problem or wishes and background information in simple words. You can even use this storytelling strategy for the development of prototypes. (For more on prototypes, see Chapter 13.)

The sentence that captures the right point of view should stimulate discussions and be permanently visible in the room during the course of any subsequent steps as you move toward a solution. Then you can repeatedly refer to it while working. The sentence also enables you to measure the results of the subsequent steps against it. You can evaluate whether the idea you found can solve the problems formulated in the point of view or satisfy those wishes.

**WARNING**

Avoid formulating a single task for multiple different target groups. Likewise, don't cram into a single task all the insights you have collected so far about the person and their problems and wishes. That would only serve to overload your task. To be sure that your point of view is clear, you have to condense the information and be able to express it in just one sentence. However, you have to eliminate any trace of conventional wisdom or stereotypical pronouncements from this sentence. Focus on what's special about the person and their problems or wishes, or on the special aspects of the situation. Here's a sample sentence: "How can we help students with a migration background so that they can fully reproduce the educational material in an upper-level English class within six weeks, without a personal tutor, and improve their results by one letter grade?"

# 3

# The Solution Phases

Open up sources for new ideas and use the principles of creative thinking.

Apply various creativity techniques and consider your question from different perspectives to find a solution.

Assess your ideas with several methods by selecting and applying appropriate criteria for evaluation.

Create prototypes for potential customers to try.

Test your assumptions and ideas with feedback from your target users and continue to refine your idea.

Chapter **10**

# Finding Ideas

You've come to the phase of the design thinking process where you actually develop ideas. Your goal must be to generate as many ideas as possible. In this chapter, you find out how the creative process works and which principles you can use for this process. Your task is to identify sources for new ideas so that you can uncover innovative approaches. To prepare for your creative work, first familiarize yourself with the factors for success, and then scout out which creativity blocks might exist and how you can overcome then. Ultimately, you'll get to know the systematics behind the techniques designed to further creativity and then be able select the right methods for your task.

## Mastering the Creative Process

Being creative means that you think of something new. Being innovative means that you implement something new. This is why creativity is a fixed component of any innovation project, regardless of whether you're aiming for a new product, service, process, social and organizational change, or business model.

Creativity is not an event — you should see it as a process. This process can sometimes take days, weeks, or months. Figure 10-1 gives an overview of the creative process. Graham Wallas already described this process, back in 1926, and it still remains universally applicable.

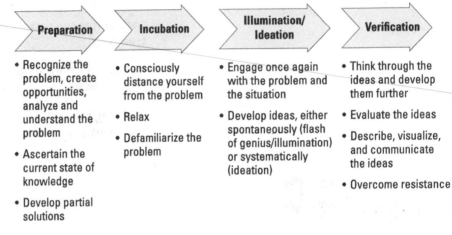

**FIGURE 10-1:**
The creative
process.

To develop an idea, you first have to engage intensively with a problem or an opportunity. Above all, you have to investigate the current state of technology. You can develop the first partial solutions on this basis. All this comprises the preparatory phase. (You can also create the entrepreneurial opportunity yourself.) In the second step, you have to distance yourself from the task. To gain mental distance from your task, you can also defamiliarize it. (For more on defamiliarization, see Chapter 11). You have to ponder on the task, so to speak, and relax at the same time. That's the incubation period.

TIP

Gain distance from your problem or question. You don't have to concern yourself about the task every minute of the day. Do something else between the times that you think about it. Busy yourself with other activities. Engage in sports. Take a vacation. When you mentally return to the task and grapple with it again, you'll have created new ideas and will have a new perspective.

After the incubation period, start dealing with the question and problem again. Only now does the generation of ideas take place. Ideas can arise spontaneously in the form of a flash of genius — this is referred to as *illumination*. But an idea can also be developed systematically. This is called *ideation*. Your idea is never finished. You subsequently have to further develop, test, implement, describe, and communicate your idea. (Expect it to encounter some resistance at the company as well.) This step is the *verification*. These phases don't happen sequentially in actual practice, as you might assume from viewing Figure 10-1. Instead, you'll find that numerous and varied feedback and reflection loops occur in this process. The design thinking approach is based on this creative process.

# Opening Up Sources of New Ideas

Becoming aware of possible sources of ideas and systematically searching these sources for information and inspiration is sure to help the creative process. Depending on the range of tasks, a variety of information sources are available to you. You'll find out about a few particularly important sources in the following subsections.

## Taking advantage of employee skills and knowledge at your own company

It seems a given that you can get information and inspiration about possible solutions from employees at your own company, but especially in larger companies with different business areas, knowledge regarding the skills of colleagues in other departments and sharing information across various divisions often leaves something to be desired. You should systematically establish a knowledge management system at your company that promotes the sharing of information.

Establish a few knowledge management tools at the company. Here are two approaches that are particularly relevant for finding ideas:

>> **Yellow Pages:** This idea, borrowed from old-style paper telephone books, features expert directories that list contact information and descriptions of the employees' skills. Moving down the list, this information might include a person's name, position, area, department, phone number, email address, work areas, project experiences, special areas, special know-how, and specific skills. The competence profiles can be created by the employees themselves in a standard format and potentially be edited by a staff member.

>> **Knowledge map:** This item makes it possible to visualize knowledge areas or knowledge carriers (experts) for your innovation activities. The relationships between individual knowledge areas or knowledge carriers can be clearly represented in the form of a mind map. In addition, these knowledge maps can be supplemented with graphical elements for more clarity. Additional background information, method descriptions, or contact persons for particular knowledge carriers can be filed away under either the individual knowledge areas or the carriers themselves. When you design a knowledge map, the guiding questions you want to pose should concern themselves with which knowledge areas are required and what knowledge in particular someone has to have about an area.

## Surveying and observing customers and involving them in developing solutions

You can survey and observe customers with not only the goal of getting information about their problems and wishes but also in the hope that customers will give you information about solutions. Customers who are particularly invested in the product area — the ones referred to as *lead users* — provide information about not only requirements but also solutions in some detail, because they're personally interested in a solution and have the necessary competencies. You should therefore systematically search for such customers.

Lead users like to share information in specialized online communities, publish blogs on the topic, or comment about previous products on comparison portals. Approach these customers and win them over to your search for ideas. One option might be an invitation to a joint idea workshop. You can also involve customers by way of innovation competitions, using your own website or external providers to make fixed-term requests for external partners to submit ideas about a particular question in a competitive process. You can offer rewards for the best ideas.

## Surveying and working with suppliers

You can systematically integrate suppliers into your design thinking process, just as you can do with customers. Suppliers have high (technical) competencies in the area of your task and will be glad to support you as their customer with the development of new products and processes. In addition to personal talks and surveys with the suppliers' employees, you can hold joint workshops or call for their participation in innovation competitions.

## Keeping up with what the competitors are doing

An analysis of competitive activities can give you suggestions for future products and services. Analyze your competitors' new developments and products. You can acquire information by way of patent-pending inventions, publications in trade magazines, brochures, press releases, and trade fair appearances. Buy your competitors' products and take them apart so that you can see the (technical) innovations — this is called *reverse engineering*. In addition to the direct and potentially new competitors, you have indirect competitors. These companies offer the same customers other types of products or services. For the maker of an MP3 player, for example, smartphone manufacturers and music streaming services are indirect competitors because they offer music for mobile use. Look at other industries to see which alternative trends, developments, and new products and processes you can find there.

# Evaluating publications and patent information

Before starting your ideas search, you should research articles in trade magazines as well as the descriptions found in patent applications. In addition to general Internet research (websites of the relevant researchers, institutions, and companies), as well as a scientific research through databases, you should research particularly in patent databases. Patent research is a useful tool to determine the state of technology, detect technological breakthroughs, find cooperative partners, and gather suggestions for new ideas. Some of the largest free patent databases in the world include ones run by the European Patent Office (https://worldwide.espacenet.com) and the US Patent Office (www.uspto.gov). The Google Patents search engine (https://patents.google.com) is another resource you should definitely use for your patent research.

TIP

When doing patent research, define possible keywords with reference to your task and the technology area of interest. The keywords shouldn't be too specific, since patents deliberately encompass broad (specialized) terms. Always research for synonyms, too. Read relevant patent documents so that you become familiar with the expressions used for specific technical terms. You can also use the names of the relevant persons and companies working in this area.

## Participating in trade fairs and conferences

You can locate interesting partners for finding ideas through discussions or by participating in technical presentations at trade fairs and conferences. You'll get to know new customers, suppliers, and representatives from the scientific world. Search specifically for trade fairs and conferences where you will encounter new partners in science and industry. You can also visit events in other sectors so that you discover new trends, developments, and products in other areas that can be used as a source of inspiration for your own project.

## Collaborating with experts

Experts in science and industry who have gained in-depth specialized knowledge from their work can be integrated into the design thinking process in the form of workshops, oral or written surveys, and project work. You can find experts through publications in trade magazines, patent research, social networks and specialized online communities, or at trade fairs and conferences. Approach the experts and describe your task.

You can find ideas for your task with the help of these sources of information. After the incubation period, you're in a position to develop a creative solution during the phase of illumination or ideation based on this foundation.

# Understanding the Creative Principles

I have come up with a few general basic principles for the illumination/ideation step after many years of experience with the creative process. The following creative principles don't occur independently in the real world; their potential actually unfolds when they're combined with each other. For that reason, you should combine the principles for your task.

## The decomposition principle

Following the decomposition principle, you disassemble the problem, task, process steps, or the redesigned product into its parts and then vary or combine these parts in a new way. Many multifunctional devices were created by following this principle. By using what is referred to as a *morphological box*, you break down individual products into their various functions. Vary the distinct form of this function, and then combine the functions and their forms in a new way.

## The associative principle

With the associative principle, you link ideas, information, perceptions, and emotions. You can make this connection without a fixed target in mind. (We're talking free association here.) One example is brainstorming, but it's also possible for you to proceed in a particular order or sequence in which you link something together. (This is known as *structured association*, and you can find out more about it in Chapter 11.)

## The analogy and confrontation principles

Analogy and confrontation, which are specific changes in perspective, are based on comparisons to different kinds of areas (also referred to as *bisociation*). This allows you to form relationships that had not existed earlier. Using analogies, you compare your task with another area. The identified commonalities and differences will offer you a stimulus for new ideas. By applying analogies, you can achieve positive effects for idea development and their subsequent implementation, such as greater originality, reduced risk, shorter development times, and low development costs.

In confrontations, the selected area is intentionally posed in contrast to your task. There can be different kinds of confrontations: With an inversion, you consider the problem from a reverse perspective. Rather than ask "How can we solve the problem?," you ask "How can you make the problem worse?" This principle is based on the brainstorming variant of the Headstand technique. (I tell you more about that topic in Chapter 11.) However, you can also create a deliberate provocation to stimulate the flow of your ideas. "How could we solve our problem if we were ten times as rich as Jeff Bezos, Bill Gates, and Warren Buffett combined?"

## The abstraction and imagination principles

With the basic principles of abstraction and imagination, you solve a problem on a higher or simplified visual level. Get as much distance from the problem as possible so that you can understand the problem from a birds-eye view and come up with ideas for solutions. From a higher-level perspective, you can also look for typical patterns of successful innovations. With imagination, you think primarily in images. You approach the problem or question as an object or a situation. Visualizing your own thoughts or using metaphorical thinking support this principle.

**EXAMPLE**

The chemist Friedrich August Kekulé spent a long time working unsuccessfully on one of the greatest unsolved mysteries in chemistry — the structure of the benzene molecule. One day, he pictured the molecule as a snake that was biting its own tail. That was the solution: As a molecule, benzene forms a ring structure.

# Know the Success Factors for Increasing Creativity

In addition to the basic principles, you'll discover that other success factors contribute to the creative process. Take a look at your task and ask yourself whether you can use any of the individual factors described in the following sections.

## Questioning the conventional wisdom

Don't take anything for granted. Ask the following questions:

>> Why is it like this?

>> Why *isn't* it like this?

>> Why should it be like this or not be like this?

>> How could it also be different?

You can mentally change everything. Take different paths. You should understand this in both the actual sense and the figurative sense. Question the conventions and assumptions in your industry.

**EXAMPLE**

For a long time, it was a convention in the furniture industry that customers can't assemble furniture and don't want to assemble furniture. The founder of IKEA, Ingvar Kamprad, successfully broke with this convention. The Canadian entertainment company Cirque du Soleil broke with the convention that a circus must have performances by animals and clowns and be designed for children. Using the concept of combining elements from opera, musicals, and rock music with a circus for adults, the company was able to create a brand-new market.

## Simplifying products and processes

Successful product and process innovations aren't distinguished by being particularly complicated. Quite the contrary: Customers appreciate being able to operate something easily, not being overwhelmed by the functionality, or not having to think while using it. There are numerous examples of how *streamlining* — the simplification of products and processes — is a formula for success.

**EXAMPLE**

The great initial success of Instagram is based on its simplicity. Editing and sharing photos without having to expend much effort was the idea behind that success. The McDonald brothers, of fast food fame, reduced their menu by half in order to serve their customers more efficiently. The first iPod had far fewer features than competing models. It impressed users with its high storage capacity, appealing design, and combination with iTunes, an innovative service at the time. Southwest Airlines cut services like on-board meals, lounges, and seat reservations, which allowed it to reduce its prices. The winning formula of this inexpensive airline was born from these simplifications.

Remove or reduce all process steps, characteristics, or functions that aren't relevant for the customer or that the customer doesn't perceive and acknowledge. Also focus on only the absolutely necessary functions. Streamline the products and their functions, standardize, and automate your processes.

## Starting where others left off

This quote is from Thomas Edison: "Most of my ideas belonged to other people who never bothered to develop them." Innovations aren't created in a vacuum; they're based on experiences, insights, knowledge, and the approaches of other people. Nothing is perfect, which means that everything can be done differently, used differently, or combined differently. Modify the existing state of affairs, deliberately falsify it, or use it for completely different applications. Never consider your initial ideas to be the be-all and end-all. In this context, successful inventors are characterized by persistence and endurance.

## Observing everything and everyone in every possible place

You can get myriad suggestions for new ideas from systematic as well as random observations of ordinary or unusual situations. Don't hesitate to analyze even trivial situations. Start with yourself. Observe your own habits and business processes. Curiosity and attentiveness are prerequisites for successful observations. (For more on the potential found in observations, see Chapter 8.) A good exercise for training your observational skills is watching an object or a situation calmly for 15 minutes and looking precisely at every detail without getting distracted. Then try to remember as many details as possible and describe them in your own words.

## Experimenting with ideas

Numerous innovative ideas have originated from the trial-and-error approach. This approach is expedient not only in research-and-development for technical products and process innovations but also for all kinds of innovations (product, service, social, and business model innovations). Think in terms of experiments: Experiments allow you to select from multiple — even competing — alternatives. Creative ideas, in the sense of feasible and desired innovations, can be developed or selected only to a certain degree using purely logical thinking spun out while sitting at a desk. An approach that relies on real-world experimentation — one that tests your own ideas and assumptions — offers a reality check as well as new suggestions. For such experiments to succeed, you have to create the necessary breathing room *and* tolerate mistakes. Any experiment can fail. The trick is to learn from these mistakes and develop new ideas.

EXAMPLE

The founding idea of Zappos is an example of an experimental approach. The founder, Nick Swinmurn, experimented with his business model. Based on an experiment, he developed the successful online shop, which focuses on the sale and shipping of shoes and fashion items. He visited various shoe stores, took photos of the shoes, and then offered them for sale in an online shop. This experiment taught Swinmurn that the idea was working and showed him how he could further develop it.

# Networking

Search for and promote exchanges with others. Networking is the shortcut you can take so that you can come up with a new idea faster. Take an interest in discussions with people from other disciplines, cultures, business areas, departments, or external partners (customers, suppliers, business partners). Collaborate with diverse teams in workshop formats. Spring your idea for a solution on other people. Thanks to the different perspectives you'll encounter, this interaction will offer you new suggestions.

# Overcoming obstacles to creativity

Another crucial success factor for the creative process is overcoming the multifarious blocks to your creativity that you will encounter. Such blocks, which appear in various guises, can be divided into physical, environmental, sociological, and psychological blocks. Get to know these blocks in the following sections, and learn to overcome them.

## Overcoming physical and environmental barriers

Possible physical barriers can be represented by fatigue, stress, or burnout symptoms. For that reason, avoid stress and unhealthy behavior on a personal level because this can also influence your creativity. On a company-wide level, you should introduce a health management system and support your employees in activities that allow them to have a healthy and stress-free lifestyle.

The environment in which you work also influences creativity. The environmental blocks that you should remedy immediately include non-ergonomic workplaces, inadequate work equipment, noise, and rooms that are too cold or hot. You also have to find a suitable time for your creative work. Shortly after lunch or in the late afternoon is often an unfavorable time. Avoid disturbances and interruptions because you can develop creatively only if you can focus.

## Removing sociological blocks

Sociological blocks refer to barriers related to the corporate culture, the type of collaboration at the company, and the degree of formalization of processes and structures. At a company that doesn't acknowledge creative services and where mental blocks take the form of sacred cows, creativity has a fundamentally difficult time. The main revenue generator at a company is often an example of such a sacred cow. If you want to replace this revenue generator with something completely new, you must expect resistance at the company. Make it clear to the company as a whole that innovations are necessary for sustainable success. Introduce incentives at the company so that creative thinking and creative actions are worthwhile.

Creativity thrives on group work, but it also thrives when your teams feature diversity. If the company experiences conflicts, tensions, or rivalries, they negatively influence the creative process. Formulate clear and challenging goals for the team — goals that strengthen the communal spirit. Rigid and strict controls and numerous regulations and formalisms contribute to a bureaucracy that limits the flourishing of creativity. Scrutinize your regulations and formal procedures. Create breathing room where these regulations don't apply.

## Overcoming psychological blocks

Psychological blocks appear in numerous forms, such as closed-mindedness, which manifests itself in the rejection of outside ideas. Accept and honor the ideas of other people. If you pick up ideas from others, it isn't a weakness — rather, it's a special strength.

Another form of psychological block is the mental rigidity shown by clinging to well-established habits. If you can change these habits, it's a success factor for innovations. You generally pursue habits subconsciously and thus form mental blocks that are difficult to change.

**TIP**

You can overcome psychological mental blocks on your own. Here are some tips on how to release the "hand brake" that's in your head:

>> **Demand a minimum of new ideas from yourself.** Put pressure on yourself. Try to develop a certain amount of new ideas for one or more problems per day or week. This strategy is meant to force the issue. The generation of ideas starts off slowly, but don't just give up right away. Neither do the ideas have to be of the highest quality. It's about getting stimulation from a flow of ideas.

>> **When you read books or articles, pause your reading and ask yourself how the story or the article might continue.** Imagine the continuation of novels, or think about what a solution might look like when you read articles offering advice. Compare your ideas with the actual continuation of the book or article.

>> **Ask yourself "When was the last time that I did something for the first time?"** If this activity took place more than a week ago, you should promptly do something new or unusual.

>> **Start with yourself and change your personal habits.** This strategy resolves mental blocks at work that were created by routines and habits. This process starts on a small scale, such as in these examples:

  - *Take a different route to work.*

  - *As a right-handed person, use your left hand.*

- *Change your eating habits and eat at different times.*

- *Read novels and science fiction instead of nonfiction books.*

- *Take a bath instead of a shower.*

- *Read various newspapers.*

- *Listen to another radio station.*

- *Change your working hours.*

- *Arrange meetings with people you barely know from other departments.*

# Selecting the Appropriate Creativity Techniques

Creativity techniques can be divided into methods that are intuitive-creative or systematic-analytical. By applying the intuitive-creative techniques, usually in a group, you can stimulate spontaneous ideas, associations, and analogous conclusions in order to overcome mental blocks in the form of a much freer configuration. Intuitive techniques are particularly suited for problems that are tough to solve as well as for tasks that are still unclear. (For more on spontaneity in the creative process, see Chapter 11.)

TIP

Not every technique designed to improve creativity is suitable for every question and for every team. Creativity is highly individualistic: Everyone has their own experiences, habits, preferences, strengths, and weaknesses. This is why you should experiment with various techniques for spurring creativity and test multiple techniques in a team. Avoid using the same methods all the time. In any workshop, vary the use of creativity techniques frequently. Ideally, you combine different techniques in order to get new impulses for the generation of ideas.

The principles of decomposition and abstraction are increasingly used in systematic-analytical techniques. If you want to improve products with a modular structure or solve technical problems, systematic-analytical creativity techniques are recommended. Two helpful systematic-analytical methods that you can combine with brainstorming are mind-mapping and the morphological box, as described next.

# Structuring the topic with mind-mapping

*Mind maps* are graphical representations of a problem and the various aspects of its solution. The problem or question is written down in the center of a large sheet of paper or on a white board, and the solutions are spread out over the entire surface. The idea is to write down the topic or question in a cloud in the center of the sheet, as shown in Figure 10-2. Branches that divide and fan out from the topic into different areas emerge from the cloud. When you develop a culture of innovation, these areas are strategy, leadership, processes, structure, and competencies. (For more on developing a culture of innovation, see Chapter 16.) Keywords are written on the branches. The main branches represent the top themes. Details are written on the twigs. Make the mind map even more expressive by using color, images, or symbols. After creating a mind map, you can summarize the branches and twigs again, or you can combine branches that hadn't been connected before.

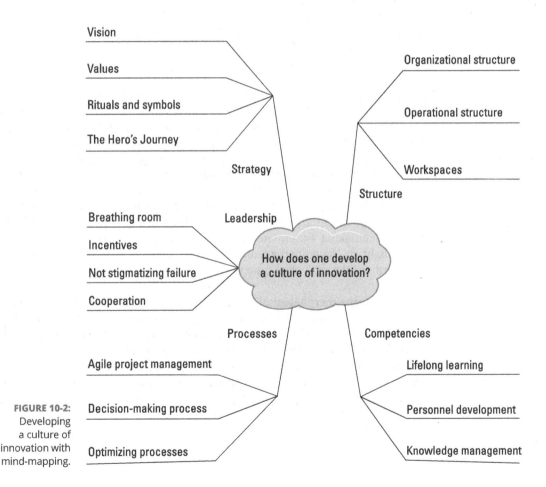

**FIGURE 10-2:** Developing a culture of innovation with mind-mapping.

Specifically search for missing branches or twigs so that you can detect gaps in your problem-solving process or your generation of ideas. There are also software programs for mind-mapping. You should note the following rules for mind-mapping:

>> Only use nouns

>> Write in block letters

>> Use symbols (arrows, emojis, figures) and images

>> Write the labels horizontally for legibility

>> Use W-questions for the structuring (Who? What? Where? Whereby? When? Why?)

## Systematically finding solutions with a morphological box

With a morphological box, you first mentally break down a product, process, service, or your entire business model into its components or functions. You then search for different characteristic forms for each component or function. These variants are combined in order to generate new ideas for solutions. The creative approach of the morphological box is shown in Figure 10-3, with the example of an alarm clock. In the first column, write down the individual functions of an alarm clock, such as the alarm itself, the alarm reminder, or the setting of the wake-up time. For each of these functions, think about how you might express this function differently. You can generate an alarm signal by ringing a bell, playing music, making an announcement, shaking an object thoroughly, shining a bright light, or changing the temperature. Then combine the different characteristic forms of the individual functions with each other.

You can use the morphological box for more than just technical devices. Imagine that you want to write a thriller. A thriller has a perpetrator, a motive, a victim, a detective, a witness, a crime scene, a time of the crime, and other characteristics. Then list how you would realize each individual component. The perpetrator can be a professor, a book author, a soccer player, a butcher, or a gardener. These are the characteristic forms of the perpetrator component. In the end, combine the selected characteristic forms of the various components with each other. Your screenplay for a new thriller is complete!

| Functions | Characteristics | | | | | |
|---|---|---|---|---|---|---|
| Awakened by | Alarm ringing | Music | Announcement | Shaking | Bright light | Change in temperature |
| Shutting off alarm | Passing through a photocell | Voice | Switch | Releasing weight | Adding weight | |
| Reminder | none | Telephone rings | Another signal | Repeating the signal louder | Inflict pain | Jet of water |
| Setting the wakeup time | Setting the clock hand | Keypad | Voice input | Written input | Running a search | |
| Time display | Clock face | LCD/LED | Acoustic announcement | Mechanical counter | | |
| Wakeup time display | Setting the clock hand | Acoustic announcement | LCD/LED as needed | Permanent LCD/LED | Printout | Write down by hand |
| Energy source | Manual | Vibration | Radiant energy | Power grid | Battery | |
| Energy storage | Weight | Spring | Bimetal | Pressure tank | Magnetic storage | none |

**FIGURE 10-3:** An example of the development of an alarm clock with a morphological box.

# Chapter **11**

# Developing Ideas Intuitively and Creatively

I f you want to resolve questions that seem especially murky, you might find that intuitive techniques designed to boost creativity are especially helpful. Brainstorming is the basis of finding ideas and a component of many creativity techniques. In this chapter, you find out how to successfully apply brainstorming techniques and learn what their variants are. For example, I introduce an option that lets you integrate the creative potential of reticent team members, in the form of written brainstorming, known as the *635 method*. You also find out about methods you can use to develop innovative solutions through confrontations with outside areas. And finally, you can systematically adopt various points of view by using the Walt Disney method and the Six Hats method to develop new inspirations for generating ideas.

## Solving Difficult Problems Intuitively and Creatively

Design thinking is a good way to master problems and tasks that prove murky or especially hard to solve. The main characteristic of such problems — known affectionately as *wicked* problems — is the presence of incomplete or contradictory information and the absence of simple, obvious approaches. The problem or question can partially change over time.

EXAMPLE

One example of a difficult-to-solve problem is how to provide energy and resources for humans in the face of a constantly growing population. This problem is associated with numerous dynamically changing influences on a social, political, legal, environmental, and economic level. But this kind of problem can also arise on a small scale. The development of a certain material that's simultaneously stable, light, and flexible can be a problem that's difficult to solve on a technical level, as is developing software that can be used easily and intuitively by many different people with various personal requirements. Creativity techniques can help you with these kinds of tasks so that you can creatively and intuitively generate new ideas for solutions.

Intuitive creativity techniques are based on forming a mental association between different subject areas — the associative principle, which I discuss in Chapter 10 — as well as bringing to the surface knowledge that you're not consciously aware of. Such techniques allow you to discard traditional entrenched thought patterns and gain new perspectives.

# Generating Ideas by Brainstorming

*Brainstorming*, which is the mother of all creativity techniques, involves spontaneously expressing ideas about a question or the solution of a problem in a group setting. You should take the following rules into account during brainstorming; you'll be more productive and generate better ideas (and more of them) if you stick to them:

>> **No criticism:** Postpone any criticism or evaluation to a later phase. You must strictly prohibit any killer phrases, such as "This won't work" or "No one wants this" or "We already tried this several years ago, without success." Holding to this no-criticism rule keeps the flow of ideas from being interrupted or the participants from being blocked. Comments are also prohibited.

TIP

Use the yes-and technique during brainstorming to avoid negative criticism and to constructively pick up the ideas of others. The brainstorming participants may not start with "Yes, but . . . ," but with "Yes, and . . ." instead. This technique is meant to support the ideas of others in line with compiling feedback and encouraging the further development of the ideas.

>> **No copyright:** Ideas by others can and should be picked up, modified, or refined.

>> **Free expression of ideas:** The participants should give their imagination free rein in order to find new and original ideas. Even the craziest ideas are welcome. The free expression of ideas also stipulates that only one person speaks at a time.

>> **Quantity precedes quality:** The point is to produce as many ideas as possible in as short a time as possible. This rule ensures the spontaneity of the expressed ideas.

Many participants of a brainstorming session have trouble sticking to these rules. Write down the rules on a flip chart and hang it up so that everyone can see it during the brainstorming session. You can also issue yellow cards (as in soccer) when someone breaks these rules.

TIP

Although brainstorming is simple enough, thorough preparation is important. Here are a few suggestions for the preparation:

>> Take the time to define the problem or question beforehand. (For more on these preparatory steps, see Chapter 9.)

>> Communicate the issue that you want to brainstorm, along with the initial invitation and request for participants to think about possible ideas for solutions beforehand.

>> Limit the group size to 12 people. (Having 5 to 7 participants is ideal.)

>> If some participants don't already know each other well, start by asking everyone to introduce themselves.

>> Set a time limit for the brainstorming session.

## Giving the flow of ideas a new boost

After a productive initial phase in brainstorming, the flow of ideas is often quickly depleted. Always ask all participants to actively contribute. Above all, you should provide new stimuli with *trigger questions,* or *tuning questions.* Doing so lets you keep up the flow of ideas and bring new perspectives to the session. You can ask some of the following questions:

>> How can the idea be fun for the customer?

>> How can you turn the idea into an adventure?

>> How do you turn the idea into a big secret?

>> How would a child solve the problem?

>> What could an automated solution look like? How would a robot solve the problem?

>> What would happen if you remove, add, replace, or change the sequence of elements in the idea?

>> What would happen if you were to use the idea exactly in reverse or flipped into its opposite?

>> What precisely should the idea *not* be?

>> What would the advertising message be if the most important aspect were to be concealed?

>> What would the idea look like in 2050?

>> What would the customers be doing shortly before or after they used the ideas?

>> What happens in the vicinity of 10 meters around the idea?

>> Can ideas be combined? Can the ideas be integrated into a larger whole?

>> Can a service (an additional one) be offered, aside from the product idea?

Another approach is the question of how a certain company or person would develop a solution. When searching for a solution, put yourself in the shoes of another person or another company. Using analogies, an idea can be developed or enhanced. This *analogy method*, known as the what–if technique, asks the question "What if we . . . ?"

>> **"What if we were billionaires?"** A billionaire should symbolize infinite riches that would be available for the solution to the problem.

>> **"What if we were Scrooge McDuck?"** The problem has to be solved with little money, just like the stingy Scrooge would do it.

>> **"What if we were IKEA?"** IKEA should represent the principle of self-service. Customers help themselves from a wide range of offers and assemble the solution for themselves.

>> **"What if we were Apple?"** The solution should be distinguished by an attractive design and ease of use.

>> **"What if we were Google?"** The problem should be solved by analyzing enormous amounts of information.

>> **"What if we were Lego?"** The solution should have a modular structure.

>> **"What if we were LinkedIn?"** The problem should be solvable by connecting people.

>> **"What if we were Airbnb?"** The solution follows the principle of sharing.

You can also use living or dead persons in business (Steve Jobs, Bill Gates, Mark Zuckerberg, Thomas Edison), from sports, art, or culture (Goethe, Picasso, van Gogh), or from society or religion (Mother Theresa, Pope Francis) to provide a stimulus. These persons stand for particular characteristics, personalities, or principles of action.

**WARNING**

Here are a few notes on how you're guaranteed to destroy a brainstorming session:

>> Letting the boss speak first and set the goal and the requirements

>> Insisting that the contributions should be made in order

>> Stating at the outset that only experts may offer ideas

>> Forbidding silly ideas

>> Insisting that everything be written down

## Getting to know the different brainstorming variants

During a brainstorming session, you run the risk that the participants will consider the method boring and that it will become routine. You can bring some variety into the idea-finding process and create new stimuli by using other forms of brainstorming. Try some of the following variants, and then evaluate each method's success, the degree to which the participants found the method inspiring, and the quality of the ideas:

>> **Step-by-step brainstorming:** Following the first brainstorming session, the most interesting idea is used as a starting point for additional brainstorming. With this method, it's possible to find ideas ranging from a general solution to a specific one. In the case of large groups, it's also possible to divide into smaller groups that either work on a different aspect of the problem or solve the same question in a competitive environment.

>> **Anonymous brainstorming or writing:** The participants write the ideas on brain cards, which are sticky notes in block letters. A moderator reads the ideas out loud as a basis for further brainstorming in the group, or the ideas are subsequently compiled into similar theme blocks and evaluated.

>> **Visual brainstorming/brainpainting:** The ideas are captured visually by using paper and pencil (or digitally). This creates sketches in the form of spontaneous scribbles, which don't have to be perfect.

>> **Blindstorming:** The brainstorming takes place in complete darkness or while participants wear facial masks so that the participants don't get distracted by visual stimuli or the gestures and facial expressions of the others.

>> **Brainwalking:** The participants' spontaneous ideas are written down on whiteboards or posters that are distributed throughout the room. The movements of the participants in the room as they move from poster to poster or from whiteboard to whiteboard are meant to trigger movement in the mind. In line with the brainstorming rules, the ideas can also be immediately supplemented or changed during the session. Small talk about the idea on the poster or whiteboard is also desirable.

>> **Speedstorming:** Here, the participants share thoughts about the question in pairs for a few minutes and then switch chairs. This results in discussions with new, rotating partners.

>> **Stop-and-go brainstorming:** The brainstorming session is intentionally ended after defined time periods, and the interim periods are filled with breaks or other techniques. These periods can also alternate between phases of idea generation and evaluation.

>> **Bodystorming/rolestorming:** During the brainstorming session, the participants should occupy a certain role and formulate their contributions or ideas from this perspective. The roles might be particular customers, users, competitors, or famous personalities in another area (politicians, athletes, artists, historical persons).

>> **Brainshaping:** The ideas are depicted in the form of clay models.

>> **Brainstation:** At different stations (rooms or separate work areas), groups of participants work on different questions by brainstorming. The participants change stations after defined time periods.

>> **Electronic brainstorming:** Ideas are shared electronically via chat or instant messaging systems in order to also include participants in different locations.

>> **Imaginary brainstorming:** The actual question is disassociated and relocated into a completely different imaginary area (outside the sector). The imaginary area should have certain similarities to the original problem but be different or absurd. The first step of this imaginary problem is to search for ideas, which are transferred back to the original problem in a second step. The original problem can be completely unknown to the participants.

>> **Object brainstorming:** In this variant of imaginary brainstorming, the participants are confronted by objects that seem to be unrelated to the problem or question and that come from very different areas (sports equipment, household appliances, tools, toys, containers, office objects, computer peripherals). From the visual and tactile confrontation, they should develop ideas about how these objects can contribute to solving the problem.

>> **Didactic brainstorming (or little technique):** The participants receive only abstract information about the topic, in the form of a general question, such as how to form customer loyalty for a company. Only the moderator knows the specific problem or question. Incrementally, when the flow of ideas decreases, the participants gain more information about the specific problem. The question about customer loyalty is focused on the existing bonus program, for which ideas for improvement should be found. This makes it possible to prevent participants from narrowing the search for ideas too much at the start.

>> **Question storming:** Rather than search for answers, participants come up with questions about the problem.

>> **Big brainstorming:** The brainstorming session takes place with several people. The participants can be divided into subgroups that compete for the most or the best ideas.

>> **Reverse brainstorming:** In this method, only negative aspects are discussed. Various aspects of the question or problem can be considered here: What is bad about the situation? Why can't the problem be solved? What are all the things that could go wrong? This reverse brainstorming approach is also a good option to let off some steam first. However, this destructive phase should quickly be followed by a constructive approach.

>> **Headstand:** In this method, the question is completely reversed: How can we make the problem worse? Or make it as complicated as possible? Or make it more expensive? Or scare off customers? In the next step, all ideas can be returned to the positive view.

>> **Pre-mortem:** In this approach, similar to headstand, you look into the future and ask the question of why the developed solution failed disastrously. The idea is to find possible reasons for the failure of a solution that hasn't been developed yet.

# Written brainstorming

One frequent problem with brainstorming is that some participants dominate and others hold back. To activate the quieter participants as well, you can apply *brainwriting*, also called the *635 method*, in which six participants all write down three ideas in periods of five minutes each. Ideally, the 635 method is finished after 30 minutes and produces 108 ideas. This process is divided into six steps:

**1.** **A moderator introduces the problem or question.**

If anyone has difficulty understanding the problem, you have to resolve it. (For more on how to define a specific task, see Chapter 9.)

2. Within five minutes, all participants enter, in the top row of a form, three ideas in keywords or a short sentence.

   Figure 11-1 shows a template for the form. In this template, the six participants are labeled A, B, C, D, E, and F. In the columns, the ideas have the numbers 1, 2, and 3.

3. The forms are subsequently exchanged between the participants in a clockwise rotation.

4. The participants look at the ideas from the previous person and then write in turn, in the second row, three ideas that supplement the preceding ideas.

   Such ideas can further develop the preceding ideas or can be completely new and different.

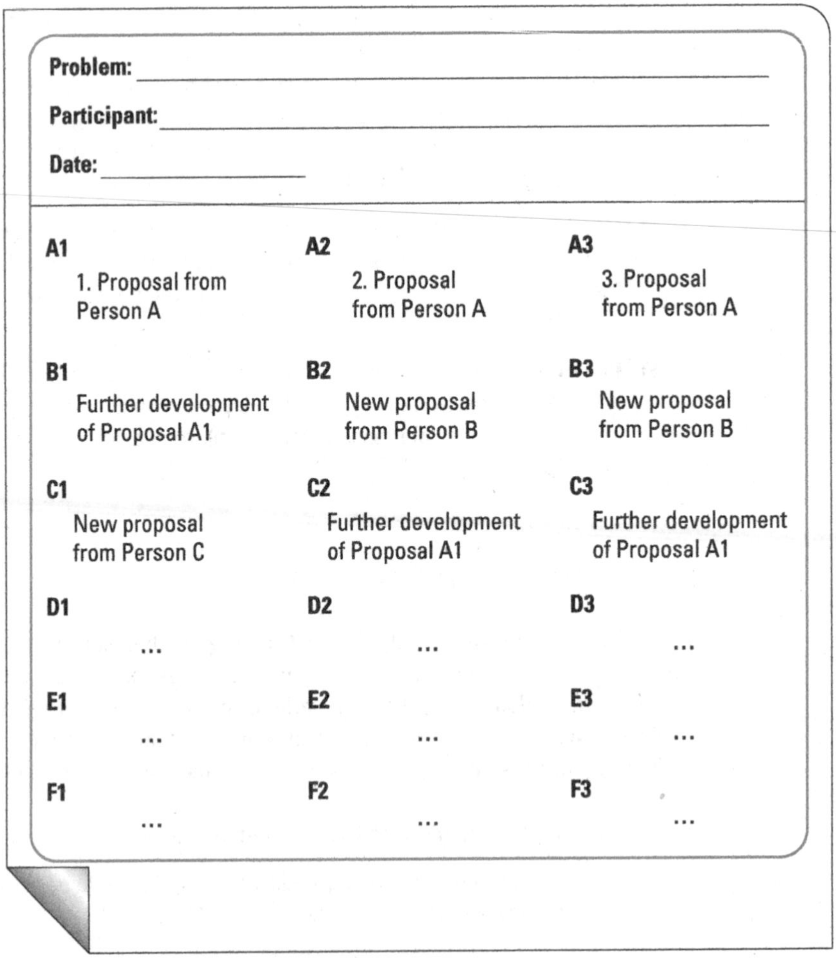

| A1 | A2 | A3 |
|---|---|---|
| 1. Proposal from Person A | 2. Proposal from Person A | 3. Proposal from Person A |
| **B1** | **B2** | **B3** |
| Further development of Proposal A1 | New proposal from Person B | New proposal from Person B |
| **C1** | **C2** | **C3** |
| New proposal from Person C | Further development of Proposal A1 | Further development of Proposal A1 |
| **D1** | **D2** | **D3** |
| ... | ... | ... |
| **E1** | **E2** | **E3** |
| ... | ... | ... |
| **F1** | **F2** | **F3** |
| ... | ... | ... |

Problem: _____

Participant: _____

Date: _____

FIGURE 11-1: Template for the 635 method.

**5.** The forms are passed to the next person again after five more minutes.

**6.** When the forms have completed the circle once, the method is finished.

**EXAMPLE**

A group of students uses the 635 method to develop ideas for how to make the first weeks of studies in an unfamiliar environment easier for new students. Their initial ideas comprise a workshop, together with students in a higher semester, a mentor system, and a survival kit. The participants pick up the survival kit idea and then supplement it several times. At the end of the brainwriting session, the survival kit consists of these elements:

| | |
|---|---|
| City map | Apple |
| Travel guide | Energy drink |
| Writing utensil | Alphabet soup |
| Tips for going out | Recipe book |
| Appointment planner | Pizza cutter |
| USB stick | Bottle opener |
| Power bank | Plastic can |
| Vouchers from local companies | Bookend |
| Collection of the best apps for studying | Laundry bag |
| | Anti-stress ball |
| Literature tips | Coffee cup emblazoned with the semester schedule |
| Crossword puzzles with the most important terms from everyday college life | Earplugs for the library |
| Care products | Copy of *Study Skills For Dummies* (Wiley), of course |
| Nuts | |

A variant of this brainwriting method is the *collective-notebook* method, where participants briefly write their ideas in a notebook over the course of several weeks. Everyone can create a suitable notebook for themselves or as a group, which the specification that the notes resemble those in a diary. In other words, you should address the problem or question once a day. After a certain period, the notebooks are exchanged among the participants (randomly or according to a predefined method) and — as in the 635 method — the ideas from the notebook are supplemented or developed further, or new ideas are described. In principle, this can also take the form of a virtual notebook. In the end, the participants can discuss, develop, evaluate, and rate the ideas in a joint workshop.

# Inspiring with Random Words

Using the *random-word* technique, you name the question or problem after a randomly selected word in order to create a new perspective. After the question or problem is defined, an arbitrary word that describes an object is picked from the dictionary. For the random-word search, you can also use glossaries, newspapers, magazines, catalogs, brochures, or books on particular topics. Where appropriate, a moderator can also prepare suitable lists of random words. Even if the word seems inappropriate, don't discard it too soon. First, every participant considers or writes down everything they can think of pertaining to the random word. The idea is to create an association between this random word and the question or problem. You can use the following questions to accomplish this goal:

>> Which characteristics or properties does the random word have?

>> How does the random word function?

>> Where and by whom is the random word used?

>> Which feelings and emotions does the random word trigger in you?

>> What do you associate with the random word?

>> What are the commonalities and differences between the random word and the question or problem?

>> How can the random word be used to solve the problem?

In addition to emotive words, it's possible to use randomly selected photos, drawings, music, or objects.

**EXAMPLE**

Imagine that you want to develop a new app that advises customers about the selection of financial products and suggests financial and capital investment options. You open the dictionary and your random word is *theater:* You ask yourself what an app for financial products has in common with a theater. You assume that some major overlap occurs in the customer groups — this insight might be helpful for the subsequent marketing. Theater is fun but can also encompass serious messages. It creates tension and proceeds according to a certain dramatic composition. For consultations about financial products, you ask yourself whether and how you can incorporate the fun factor and dramatic structure similar to a theater.

# Getting New Stimuli through Provocations

With the provocation technique, the ideas or solutions are formulated as provocative statements in order to get new stimuli from exaggerations, contradictions, or wishful thinking. Statements for finding ideas or solving the problem are worded provocatively by design, in the style of brainstorming. The type of provocation can be quite different, as I describe in this list:

>> **Wishful thinking:** Money and time don't play a role, and everything is technically possible. You can downplay or exaggerate various factors. The idea can be much faster or slower, much larger or smaller than usual, or offered much more expensively or for free.

>> **Reversal:** The exact opposite of what is desired is formulated.

>> **Breaking the rules:** Assumptions or conventions that are taken for granted are denied, or they're completely eliminated.

>> **Compare the incomparable:** You go out of your way to compare your solution with other products or services that are deliberately incongruous.

To introduce your provocative statement, the term *PO* can be used to stand for *provocative operation*. For example: "PO, if we had as much money as Bill Gates, we would. . .." This statement is intended to point out the provocation while also lowering inhibitions among the participants for formulating absurd statements.

**EXAMPLE**

You want to develop ideas for a new e-bike that has a large range and is light and suitable for off-road terrain. The wishful thinking is this: "PO, our e-bike can go around the earth ten times without recharging." Think about whether you can use solar or wind energy for an e-bike. A reversal in the form of an understatement is this: "PO, our e-bike is as light as an ant." Ants can carry loads that weigh 40 times their own body weight. You get rid of an assumption by saying, "PO, our e-bike has no wheels." Ask yourself whether an e-bike with air cushions is possible in the future. A ludicrous comparison is, "PO, our e-bike should look like a fish." In this case, think about whether you can find applications for underwater e-bikes.

# Changing Perspectives with the Walt Disney Method

The Walt Disney method is a creativity technique based on a role-playing game in which one or several people consider and discuss a problem from three perspectives. The method alludes to the famous film producer and animation pioneer

Walt Disney, who was said to systematically assume three roles for his creative ideas: In succession, he took on the roles of the dreamer, the realist, and the critic by mimicking them in three different rooms. This is also how the method named after him functions.

The perspectives of the dreamer, the realist, and the critic are assumed one after another. The separation of these three roles is symbolized by three different rooms — or, more simply, with three chairs. A location–based, or at least visual, separation helps you mentally slip into the different roles. Someone who sits in the dreamer's chair, for example, must argue from that perspective. For the actual problem, the perspectives for the three roles should be used successively as an aid:

>> **The dreamer:** Think about how the ideal solution to a problem might look. Time and money or technical limitations play no role in your visions. The thoughts can be offbeat, crazy, or illogical. Think about what you've always wanted to have.

EXAMPLE

Imagine how you might simplify the purchase of food for people with 9-to-5 jobs. You dream about a future 3D printer for food. Each food item can be made at home with the push of a button.

>> **The realist:** In this role, you ask what must be planned and realized for the project's implementation. Provide logical and fact-based arguments. Summarize the current state of the basics that are available for the realization. Compile a list of resources (personnel, knowledge, material, devices) that are required to get the project off the ground. Think about whom can help you with its implementation. Consider whether and how the idea is being tested. Plan the required steps and their sequence. Formulate interim goals and milestones that you can reach as part of the implementation. Estimate the timeframe and budget you'll use to actually realize the idea.

EXAMPLE

For the idea of food products from the 3D printer, the realist names the foods that can realistically be executed. This also involves listing the necessary resources for this process and collecting the names of potential cooperative partners in food processing, 3D print manufacturers, and scientific establishments. The realist suggests that you first test individual foods and gain customer feedback about the development results at an early stage.

>> **The critic:** In this role, you take on a constructive and critical attitude. Question the feasibility, economic viability, sustainability, and usefulness of the idea. Think about how you can improve or change the idea. Point out whether others have forgotten anything. Name the strengths and weaknesses of the idea. List the possible risks, and assess the probability of the occurrence of these risks and their potential to cause damage.

**EXAMPLE**

The critic initially questions the technical feasibility of foods made from a 3D printer and wants to see studies or prototypes of similar technical developments. The critic also mentions the trend toward organic products and natural food processing in the food area. 3D printing, in contrast, represents a high degree of artificiality and chemical additives. Furthermore, it will never be possible to make food products economically in this way. The customers are also overwhelmed by this aspect on a technical level.

After the first pass, continue with the dream role again, and pick up on the previous suggestions and questions from the other two roles. Expand, supplement, or change your idea in line with what has previously been determined. Address the suggestions from the realist and objections by the critic, point-by-point. Stop the method as soon as you stop developing new ideas and thoughts and after all open questions from the three perspectives have been answered.

Schedule at least 15 minutes for each role during the first pass. If possible, no perspective should be dominant in terms of time. Initially, you can plan for a period of five minutes for the participants to think about the perspectives during individual work. Theoretically, you can perform this method alone, but you're sure to get more suggestions in a group from five to seven people. I recommend that all participants assume all roles rather than divide the work.

**TIP**

Before you delve into the various roles, do a test run, in which you assume all three roles:

>> **Dreamer:** Recall a pleasant situation in your life. For this process, you can also visit a location where you know you'll develop positive feelings. for example, go for a walk in the park or to your favorite café.

>> **Realist:** Remember a situation that you solved in a practical way. Recall what the situation was like, how you proceeded, and what you felt.

>> **Critic:** Think back to a situation in which you analyzed a situation critically. Ask yourself how your constructive criticism contributed to a substantial improvement.

# Assuming Different Mindsets with the Six Hats Method

The Six Hats method, by the British creativity researcher Edward de Bono, should inspire you to assume different perspectives while you consider a problem or find ideas. This method enhances the Walt Disney method with additional aspects. In a creative workshop, the participants put on hats in different colors that represent different mindsets, such as functional, emotional, negatively or positively critical, creative, or moderating. A total of six hats are available. When the participants are asked to analyze and solve a problem, they can put on all six hats in succession and then write down their thoughts and analyze them.

Here's a good idea: Have the wearer of the blue hat first introduce the task as the moderator, followed by the wearer of the white hat, who collects the facts about the current situation. The following list tells you more about the meaning of the six hats and the perspectives assumed by their wearers:

>> **Blue hat:** The wearer of the blue hat is the moderator. This person introduces the problem or question at the beginning. In the end, they summarize the results. During the creative workshop, the moderator structures and evaluates the words contributed by the other hat wearers. The moderator asks that the rules be followed and compiles the contributions as an interim conclusion every time a hat wearer is switched. This person moderates without integrating their own ideas.

**EXAMPLE**

A group of participants from a company's various departments (research, development, production, marketing, sales, controlling, and accounting) discusses whether and how the introduction of innovation management can be realized. The wearer of the blue hat presents the task and clears up any comprehension questions.

>> **White hat:** With the white hat, you're the neutral objective person. As such, you're tasked with objectively and neutrally describing the current status of the problem. That means compiling numbers, dates, and facts (NDF), presenting statistics in the form of images, and considering which important information is missing and how this information can be obtained. Never evaluate.

**EXAMPLE**

The wearer of the white hat presents the current situation at the company related to how the company handles innovations. The process is characterized by a work division in which the research-and-development department initially develops new ideas until a functional draft is completed. Then the production department handles the creation and subsequent testing of a prototype and establishes the manufacturing process. Shortly before the market launch, marketing and sales gather information about the new product and plan and implement its introduction to the market. Numerous problems usually occur in this process, such as redundant work, a lack of coordination between departments, and no early consideration of customer requirements.

>> **Green hat:** When you wear the green hat, you assume the role of the spontaneous creative person. You develop spontaneous ideas for solving the problem and ask yourself which other ideas you might add. Never express yourself in a critical manner.

The wearer of the green hat suggests that an independent group is formed for the innovation management. This group consists of representatives from the various departments that have previously been involved in the innovation process.

» **Red hat:** The wearer of the red hat is the emotional person. Express your feelings when you evaluate the problem or idea. Describe what you like about the challenge or idea and what you consider threatening. Formulate your hopes as well as your fears regarding the idea or problem.

The wearer of the red hat thinks that the idea is great — innovations are just too important. An independent group brings more visibility to the subject of innovations at the company. The employees in the innovation management group have an interesting, challenging task.

» **Black hat:** When you wear the black hat, you're the negatively critical thinker. Critically analyze the problem or idea. Argue why the problem or idea isn't, in your opinion, solvable or feasible. Clarify which errors and dangers the problem or idea has and why this is the case.

The wearer of the black hat criticizes the idea. A separate group for innovation management has no authority to instruct other departments. Nor does the innovation management staff have any idea about the tasks in the various areas. Innovation management only leads to more bureaucracy at the company.

» **Yellow hat:** The positively critical thinker wears a yellow hat. Argue why you think the problem or idea has a chance to be realized or has advantages. Objectively show the chances of success of the problem or idea. Always be logical and rational.

The wearer of the yellow hat points out the chances. The innovation management group finds high acceptance at the company because the employees are sent there from the various departments. The group can maintain much closer contact with the management board and offer advice on strategic questions. Additionally, you get contact persons for external inquiries from other companies or scientific establishments.

Based on the contributions by the individual hat wearers, the person wearing the blue hat summarizes the results and asks the participants to address the positive and negative points of criticism. In the end, a joint proposal is adopted.

The workshop participants determine the precise tasks, competencies, and areas of responsibility for the innovation management group so that the critical points by the wearer of the black hat are taken into account. The innovation management doesn't lead to additional reporting duties at the company. In line with recommendations by the wearer of the yellow hat, the innovation management group is directly supervised by a board member at the organization. The group is named as the first contact point for external partners.

Chapter **12**

# Evaluating Ideas

This chapter is all about how you, along with your team, can select the best ideas from among all those that you have gathered so far. In general, you can take a number of different approaches for such an evaluation, but my goal here is to provide you with an overview of which methods are best suited specifically for the evaluation of ideas in design thinking projects. You'll find out how to apply these methods with your team and how you can assess the chances for success from various perspectives.

## Selecting the Right Evaluation Method

The path from defining the task to finding ideas designed to solve that task to ushering in a successful market launch is a long one. After finding ideas, you'll still be in an early development phase, where you'll see a great deal of uncertainty about the feasibility, economic viability, and acceptance of the idea by the customer. You don't know whether the idea can be implemented yet and whether it will position itself successfully in the market. In cases of uncertainty, always apply evaluation methods that consider ideas from various perspectives. There's no single correct method here — each method has its strengths and weaknesses. Not every evaluation approach can be used for various thematic tasks.

**TIP**

Discuss the evaluation methods in your team and decide on the right technique. Use several kinds of evaluation so that you form a comprehensive image of your idea. By evaluating an idea from various perspectives, you also get a chance to see which areas of the selected idea can use improvement.

The methods presented in this chapter are also relevant for the later phases of creating prototypes and testing your product, service, or business model idea with the customer. You have to perform evaluations in these phases as well. (For more on those evaluations, see Chapters 14 and 15.)

# Relying on Diversity in the Team for Your Evaluations

It's important that you discuss, weigh, and then decide on your ideas from different perspectives — whichever method you choose isn't as relevant. For this to happen, you need diversity on your team. Employees from different specialized areas such as research, production, marketing, sales, financial control, quality assurance, as well as the legal and patent departments, are sure to assess the opportunities and risks of potential solutions in quite different ways. They add various perspectives, backgrounds, and values to the project. Take advantage of this fact and rely on variety in your team. (For more on team diversity, see Chapter 5.)

**TIP**

It makes the subsequent implementation easier if you integrate persons from different departments at the company into the work of your team. The sooner that people in other areas learn about the idea and get involved in the selection process, the more approval the suggestion will garner at the company. The idea of your team becomes the idea of the entire company. This means that, at an early stage, you already have the required support when you want to turn the idea into a new product, new service, or an entire business model that you want to successfully launch in the market.

# Quickly Selecting Ideas

Using an array of creativity techniques, it's quite possible to generate quite a number of new ideas for solutions to your task in a relatively short time using a workshop format. If you pursue each of these possible solutions, you'll soon reach your limits because you probably have a fixed budget and there's often great urgency for the eventual implementation. That's why it's crucial for you to make a selection in the team at an early stage. You can choose from different approaches for a fast evaluation:

>> **Dot-voting:** With dot-voting, every participant distributes five adhesive dots to the individual ideas you have written on a screen, poster board, card, or sticky note. One idea can receive multiple dots. You sort the ideas according to the number of adhesive dots they've accumulated.

>> **Thumb method:** The ideas are briefly presented in random order. Following a sign, everyone points a thumbs-up or thumbs-down. Thumbs-up means that the idea will be pursued. Thumbs-down means that the idea will be rejected. Order the ideas according to the number of thumbs-up.

>> **Five-finger method:** The ideas are briefly presented in random order. Following a sign, everyone shows a number of fingers on the right hand. The number of fingers corresponds to the following rating: Five fingers: "The idea is great." Four fingers: "The idea is good." Three fingers: "The idea is interesting." Two fingers: "The idea has weaknesses." One finger: "The idea should be rejected." You sort the ideas according to the number of fingers shown.

>> **Card sequence:** Write the idea on a card or sticky note in keywords. After a discussion among team members, sort the cards or notes from left (very good idea) — to right (bad idea). Ideas with the same rating are positioned on top of each other.

You can use these approaches to weed out ideas that everyone views critically or considers less interesting. Give the remaining suggestions a detailed evaluation.

# Evaluating the Advantages of (and Barriers to) Ideas

After completing your rough selection, you need to look at the advantages and opportunities posed by your proposed solutions as well as the barriers to implementing them. The PPCO method can assist you in evaluating your suggestions. The abbreviation PPCO stands for Pluses (positive aspects of the idea), Potentials (potentials of the idea), Concerns (concerns about the idea), and Overcoming concerns (ideas for ways to eliminate these concerns). These four aspects are meant to briefly and clearly summarize the advantages, potentials, and barriers to an idea as well as the approaches for overcoming these barriers. Figure 12-1 shows a matrix with the four fields of the PPCO method.

| Pluses | Potentials |
|---|---|
| What do you like about the idea? | What future possibilities do you see with this idea? |
| **Concerns** | **Overcoming Concerns** |
| What concerns do you associate with this idea? | How could you overcome these concerns? |

**FIGURE 12-1:** In the PPCO method, the advantages, potentials, barriers, and approaches for overcoming these barriers are clearly summarized.

Brainstorm (more about this topic in Chapter 11) and then compile the positive aspects of this idea that you and your team can spontaneously think of. For the *Potentials* keyword, consider which future developments and trends will support this idea and whether there might be additional possibilities for application. These developments can come from the economic, political-legal, social, or technological environment and constitute a lasting trend. (For more on analyzing trends, see Chapter 6.)

The idea of a vegetarian hot dog made of plant-based products fits the trend of an increased interest in healthy and environmentally conscious food. Consider new types of applications for your idea during the evaluation of the potentials. After you have compiled the advantages and possibilities, assume the role of the devil's advocate — the one who opposes your idea and raises concerns. Name reasons why the idea isn't feasible (or can't be implemented at the company), why it isn't economical, why it's too complicated, or why it won't get approval from the customer. On this basis, you can develop suggestions for measures to invalidate these concerns and overcome the barriers to its implementation.

Write your team's thoughts on the four dimensions — Pluses, Potentials, Concerns, and Overcoming concerns — in keywords on a card, and stick them into the matrix for the PPCO method. Use this compilation to discuss the evaluation of your idea. The advantage of this evaluation approach is that you consider the positive and negative perspectives of an idea and have to think about how to eliminate objections and overcome any barriers to implementation.

**WARNING**

When the problems and risks of innovative ideas are mentioned at an early stage, often the idea gets rejected before it was even truly discussed. People often don't consider that every innovation can show risks at first and that such risks can in fact be mastered. The PPCO method encourages you to develop measures for risk management and take them into account during the evaluation.

# Evaluating Ideas with Checklists

With checklists, you can test whether the idea will meet your requirements. You can formulate the requirements in the form of questions ("Can the idea be technically implemented?") or as a statement ("The idea is user-friendly from a customer's view"). Design this review as a yes-no evaluation, or use a rating scale based on school grades.

Use the checklists detailed in the next several sections to review the following six areas:

>> **Feasibility:** Check whether the idea can be implemented. Your approach should be doable as a product, process, service, or business model and applied by customers or users.

>> **Strategic and cultural fit:** The idea must fit the vision, strategy, and culture of the company. The fit ensures that you attract the support you need for implementation at your company.

>> **Desirability:** Your idea must have a customer benefit. Check whether your idea offers the solution for a wish or a problem.

>> **Business viability and scalability:** An idea with business viability is one where the revenue is higher than the expenses. Scalability refers to the idea's ability to accomplish high growth with relatively little effort.

>> **Sustainability:** Your idea must be successful in the long run. You have to assess whether your offer can exist on the market for the long term.

>> **Adaptability:** In a dynamically changing environment, your idea must be adaptable. Customers' wishes can change over time, which means that your product, service, or business model has to adapt in order to remain successful.

For these areas, you should also formulate disqualification questions that you must definitely answer with a Yes — otherwise, you discard the idea. If your idea violates legal regulations, this can be a reason for disqualification.

## Determining feasibility

*Feasibility* describes whether and to what degree your idea can be used to successfully introduce a product, service, or business model in the market. If you realize that your solution can't be executed when you're already in the implementation phase, the time and money you've invested already would have been for nothing.

**WARNING**

Feasibility can also refer to the available resources. Maybe your suggestion can be implemented in principle, but your company lacks the financial means or skills to execute it. If the developments are technical in nature, you may also need licenses or the technical expertise of other companies.

Thoroughly check an idea's feasibility at an early stage. You can ask the following questions to check whether the idea can be implemented:

>> Are licenses or technical knowledge of external parties necessary for the implementation?

>> Is the idea technically easy to realize?

>> Does it require high investments for development, production, marketing, or sales?

>> Does the company have the required means and capacities for the implementation? If not, can they be acquired easily and quickly?

>> Are partnerships with others (other companies, colleges, or research institutes, for example) necessary or possible? Can these partnerships be established quickly?

>> Are there high barriers for a launch on the market?

>> Can the legal requirements or industry standards be adhered to in the implementation?

Depending on the product, you have to check additional criteria that influence the feasibility:

>> Are the materials offered on the market robust and consistent? Do they have the required quality?

>> Can the necessary materials be acquired easily, quickly, and inexpensively?

>> Is the product safe and reliable?

You can answer and evaluate these questions only if your idea is clear, comprehensible, and understandable. Otherwise, you should limit the level of your investment —in both time and money — if you decide to further develop the idea.

**TIP**

Technical inventions might need further experiments or tests in order to check an idea's feasibility. Proceed gradually by setting the minimum information as a milestone. If you have received the information from experiments or tests, evaluate the technical feasibility.

# Estimating the fit

You need support from various departments and employees at the company for your idea to succeed on the market as a product, service, or business model. The idea must be developed into a market-ready product by the research and development departments. The production department has to ensure the manufacturing process. The marketing and sales departments have to be prepared and motivated for the market launch. The company management has to support your project. (For more on getting this support, see Chapter 3.) Your project can't become successful without support. Clarify early on whether your idea fits the company's strategy and culture. You can test the fit by asking the following questions:

>> Does the idea fit the company's innovation strategy, and can it make a significant contribution to that strategy? Does the company management want this idea?

>> Is the idea appreciated at the company? Does it fit in with the corporate culture?

>> Are there positive effects on other products or competencies at the company?

>> Could this lead to learning effects at the company?

## Testing your idea's desirability from the customers' perspective

One criterion for your decision is the question whether — and to what degree — the idea creates a benefit for the customer. To determine that, you need to come up with target users who actually derive added value from the idea. The benefit for these target users can lie in your idea's satisfying a wish that was barely fulfilled before, if at all, or in solving a problem.

This desirability can take on various forms. For example, the product or service might be useful for the customer because it performs a specific function or solves a specific task for the customer. Perhaps your idea for a solution has high user-friendliness, making it easier to use. Maybe your online shop lets the customer see and compare, at a glance, all product information relevant to the buying decision. Last but not least, perhaps your idea generates a positive emotional reaction on the part of the customer. You can test the desirability from the customer's perspective in more detail with the following questions:

>> Can you identify people who receive a benefit from your idea and who therefore can serve as your target users?

>> Can your target users save time with this idea?

» Can the target users reduce their effort with this idea?

» Would your target users consider this idea trustworthy?

» Can the target users quickly acquire the product resulting from your idea? (Would it be available and easy to find, in other words?)

» Is the idea valuable from your target users' perspective?

» Is the idea cost-effective from your target users' perspective?

» Is the idea user-friendly from your target users' perspective?

» Is the idea ethically desirable?

» Does the idea convey prestige from your target users' perspective?

» Does the idea offer entertainment value from your target users' perspective?

» Does the product have an appealing design?

» Can your target users service the product easily and inexpensively?

**TIP**

You don't have to find the answers to all these questions. Depending on the application area, some questions aren't relevant. When it comes to systems for mechanical engineering, for example, the design or entertainment value of the product is secondary or insignificant.

## Considering the economic viability and scalability of your idea

A solution desired by the customer isn't necessarily economically worthwhile. The costs of development, manufacturing, or sales may be so high that you can't make any profit. In consideration of your costs, you have to assess whether the number of customers ready and willing to pay is sufficient.

You can estimate the economic viability of your idea by asking using the following questions:

» Does the customer have high purchasing power and a willingness to buy?

» Is the market attractive and growing (dynamically and on a long-term basis)?

» Is the expected yield worthwhile?

» Are the economic risks determinable, quantifiable, and acceptable?

It's difficult to evaluate the economic viability at an early stage — it's possible that the market for your product, service, or business model idea doesn't exist yet. The more innovative your idea, the more difficult it can be to find reliable information about the market size and your company's potential revenue growth. After the market launch, it still takes some time for your product or service to be economically viable. When the first microwave ovens came on the market in 1970, it took six years before sales generated significant profits.

In addition to the economic viability of your product, check its scalability. The scalability of a product means that you can reach a relatively high amount of potential customers or users with only little additional effort. If you developed software that you want to distribute from an online shop, you can reach an almost unlimited number of customers with low additional marketing costs. The scalability is high. If you want to offer individually made bicycles, you have to account for the same effort for each customer. The scalability is low. You can estimate scalability using the following questions:

>> Are high costs required for production facilities? (High costs are an indication of low scalability.)

>> Are the capacities of the production facilities limited? If yes, can they be easily expanded? (If the production capacities are limited or difficult to increase, that indicates low scalability.)

>> Do you need many employees for the production or sales, and does the personnel need to be expanded proportionately to the customer growth? (Yes means low scalability.)

>> Do the costs increase proportionately with the sales growth? (Yes means low scalability.)

>> Can the product or its production process be standardized? (Yes indicates high scalability.)

>> Do the development, marketing, and sales require low costs? (Yes indicates high scalability.)

>> Can the production or sales be automated? (Yes indicates high scalability.)

>> Can important lessons be learned in the implementation of this idea over time so that the costs can be reduced? (Yes indicates high scalability.)

>> Can additional applications and markets be developed with low additional effort? (Yes indicates high scalability.)

For investors who have a financial participation in a company, scalability is a criterion for the decision for or against an investment. Companies with products or business models that quickly reach a high number of customers or users with limited effort are attractive investment options. Scalability can make any initial concerns about the economic viability of a product recede into the background.

EXAMPLE

Companies like Google, Facebook, Instagram, Snapchat, Netflix, and Twitter quickly reached a high number of users after they were founded. For these companies, the economic viability was sometimes consistently negative for years. It becomes a top priority in the later course of the company development.

In the evaluation of your idea, you have to consider whether high scalability is initially more important than the question of economic viability.

## Ensuring sustainability

Keeping sustainability in mind, evaluate whether your idea is manageable on a long-term basis. *Sustainability* means that something has a long-term economic, social, and environmental benefit.

WARNING

When you assess sustainability, you have to differentiate — not every idea has a long-term economic, social, and environmental benefit. You have to determine whether all three aspects are important for your idea. It's difficult to associate environmental benefits with a new service concept for financial consulting.

During the evaluation, check the sustainability of your idea using the following questions:

>> Is the idea manageable on a long-term basis?

>> Are there advantages compared to existing competitive products?

>> Are the potential customers willing to pay for it over the long term?

>> Does the idea have environmental and social benefits?

>> Can the invention be patented? Is it easy to imitate? Can you protect your idea from the competition?

Sustainability is a trend with long-term effects in society. (For more on analyzing trends, see Chapter 6.) If your idea contributes to sustainability, you can benefit from this trend on a long-term basis.

## Determining adaptability

The market for your new product, new service, or new business model will change over time. The customers' quality requirements are permanently fluctuating. The legal framework conditions can change. New competing products are entering the market. Technical progress will influence your market. Your target group will change. You can test the adaptability with the following questions:

>> Can the idea be individually adapted to customers' wishes? Is it flexible?

>> Can the idea be adapted to the dynamically changing state of technical progress?

>> Can the idea be adapted to the political, social, economic, and legal requirements?

>> Can your idea lead to follow-up products for changing situations?

An idea that is truly promising can always be quickly and easily adapted to dynamic changes in the requirements.

# Making the Chances for Success Measurable

One particular scoring method — also known as benefit analysis — will help you make the chances for success for your proposed solutions measurable and comparable with each other. When using this method, you apply different criteria to compare several ideas with each other.

The scoring method is applied in four steps:

1. Specify the evaluation criteria.

2. Specify the weighting factors.

3. Evaluate the ideas based on the criteria.

4. Determine the ranking and the final selection.

After you specify your evaluation criteria, create a matrix listing the (most important) criteria. Write the criteria into the first column and the individual alternative ideas in the first row. Write the weighting factor of each criterion into the second column. Table 12-1 shows an example.

**TABLE 12-1**   **Example of a Scoring Method**

| | | Idea 1 | | | Idea 2 | | | Idea 3 | | |
|---|---|---|---|---|---|---|---|---|---|---|
| | Weighting | Evaluation | Partial Use Value | | Evaluation | Partial Use Value | | Evaluation | Partial Use Value | |
| **Probability of implementation:** | 4 | 5 | 20 | | 2 | 8 | | 5 | 20 | |
| **Strategic significance** | 3 | 4 | 12 | | 4 | 12 | | 4 | 12 | |
| **Synergy effect** | 2 | 4 | 8 | | 3 | 6 | | 3 | 6 | |
| **Perceptible benefits** | 5 | 3 | 15 | | 2 | 10 | | 3 | 15 | |
| **Image effect** | 1 | 4 | 4 | | 4 | 4 | | 3 | 3 | |
| **Market size** | 3 | 4 | 12 | | 3 | 9 | | 3 | 9 | |
| Total utility value | | | 71 | | | 49 | | | 65 | |
| **Ranking** | | | **1** | | | **3** | | | **2** | |

*(Left vertical label: Evaluation Criteria)*

# Finding and weighting appropriate evaluation criteria

You can select criteria for estimating the chances of feasibility, fit, desirability, economic viability, sustainability, and adaptability. You have to define a standard rating scale so that you can apply various criteria. I suggest selecting a scale from 0 to 5, where the 0 value means that the criterion is not met. Arrange the values from 1 to 5 so that the best evaluation is communicated with the number 5. Set up a scale from 0 to 5 for each evaluation criterion. This is how you make the criteria measurable and can compare various ideas with each other.

When you assess feasibility, ask yourself whether you can implement the idea and successfully introduce it on the market. You can assess the feasibility with the following criteria:

>> **Probability of implementation:** If you estimate the probability with over 90 percent, assign the value 5. If you estimate that the implementation isn't possible, assign 0.

>> **Development period:** In the team, determine how many weeks or months correspond to each of the values from 0 to 5. For the 0 value, determine the number of weeks or months that are no longer manageable for you as a development period.

- » **Development costs:** Specify in the team how high each of the investments is for the values from 0 to 5. At the 0 value, the development costs are so high that you wouldn't implement the idea.

- » **Complexity:** Evaluate whether you have to consider interdependencies during the implementation. The more interdependencies there are and the stronger the interactions, the more difficult the implementation will be.

**EXAMPLE**

A product that's assembled from several dozen individual parts using various materials (plastic, aluminum, steel, glass) can be difficult to make. Assign values 1 or 2 to the complexity.

Make sure that the idea has support at the company. This is possible only if the idea fits the strategy and culture of the company. You can evaluate this using the following criteria:

- » **Strategic significance:** Use the scale from 0 to 5 to rate the strategic significance this idea has for your company.

- » **Strategic fit:** With the scale from 0 to 5, measure the degree to which your idea corresponds to the company strategy.

- » **Cultural fit:** With the scale from 0 to 5, measure the degree to which your idea corresponds to the company culture.

- » **Synergy effect:** Your idea for a solution may result in positive effects on other products or projects at the company. Use the scale from 0 to 5 to rate the strength of these effects. If your idea contributes to a significant increase in sales of products already on the market, assign a 5.

An important area for your evaluation is how attractive your idea is to customers or users and the advantages compared to competitive offers. You can use several criteria for ratings in this area. You can make the product's appeal and its competitiveness measurable with the following criteria:

- » **Recognizable benefit (value proposition):** Rate how much added value you create for customers or users with your idea. The value 0 expresses that there's no recognizable benefit for the customers or users. The value 5 means that it inspires enthusiasm on the part of the customer.

- » **Significance for the customer:** If your idea has very high significance for customers, they'll want to have a market-ready product as soon as possible. The value 5 reflects this situation.

- » **Alignment with trends:** Your idea is particularly attractive to an older target group. The growth of this target group is a trend in many industrial countries.

(I tell you more about the individual trends in Chapter 6.) Rate the appeal of your idea with a value between 4 and 5.

>> **Image effect:** Your idea can also play a key role in creating a positive image effect for your company. You can use the value 0 for ideas that generate no image effect or even a negative one. Ideas with the value 5 have an extraordinarily positive effect on the reputation and prestige of the company.

>> **Differentiation advantages:** Your idea must distinguish itself in a positive way compared to competitive offers. With the value 0, your idea offers no added value compared to other products or is actually inferior. The value 5 would refer to a unique selling point.

>> **Sustainability of the competitive advantage:** If you can protect your idea against imitations for the long term, you achieve sustainable competitive advantages. Rate with the value 5 a patent that has a comprehensive scope in terms of patent protection. If there are no legal protection options and a quick entry of established competitors is possible, set the values between 0 and 2.

A product with a clear use for the customer and advantages compared to competing products is sure to be of interest — if the market is attractive. Such attractiveness is determined by the size and sustainable growth of the market. Rate the market attractiveness using the following criteria:

>> **Market size:** Your idea taps into an attractive market if it includes a large number of potential customers with great purchasing power. You can estimate this based on the potential number of customers or potential sales volume and incrementally assign the values from 0 (very low sales volume) to 5 (very high sales volume).

>> **Market growth rate:** Assign the value 5 to a market that's rapidly growing over 10 percent per year. If the market is stagnating or even shrinking, values between 0 and 2 are appropriate.

>> **Market entry barriers:** There might be many obstacles to the market launch. If you have to make high investments for the production or marketing and sales for the market launch, you first have to overcome this obstacle. Use the values from 0 to 5 to estimate how easily you can tap into the market with your idea. If the barriers are so high that you can't overcome them, assign 0 to this criterion.

TIP

You don't have to use all criteria for each evaluation. In the team, select the criteria that are relevant for your task. From the various evaluation areas, such as feasibility, fit to strategy and culture, product appeal, competitiveness, and market attractiveness, select at least one criterion in each case so that you can evaluate the ideas from different perspectives.

# Weighing criteria against each other

After you select the criteria, you have to specify their significance. Compare the criteria with each other and determine a sequence. You can assign a sequence in the team by using dot-voting, the thumb method, five-finger method, or card sequence.

You can also make a pair comparison. For that purpose, write each criterion in the rows and columns of a table. (See Table 12-2.) Compare the individual criteria with each other and assign the following values:

>> **0:** Criterion in the row is less significant than the one in the column.

>> **1:** Criterion in the row is equally significant as the one in the column.

>> **2:** Criterion in the row is more significant than the one in the column.

**TABLE 12-2**     ## Pair Comparison

| # | Implementation probability | Strategic significance | Synergy effect | Perceptible utility | Image effect | Market size | Sum | Sequence |
|---|---|---|---|---|---|---|---|---|
| Implementation probability | – | 2 | 2 | 0 | 2 | 2 | 8 | 2 |
| Strategic significance | 0 | – | 2 | 0 | 2 | 1 | 5 | 3 |
| Synergy effect | 0 | 0 | – | 0 | 2 | 0 | 2 | 5 |
| Perceptible utility | 2 | 2 | 2 | – | 2 | 2 | 10 | 1 |
| Image effect | 0 | 0 | 0 | 0 | – | 0 | 0 | 6 |
| Market size | 0 | 1 | 2 | 0 | 2 | – | 5 | 3 |

Transfer the sequence into a scale ranging from 1 (very low significance) to 5 (very high significance). The values from 1 to 5 are the weighting factors.

**TIP**

Make sure that the contents of some criteria overlap during the weighting. The strategic significance criterion and synergy effect criterion are closely related. If your idea leads to further sales growth of existing products, this also means it has high strategic significance for the company. In the weighting, this means that if you use both criteria, the same benefits of your idea will flow into the evaluation disproportionately. You have no way to completely avoid overlapping evaluation criteria. Discuss the individual weighting factors in the team, and make changes by selecting a lower weighting factor if you think the criteria overlap too much.

## Evaluating and selecting ideas

Rate the ideas with the help of the selected criteria by using the scale from 0 to 5. Multiply the value for each individual criterion with the corresponding weighting factor from 1 to 5. This multiplication yields the partial use utility. When you add these, you get the total utility of the individual idea.

In the end, the ranking of the different ideas is assigned according to the number of the total utilities. The alternative with the highest total utility is designated as the most advantageous alternative and is thus the winner. Discuss the results in detail with your team, and select the ideas you want to continue pursuing.

Chapter **13**

# Designing Prototypes

Your plan is to expand your idea into a functional concept for a product, service, or business model. A functioning sample concept is called a *prototype* and is used as a model for subsequent product, service, or business model innovations you plan on marketing. With a prototype, you can vividly present and test the essential functions and characteristics of your idea. Along the way, you'll experiment with your prototype and gather important feedback from potential customers.

This chapter gives you an overview of the advantages offered by creating prototypes and performing experiments. The idea here is to create a prototype early on, without complex planning and with minimal means. My first piece of advice is that your very first step should consist of defining what you want to learn with a prototype. I then point out that there are different kinds of prototypes and that what you select depends on the maturity of your idea and whether you want to develop an innovative product, service, or business model. Stories that you tell or visualize in various forms will give your customers a better sense of your idea. The digital world facilitates rapid designs of prototypes. You will learn how to demonstrate your idea to your customers with prototypes and get it tested.

# Understanding the Benefit of Experiments

By creating a prototype, you're performing an experiment to see whether potential customers share your assumptions about the usefulness of your idea. Creating your prototype early on has its advantages:

>> You will overcome the mistaken belief that you know everything the customer wants. With the help of experiments you carry out, you'll verify this with hard facts.

>> With prototypes, your decisions aren't based on subjective estimates or personal preferences, but rather are supported by feedback from potential customers.

>> Prototypes let you avoid confirmation bias — a bias arising from the fact that people often err by paying more attention to information that confirms what they expect to find out or what they already know.

Prototypes are more useful if their tasks are clarified before you start testing, if simple prototypes are selected and the tests are conducted systematically. In the following section, you will learn how to proceed in the prototype phase.

# Clarifying Tasks in the Prototype Phase

First, you should clarify which target users you want to provide feedback about your idea. Describe your target users using the Persona method, which depicts people's essential characteristics, behaviors, values, and preferences. (For more on the Persona method, see Chapter 7.) After determining your target users, think about how you can visualize and pinpoint your idea in the form of a prototype. Your target users can give you helpful feedback about your idea only if they understand it and can test it.

TIP

If your timeframe and budget can accommodate it, develop further ideas for alternative prototypes, and have the potential customer or user compare them with each other.

Sharing information with potential customers or users is a decisive phase in the design thinking process. This can result in feedback to the preceding phases, if the customer's responses lead to suggestions on how to modify either the task description (see Chapter 9) or the proposed solution developed so far (see Chapters 10 and 11). Your goal is to learn as much as possible with the help of the prototype.

On the basis of your idea, decide which prototypes are best for you to use. Clarify your intended goal and then decide which parts of the design concept you want the customer to focus on when providing feedback — for example:

» Do you want to gather feedback about the usefulness of your idea?

» Do you want feedback about the user-friendliness of your idea?

» Do you want feedback on how your customer perceives your idea?

» Do you want to get feedback on individual functions or characteristics of your idea?

» Do you want the customer to evaluate the design?

You must design your prototype in line with the type of feedback you want from your customer. If your priority is user-friendliness, it must be possible to operate your prototype to the degree that your customer can actually test something. If the focus is on design issues, sketches and images are often sufficient for you to get helpful suggestions.

Ask yourself what it is that you can't find out from your customer with the aid of a prototype. You can't test the customer's willingness to pay for an idea with a prototype that features only a few characteristics of the finished product.

The maturity level of your idea also influences the kind of prototype. The less mature the idea, the simpler the design of the prototype. If the product idea is still rough, you can present drawings or simple paper models to the customer. Your timeframe and budget are additional factors to take into account when you select the kind of prototype. A prototype that's technically elaborate or made of expensive materials can quickly reach the limits of your budget.

TIP

Set limits for the timeframe and budget for the creation of the prototype and subsequent tests with the customer. Michael Schrage, from the DQ Institute of Technology, created the 5 x 5 x 5 x 5 x 5 formula: Five teams with five persons each perform five tests each, in five weeks, for a maximum of USD$5,000 each.

# Developing and Using Prototypes Efficiently

Perform experiments related to your assumptions at an early stage and with low expenditures so that you can quickly make changes. This approach corresponds to the lean start-up concept by Eric Ries, who, as a company founder and an author, coined the term minimum viable product (MVP). A *minimum viable product* is the minimally functional prototype of the product or service that makes it possible for you to get measurable customer feedback about a new feature or characteristic.

For innovation products, the creation of a minimal viable product is one option when it comes to gathering meaningful information from potential customers. Instead of *products*, one should refer to *prototypes* here because they aren't sellable products.

Apply a prototype for each development step of your idea. Be sure to answer the question about which kind of market feedback you need for the next development step. Your prototypes should be functional along the entire development phase so that customers can try them out.

**EXAMPLE**

Imagine that your idea is a new electric car with a particularly efficient drive. The classic approach is that you first create the drive and then the undercarriage and car body, and then you assemble everything into a vehicle. When it comes to the customer, the individual components of the drive, undercarriage, and car body don't mean that much. With the lean start-up approach, you would first develop an electric drive for a skateboard, and then a scooter, followed by a bicycle, and then a motorcycle, and then, finally, a car. These development steps represent functional prototypes that can be tested by customers and make it possible for you to get feedback.

You should choose the right time for the creation of the prototype. Don't start too early or wait too long. Keep in mind the following principles on how to efficiently design prototypes.

## Plan less, experiment more

When planning how to implement your idea as a prototype, don't go into too much detail; instead, focus on just those functions or characteristics that you want to test. Without spending a lot of time, create a prototype and get customer feedback early on. Learn from each customer response and pursue a fast, learning-by-doing course of action.

## Minimize effort

You're not developing the perfect product. A minimum viable product has, preferably, only the one function you want to test. When you create a minimum viable product, select the simplest type so that you can learn from it. It's not at all about testing a finished and perfect product and already engaging in sales talks; in fact, it's exactly the opposite: You're letting the customer test individual functions or characteristics of the product or service offer. If the customer wants more functions while performing the test, create the next minimum viable product for this. Look for the customer's response regarding only one function or a function change when you test the prototype.

When you create a minimum viable product, you avoid high investments in product development by investing little of your own financial means in these tests. You can borrow, lease, or use freely available items as the materials you require for the prototypes. The time factor also encourages a simple minimum viable product. You want to get fast customer feedback so that you can reduce uncertainty during the actual development process. The principle for the creation and selection of the minimum viable product is this: "As simple as possible, as meaningful as possible."

**EXAMPLE**

The idea for Twitter was first tested as a development project by the internal staff at the Odeo company without expending much effort at all. At first, they pursued only the goal of improving their internal communications. The employees were delighted by the possibility of sending brief messages via the Internet, which allowed them to save hundreds of dollars in SMS costs. Based on this positive feedback, the idea was refined and published.

## Correct at an early stage

The customers' responses regularly require smaller or larger course corrections and changes in your idea — the pivots, in other words. (The term *pivot* originated in basketball, where you change direction with the ball while still keeping a foot on the ground.) These pivots are certainly common and frequent at an early innovation stage. The function tested with a minimum viable product is accepted or rejected by the customer. In case of rejection, your direction must be changed. Adapt your idea to the customer's wishes and ideas by making the necessary changes. This lets you save money, because the continued development of a bad idea can result in costly bad investments.

**EXAMPLE**

Instagram, which originally started in 2010 as an app called Burbn, allowed users to chat with their friends, plan meetings, and edit and share images of the meeting places linked to GPS data. The users almost exclusively used the app for the feature of easily editing images with filters and then sharing the images with friends. Based on these experiences, the founders changed the app, focusing only on the photo features and calling their company Instagram. Two months later, the app already had a million users.

## Tolerate errors

Failing — which is an integral component of experiments — should be tolerated, accepted, or even expected. Mistakes found in your prototype by the customer are learning opportunities. To learn successfully, you have to answer the following questions:

>> How is the mistake revealed? Does the customer see any benefit from the prototype? Does the customer have problems with the operation? Does the customer find the design unappealing? Does the customer consider the prototype emotionally unappealing?

>> What are the causes of the mistake?

>> How can you avoid the mistake and improve the prototype?

If you receive negative feedback from a customer, you have to respond quickly and flexibly. Design a new prototype and test it again. Every discovered mistake saves the costs associated with undesired product developments.

# Using Different Prototypes

When selecting a prototype, ask yourself what would be the most easily executable test for your planned experiment. Think about what you want to find out. Then ask yourself which answers or reactions by the customer will enable your prototype to successfully pass the experiment. Lastly, clarify how you can get this information most quickly and most easily.

Set a timeframe and a budget for yourself. Your prototype experiments should last no longer than two or three months. These specifications will help you select the right form of the prototype. Not every one of the prototypes explained in following section is suitable for every task. Experiment with your selection, and familiarize yourself with the individual approaches. A combination of various prototypes for the same task could be of use.

TIP

Often, the focus quickly falls on just one favorite idea during the prototype phase — act against this situation by offering several prototypes for comparison. Go ahead and create prototypes for all the promising ideas, though it wouldn't hurt to also create a prototype for an idea that you're relatively sure to reject because of its inefficiency or risk. Mention is often made of dark horse prototypes, which are judged to be creative but also too risky. In horse races, a *dark horse* indicates that sometimes outsiders will win. This way, you avoid deciding on particular prototypes too early, so that you don't limit the search for a solution unnecessarily fast.

Prototypes are particularly well-suited for physical product developments, but with the approaches mentioned in the remainder of this chapter, service offers and business models can also become clear and tangible.

# Making Ideas Clear and Tangible

You can easily and quickly create a prototype of your idea on paper, on a whiteboard, or on an electronic device (laptop, smartphone, tablet) with drawings and photo collages. You can outline the product design; drawings of the functions and characteristics of your idea are also possible. Images from books, magazines, newspapers, advertising brochures, catalogs, or the Internet can all be used for photo collages to illustrate your idea.

Show your drawing or photo collage to potential customers for five seconds, and then ask them what they can recall and what impression it made on them. The prototypical drawings and images are indispensable at an early stage of the product development.

In addition to two-dimensional drawings and images, you can use simple model designs made of paper, cardboard, modeling clay, Styrofoam, or other foam materials to illustrate or mimic certain functions or characteristics of your idea. The use of 3D printers makes it possible to manufacture impressive prototypes with little effort.

## Telling stories

Tell a tale or perform a story about the use of a product so that you get feedback about its usefulness and ease of use along with suggestions for improvements.

With storytelling, you vividly use the narrative format to depict the usefulness or utility of your idea as a real or fictitious story. Storytelling can be used as a prototype test so that you can graphically explain your idea to customers and ask for feedback. It may be difficult to understand new ideas for products, services, and business models that don't exist yet — storytelling is an appropriate method in these cases. People like stories, and this allows them to easily relate to your idea. Stories awaken human curiosity, entertain people, and increase attentiveness.

WARNING

Don't mix up storytelling in design thinking and an advertising campaign for a mature product. In this early phase, you don't want to sell anything with the story about your idea. This is all about evaluating your idea with the help of customer feedback and receiving options for improvement. Openly communicate to the customer the goals intended with the story. The potential customers or users will talk more readily and honestly when they know that this isn't a sales pitch. Your story doesn't have to be perfect. Ask the customer whether something is missing or should be improved.

First describe the story's central message in simple words. The customer should be able to relate to the situation while using your product and understand the special benefit of your idea.

The answers to the following questions will help you find a key message:

>> Who is the target user for the message?

>> What kind of feedback do you want to get from the customer?

You're sure to call up positive emotions on the part of the customer by describing the benefits of using your idea. People search for rewards in stories. In the story, describe how your idea will give the customer a reward. Rewards can be shown in three ways:

>> **A feeling of safety and security:** People want to overcome fear and uncertainty. They look for consistency, stability, and compensation. They long for commitment, caring, home, and tradition.

>> **A sense of stimulation:** People look for new stimuli. They want to be active and break out of their routines. Rather than be bored, people look for pleasure, fun, excitement, and diversity or surprises.

>> **A sense of status and superiority:** People strive to show achievements. They want to enjoy success and superiority, prevail against others, and expand their territories. That's why people aim to avoid defeat, annoyance, anger, and dissatisfaction.

Use a typical customer or user as the protagonist of the story. Give the protagonist a name. The situation, time, and place can influence the plot. Describe them if they're significant.

TIP

Apply the Persona method to characterize the protagonist of your story — their age, appearance, characteristics, and behavior along with their values and preferences. (For more on the Persona method, see Chapter 7.)

At the beginning of your story, introduce the protagonist, place, and situation. Then build up suspense by describing the problem, deficiency, or challenge from the perspective of your protagonist. The solution of the conflict consists of alternatives that can be chosen. Briefly describe the available alternatives and their disadvantages or weaknesses. Things take a turn for the better with the introduction of your idea, which you'll describe in vivid terms. The story finishes with a happy ending — the positive solution, starring your idea with its special advantages. Your idea is the hero of the story that solves the customer's problem, remedies the deficiency, or helps master the challenge of your target users.

When you have told the story to your potential customer, ask for feedback using the following questions:

>> Is this story your story? Is it different from yours? If yes, how so?

>> What would you add to or omit from this story?

>> Did you like the story? Why?

>> Which advantages do you expect from the idea?

>> Would you want to use the idea?

>> What do you perceive with this idea?

The story enables improved communication with the customer. You'll notice an additional benefit: You too will better understand your idea if you describe it in the form of a story by using simple and clear language. You will detect flaws in your idea and gaps in the presentation about the benefits of using your idea, which in the end will help you market your idea.

## Visualizing stories

A story *pinboard* (*storyboarding* and *visual storytelling* are other terms for the same concept) is a method for vividly depicting your story. Walt Disney originally used a story pinboard for film productions. The story is schematically outlined with drawings of individual scenes.

The storyboard — with its depiction of the protagonist, the situation, the problems met, and the approaches taken to overcome them — should comprise a maximum of eight scenes. Figure 13-1 depicts a scheme for storyboarding. Outline the individual scenes with the plot activities in boxes the size of index cards or sticky notes. The sketch consists of just a few elements: surroundings, characters (customers, customer advisors), speech bubbles, thought bubbles, and relevant items (laptop, mobile phone, devices, furnishings). A drawn clock can show the respective time. No artistic skills are needed, because this isn't about drawing perfectly. Use stick figures and simple symbols (emojis).

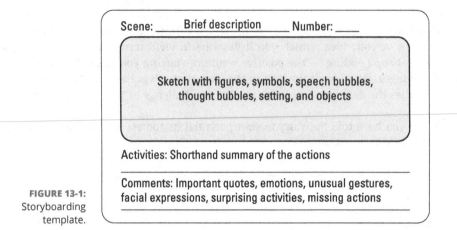

Scene: _____ Brief description _____ Number: ____

Sketch with figures, symbols, speech bubbles,
thought bubbles, setting, and objects

Activities: Shorthand summary of the actions
_____

Comments: Important quotes, emotions, unusual gestures,
facial expressions, surprising activities, missing actions
_____

**FIGURE 13-1:**
Storyboarding
template.

Show the storyboard to the customer and then ask for a response related to the
following questions:

>> Does the storyboard outline the customer's problems and activities
realistically?

>> Are the activities misrepresented?

>> Are the functions and characteristics of the idea useful for the customer?

>> Are the advantages of using the idea comprehensible and clear?

>> Is there a need for improving the idea?

Individual scenes of the storyboard may be incomplete. Ask the customer to
complete them. Thought bubbles in the storyboards can be kept blank so that
customers can use them to enter their thoughts and feelings, such as joy, annoyance, or confusion.

TIP

In addition to using the narrative form, you can make a video of the story depicting the advantages of your idea. This makes your idea more vivid. You can find
several software solutions online under the search term *explanatory videos,* which
allow you to create videos or comics for these purposes by yourself without needing any background knowledge. You'll use the storyboard to create a screenplay
that summarizes the plot of your story in individual scenes.

## Performing stories

Role-playing games allow you to perform your story realistically in ways that
illustrate the advantages of your idea. As a result, you and the customer can
relate better to the role or situation in which your idea will be used. Role-playing

games are a particularly good choice for services. Various types of customers and employees can take on different roles. You can perform the role-playing game realistically when you use costumes, props, furnishings, and devices. Afterward, the audience as potential customers and participants in the role-playing game can evaluate what they felt and how they experienced the situation, why which actions were performed, and whether one could have acted differently. An observer can also take notes and photos or make a video of the role-playing game.

You can also perform the stories or situations with Lego figures and blocks. Service ideas can be depicted with successions of individual Lego scenes. This improves clarity so that you and your customer can approach your idea for the solution from another perspective and avoid tunnel vision.

## Using digital prototypes

Wireframes can be used to depict pictorial representations of operating elements or buttons that will later be used on a website or on displays, electronic devices, or other projection screens. The operating elements or buttons are depicted only in schematic drawings and are meant to show the position and size of symbols or text in the form of placeholders.

**WARNING**

"Lorem ipsum" texts, which are filler texts without meaningful content, are often used as placeholders. This is a simple option for internal development to quickly fill and structure a presentation with text blocks. Avoid texts like this when you perform experiments, or else you will confuse the customer. Formulate short, correct texts — ones that won't take much additional effort.

Either draw the wireframes by hand, make them out of paper, or create them digitally with the appropriate software. The customer can change the position and size of the operating elements and symbols. Wireframes can also be clickable in the form of a simple website. By clicking on a button or symbol, users access additional pages or functions. You can minimize your effort by making clickable only those symbols that you want to test. The unfinished templates can motivate the customers more than perfectly designed templates, because this will give them the sense that their feedback can have an effect at an early stage.

**WARNING**

Don't use any simplified versions of the prototype — ones in which someone is prompted to click a button on a website, only for them to be notified that the offer is in development (under construction) or where they see the Page Not Found error message. This *fake door* web page, or *404 page*, though often used to test the customer's general interest, isn't something you should be pursuing. It only annoys the users; particularly, those potential customers who could recommend your offer later.

You can use extensively designed websites known as *mock-ups*. In a mock-up, you use the typography, colors, and symbols as they could be visualized in the later design. The basic structure for all the control elements is displayed without being fully functional.

**EXAMPLE**

During a large conference in San Francisco, the founders of Airbnb initially offered their own, private apartments for short-term rent and placed photos of their apartments on a simple website. That way, they tested whether there could be, in principle, an interest in inexpensive short stays outside of hotels.

You can use entire websites as digital prototypes. Create a website on which you introduce your ideas, and evaluate the user behavior on this web page.

**EXAMPLE**

The Buffer app makes it possible to schedule messages on different social networks, such as Facebook, Instagram, Twitter, and LinkedIn. The messages can thus be published at particular times of the day or at preset intervals. The prototype was a website (landing page) on which the features were presented and where interested visitors could register for initial use. The founder, Joel Gascoigne, programmed the app only after there were enough registrations. The first version could be used only for Twitter. Nine months later, the app had reached more than 100,000 users.

Mobilize visitors to your website by informing your social contacts via email or executing marketing campaigns by means of search engine optimization, advertising, or partner programs (affiliate programs). This landing page describes either only the problem or a possible solution. Depending on the development status, the website visitors can partially try out the offered product or service. Users of this website can register with their contact details. In turn, they receive more information, a newsletter, or an email message when the product is available. The registration is used to measure the conversion rate — how many of the visitors become active prospective buyers, in other words. You can evaluate the behavior of your website visitors by using different key performance indicators, such as the number of visitors, pages visited, or length of visit. (For more on performance indicators, see Chapter 14.)

## Demonstrating instead of presenting

When you're dealing with a concierge minimum viable product, a customer order is executed manually for the test phase with the intention of automating it later. Before a time- or cost-intensive (perfect) automated technical solution is created, the idea is fundamentally tested by the customer. The manual processing of individual customer orders may be complicated, but there is a high learning effect. You learn how to implement the process as well as what the customer demands and is willing to pay.

TIP

Based on its user's food preferences, the Internet platform Food on Your Table creates recipes with shopping lists based on current supermarket offers. The prototype consisted of its founder, Manuel Rosso, approaching potential customers from his circle of friends and manually creating recipes and shopping lists for them each week. He learned so much from his own observations that he later automated the process through an online offer.

The *Wizard of Oz* minimum viable product has the same approach as the concierge minimum viable product, but here the customers don't know that there's a manual process in the background. The customers think that their orders are mostly automated. Just as in the classic movie *The Wizard of Oz*, whatever is happening happens behind a screen, so to speak. The approach is this: "Fake it 'til you make it."

EXAMPLE

In 2008, Groupon was just a blog that presented coupon offers; as soon as enough buyers wanted the offer, they were contacted personally by email with the coupon in PDF format. The buyers didn't notice these manual activities in the background. Only later did the entire process become automated.

In the 1980s, IBM had already used this principle to test the question of whether there's a market for transcriptions of voice messages by computers with letter-specific precision. This wasn't yet technologically possible at the time. IBM presented a computer with a microphone at a trade fair, where visitors could see their spoken words promptly as a text on the screen. But this was a bluff: The microphone signal was transferred into an adjacent room, where someone typed it into a computer.

EXAMPLE

The first chess computer in the world was a *Wizard of Oz* prototype. In 1769 in Austria, an automaton was introduced that consisted of a life-size figure in front of a chessboard. The hands of the figure mechanically moved the chess pieces. This chess computer played against people at events and captivated the audience. No computers existed at that time. Inside the chess computer was a small person who moved the pieces and was a good chess player.

You can find several online platforms for the inexpensive creation of technical prototypes with the help of hardware or software modules. They offer standard modules for particular applications with sensor systems, motion generators, displays, and software solutions. Some of these offers are open-source programs that you can use for your experiments for free. You can take a further step with rapid prototyping, which is composed of different production processes based on your design data and is intended for the fast creation of prototypes. Mature prototypes can be developed with the use of 3D printers or laser cutters.

Chapter **14**

# Testing Ideas and Assumptions

Design thinking lives off early feedback from potential customers about your ideas and your assumptions. You can learn from this feedback, adapting your assumptions and solutions to a new reality. Think of this process as an experiment in which you make an assumption and test it through exchanges with your target users. This chapter gives you an overview of how best to test your ideas and assumptions. The steps are straightforward: Decide what you want to learn with the test method, and then formulate and check various assumptions about the behavior of your target users, their problems and wishes, as well as your ideas for a solution. You'll find out how to execute these tests using interviews and online studies.

## Clarifying Tasks in the Test Phase

In the test phase, you should proceed like a researcher — in other words, come up with a hypothesis and then check whether this hypothesis can be verified by feedback from your target users. A *hypothesis* is an unproven assumption about facts or laws whose validity you want to test. The hypothesis can be proved or disproved during the test. In design thinking, you can formulate hypotheses about the target users and about ideas on how you want to solve problems or fulfill wishes. Hypotheses about the idea in the form of a product, service, or business model can also refer to individual parts of the idea or the implementation. You want to test whether an individual function is approved by the customer or whether the customer recognizes a specific sales channel.

You can carry out your experiments using the following method:

1. Select appropriate target users who have a shared problem or need for which you want to offer a solution. (For more on selecting target users, see Chapter 7.)

2. Identify assumptions about your customers, their problems or wishes, clarify your product or service idea, or identify the components of your business model, and then use what you have learned to develop measurable hypotheses. Ask yourself which insights you must find in order to continue.

3. Create a test design in the form of a list of questions or a prototype based on your assumptions. (For more on creating prototypes, see Chapter 13.) Think about which measurement criterion to select for your test. The frequency with which various customers mention a particular problem can indicate a suitable measurement criterion.

4. Test the hypothesis in an experiment by observing or surveying customers.

5. Measure the result and learn from it by

   ● Moving on to the next hypothesis if the first hypothesis is confirmed.

   ● Either reformulating the hypotheses in cases where the results are ambiguous and testing them again or starting over from scratch and asking basic questions about the target users and their problems and wishes. (Who is the actual customer? What are their real problems?)

   ● Executing a pivot if the hypothesis isn't confirmed. (For more on pivoting, see Chapter 13.)

Perform Steps 2–5 in the form of a feedback loop. The condition for this approach is that you select experiments that are uncomplicated as well as quickly executed.

## Checking assumptions about the target users

You can use a simple set of questions to verify your hypotheses about your target users:

>> Who is acting?

>> What are they doing?

>> How often are they doing it?

>> Why are they doing it?

Table 14-1 summarizes the essential assumptions that you have to check.

**TABLE 14-1**     **Testing Assumptions about the Target Users**

| Assumption | Measurement Criterion |
|---|---|
| Your target users can be described by the following characteristics, properties, preferences, or values:<br><br>_____ | Frequency of mentioning characteristics, properties, preferences, or values |
| During the product use, your target users are influenced by _____. | Frequency of mentioning persons or media |
| The customer uses or applies the product or service _____ hours per day (your assumption). | Usage period |
| The customer is online _____ per day. | Online time |
| The customer is in X environment _____ hours per day. | Length of stay |
| The customer uses X device _____ per week. | Usage period |
| The customer visits Y city _____ per week. | Frequency of visits |

## Checking assumptions about problems and needs

The examination of the hypotheses regarding a customer's problem or needs has to focus on the customer's current situation. Avoid theoretical questions about what the customer might like in the future. With your questions, target the problem or need rather than a possible solution. The customer's problem or need can present itself in the following form:

>> **Active problem or need:** The customers know the problem or need and are looking for a solution or an appropriate offer. This is the best starting situation for you. Research the problem or need using specific questions.

>> **Latent problem or need:** The customers have a problem or need but don't know it or aren't aware of it. Through exchanges with the customers, you make them aware of the problem or need.

>> **Passive problem or need:** The customers know the problem or need but aren't willing to change anything. Think critically about whether you want to address this problem or need with your idea.

Use your examinations to help you become aware of the various forms of your customers' problems and needs. Table 14-2 summarizes sample assumptions that you have to examine for the problems or wishes of your target users.

**TABLE 14-2**     **Testing Assumptions about the Customer's Problem or Wish**

| Assumption | Measurement Criterion |
|---|---|
| The customer is most annoyed or frustrated by _____. | |
| The customer has the following problem: _____. | Frequency of mentions in interviews |
| When selecting or using X, the customer must overcome the following obstacles _____. | |
| The problem is resulting in _____ for the customer (cost or time expenditure; administrative effort). | Information about cost or time expenditure or administrative effort |
| The customer encounters this problem _____ per week. | Frequency per week |
| The customer is investing _____ minutes or hours to solve the problem. | |
| The customer currently uses _____ to solve the problem. | |
| The reason the customer's own and alternative solution is unsatisfactory for the customer is that _____. | |
| From the customer's perspective, the problem is caused by _____. | Frequency of mentions |
| The customer doesn't acknowledge this problem because _____ (your assumption). | |
| The customer is most excited by _____. | |

In addition to measurably verifiable assumptions, use contact with the customer as an opportunity to pose open questions. Because there are no predefined possible answers for open questions, you should give the customers some creative leeway for their answers. This type of question will yield findings that will lead you toward new insights.

With an open question, ask your interview partners to report about a situation in which they used a product or service. Ask the customers to detail their individual steps and have them explain how they implemented or experienced something. If the activity led to a decision-making situation like the purchase of a product, the interview partners should explain how they arrived at that decision and who was involved in the process. Ask for an evaluation about whether they had problems and whether they would have done something different as part of the process or if they had a better idea for dealing with the issue. Let your interview partners describe the surroundings in which they did or experienced something related to their problem or need. Ask them whether they used specific aids, devices, methods, or tricks to remedy their problem.

TIP

Ask your interview partners to name additional persons whom you could also contact regarding the problem or need. Inquire whether they know people who have similar problems or wishes.

If you carry out interviews with different people, report the experiences of other customers to your interview partners and ask them whether they had similar experiences. Finish the part about the problems and needs by openly asking for additional factors that are relevant for the customer.

## Testing assumptions about the benefits of the idea

For the hypotheses on the planned product or service offer, avoid speculative (or unspecific) questions about whether the customers like or would buy something that they haven't seen or tested yet. Create a prototype that makes your idea vivid and tangible. (For more on creating prototypes, see Chapter 13.) Ask the customers to evaluate an individual characteristic or individual function.

A comparison with current offers from the competition makes it possible for you to gain further insights. Ask customers whether they know current options for solving the problem and what they think about these options. If no product or service exists yet that is comparable to your idea, ask customers whether they have already looked for a solution (on the Internet, for example) and which results they found. Table 14-3 summarizes sample assumptions that you have to examine for your idea.

**TABLE 14-3**   **Testing Assumptions about the Benefits of the Idea**

| Assumption | Measurement Criterion |
|---|---|
| The customers like the following characteristics, functions, or elements of competitive offers most (or least): _____. | Frequency of mentions in interviews |
| From the customers' view, your idea is better for the following reasons: _____. | |
| The satisfaction for, or enthusiasm about, your idea is shown by _____ (customer's feedback/activity). | |
| Your idea makes it possible for the customers to do the following: _____. | |
| Your idea changes the following for the customer: _____. | |
| Your idea makes it possible for the customers to save time or money in the amount of _____ (hours/$). | Amount of money or time ($/h) |

To supplement questions about the individual advantages of using your idea, conclude by asking a general evaluation question. You can use two simple methods for obtaining the customer's overall evaluation:

>> **Net promoter score (NPS):** The net promoter score makes it possible for you to have your idea evaluated from the customer's perspective with one simple question: "How likely is it that you would recommend the idea to a friend or an acquaintance?" Assign a rating scale from 10 (extremely likely) to 0 (not likely). Depending on the answer, three groups are formed: The promoters actively support your idea and respond with a rating of 9 or 10. The passive ones are generally interested in your idea, but won't actively support it. They assign a score of 7 or 8. The detractors reject your idea and give it a rating from 0 to 6, at most. To calculate the NPS, deduct the percentage of detractors from that of the promoters. An NPS of over 50 is excellent. This NPS can be tracked over time as a key figure.

>> **Sean Ellis test:** This test, created by the American start-up coach Sean Ellis, is a simple way to have customers evaluate the overall potential of a product or service offer. The customers are asked the following question: "How would you feel if this product or service wouldn't exist?" The rating scale is divided into very disappointed, somewhat disappointed, and not disappointed or not that useful. The goal is to get more than 40 percent of the customers to answer "Very disappointed."

# Testing with Interviews

If the surroundings play a significant role in an evaluation or if the customer needs to be observed while doing a certain activity, it's useful to conduct onsite interviews. This results in a better analysis of tasks that are performed by several people at once. Just be aware that this test method takes a lot of time and money and is also difficult to coordinate. Working with end consumers can result in privacy problems, or the customers' response behavior may change because of the onsite survey.

**TIP**

You can also carry out the interviews in a neutral area. The interviews can be conducted in an undisturbed atmosphere, without distractions. However, this involves higher expenditures in terms of time and costs, and scheduling a date can be difficult.

The phone interview is a convenient method. This makes it possible to reach many professional interview partners and persons located in distant areas. You can carry out multiple interviews and take notes without interference. However, you can't observe gestures or facial expressions, which can be a disadvantage for certain product or service offers where personal feelings play a role. Nor can you show a prototype to the customer. This is possible in video calls, but not all interview partners prefer this method.

## Asking the right people

If you have no clear concept of your target users yet, you should consider a wide range of people when selecting interview partners. Focus on the potential target users as soon as possible. (For more on selecting your target users, see Chapter 9.) First, use personal friends and contacts in your social network. Ask friends of friends for recommendations. Prepare emails, suitable for forwarding, about your project accompanied by a note stating that you're looking for people to test your assumptions or idea. You can approach your employees or colleagues at your own company and survey them in the role of the customers.

Think about the location where you might find potential customers. The place might be understood as a real location (café, shop, trade show) or a virtual place (social network, trade forum). Research where your customers shop, work, or spend their time off.

**TIP**

At companies, customer service is a recommended source for contacts to potential customers. Annoyed customers can be useful. A good strategy is to include a test of your hypothesis in the customer service process. You should review the top ten customer complaints every month.

If similar products or preceding products exist, you can directly approach the customers to ask whether they're available for a discussion about your assumptions or ideas. If you want to conduct numerous customer interviews in the future, establish a customer council from which you can recruit people for the tests.

**TIP**

Look for a special group of potential customers — the *lead users*. This customer group is often the first to recognize the problem or need and considers it significant. Lead users actively look for solutions and may have already developed the first approaches to a workable solution. (For more on lead users, see Chapter 2.) They often have purchasing power and accept solutions that aren't perfect yet. This helps when you want to test a prototype.

## Asking the right questions

Good questions are those that ask about the customers' current situation and their experiences so far. Ask for stories and examples. If you want to inquire about needs, this should refer to something that the customer can specifically envision. First, describe the problem and ask whether the customer also sees this as a problem.

**WARNING**

Avoid presenting your specific business idea at the start. The interviews aren't about your self-presentation or selling an idea. You're interested in customer feedback and what you can learn from the customer's answers. Emphasize how important the interview partner's honest answers are to you, and don't hesitate to ask for advice and help.

In your interviews, focus on specific activities, events, or decisions in the present or past. You can form a comprehensive picture by using the following questions:

>> What did you use last time, or how did you use it?

>> How often have you _____?

>> What did you decide last time to _____?

>> What frustrated you?

>> What pleased you?

>> What did you spend a lot of time on?

>> What did you try on multiple occasions?

>> What do you consider important for _____?

>> What do you like about _____?

>> What do you miss or find lacking in _____?

Don't ask hypothetical questions about how much the customers would pay or how they would make that decision. Don't ask whether the customers would like something specific. Customers often lack imagination for something they don't see or can't tangibly try out. Ask your interview partner to talk about what they did in specific situations or on certain occasions. At the end of your interview, you can also ask what your discussion partner would dream of in certain situations.

WARNING

Avoid suggestive questions like these:

>> "Don't you also think that . . .?"

>> "Do you agree with me that . . .?"

>> "Wouldn't you also want . . .?"

This type of question influences the response behavior, and you won't get an honest answer. Closed questions such as yes/no questions aren't helpful because you won't learn anything from them.

If your interview partner is reserved or not forthcoming during the discussion, indirect questions are helpful. The person isn't being asked about their problems or needs but should answer from the perspective of a third person known to them. For example: "Why does your friend use product X?" or "What do you think your friend has bought recently?"

TIP

You can investigate the causes of customer problems or needs by asking the Why question multiple times. (For more on the Five-Times-Why technique, see Chapter 6.) But avoid asking the five Why questions in succession. Constant Why questions can seem aggressive and cause the customer to create a barrier. Vary your questions. Summarize the customer's previous answers in your own words and ask the interview partner to talk more about their behavior or perception.

## Asking the questions correctly

If there's an opportunity and it's not too complicated, your best option is to carry out face-to-face personal interviews The next-best option is a phone interview. Only then should you consider an exchange via electronic media (email, chat). Always use the first person singular form in interviews, and don't hide behind wording like *we* or *our company* with business contacts. Only then can you reach a more personal level that allows you to hold more in-depth discussions.

Encourage your interview partner to avoid answering generally or hiding behind the terms "one would," "we would," or, in the case of a business customer, behind "our company would" or "our company management would." Instead, ask them to respond in the first person singular from their perspective. Ask:

>> How do you personally see this?

>> What does this mean specifically for you?

>> Which experiences have you had?

Always use easily comprehensible wording, even in expert surveys. Avoid specialized terms and convoluted sentences. Speak in the customer's language. It's better for you to speak with slightly more colloquial terms than to be incomprehensible or misleading. Avoid negations and always use positive phrasing. (For more recommendations on interviews, see Chapter 15.)

# Testing with Online Studies

When you create an online prototype in the form of a web page or an app, you can examine the visitor behavior on this page. With this online prototype, you can test individual functions or the user-friendliness of these online offers. You can also provide information on this website about future products, services, or business models. The information can consist of texts, images, or videos to click on or download. You can examine the interests and preferences of your target users by researching their click behavior and input behavior. It helps your analysis if you compare the visitor behavior of various groups of users and capture a few key figures.

## Comparing user behavior

Comparing different versions of a website by means of A/B testing is a widely used evaluation method. In *A/B testing,* two groups (A and B) of users are shown different selected versions of a website or a prototype or images alternately and at random. The possible differences in the reaction or user behavior are examined in these two groups. Preferably, the differences between the versions should show up in a single characteristic or function; otherwise, the result won't be clear. Make these versions available at the same time so that you can minimize influences caused by different time periods. Software programs for A/B testing are available so that you can use them for the program's implementation or for statistical evaluation.

# Evaluating user behavior with key figures

You can use key figures to evaluate visitor behavior. With these key figures, you can measure and assess how the visitors use your online offer (app or website) and whether your assumptions about visitor behavior are applicable. First, you should clarify whether you can test your assumption about the visitor behavior with the key figure. If you want to test multiple assumptions at a time, they should each be covered by different key figures.

**WARNING**

Check whether the recording of the online visitor behavior with selected key figures can be justified legally, ethically, and in terms of your own corporate culture. If the information is person-specific, this might lead to conflicts due to data protection.

You can use the following key figures to assess the visitor behavior of online offers:

- » Number of visitors (visitors) per day, week, or month

- » Number of (unique) visitors; the unique visitors indicate the net number of total visitors

- » Number of new and returning visitors

- » Page impressions per visitor

- » Length of website visit or bounce rate (percentage of visitors who immediately leave your online offer again)

- » Number of comments or likes by your target users in individual social networks for your contributions to the online offer

You can distinguish the number of users by country, device (desktop or smartphone), or browser. This information lets you better adapt your online offer better. If your visitors mainly use their smartphones, you have to take the user-friendliness for mobile use into account. If your visitors originate mainly from specific countries, you should consider the special linguistic and cultural aspects associated with each country when you design your online offer.

**TIP**

In addition to the number of users, the *conversion rate* is quite an informative key figure — it lets you describe how many visitors actively carried out an action that you offered. If the products are already marketable, the conversion rate is the ratio of the number of buyers to the number of users. When you test ideas for a solution, you can record other actions, such as completing a form or subscribing to a newsletter or counting the number of registrations for a test version instead of the buying behavior.

The goal of an online offer is often to achieve extreme distribution on the Internet, which (hopefully) starts to spread on its own. You can use the viral coefficient to estimate whether your product, service, or business model idea has the potential of going viral (being widely viewed). It can be calculated this way:

1. Determine the average number of visitors to your online offer per time period (day, week, or month). Let's say you have 100 visitors.

2. Multiply this number by the number of average recommendations per user. Recommendations can be shown in that users share with others your posts on social networks. Assume that every user would make 10 recommendations. You would have 1,000 recommendations as a result.

3. Determine the average conversion rate in percent. The conversion rate describes how many people who have received a recommendation have actively performed an action, such as buying a product, registering on a website, or downloading files. Assume that every fifth recipient of a recommendation subsequently carried out an action, such as registering for a newsletter. This makes the conversion rate 20 percent.

4. Calculate the number of activated users that you determine with the conversion rate (refer to Step 3) from the number of recommendations (refer to Step 2). With 1,000 recommendations and a conversion rate of 20 percent, you have 200 activated users.

5. Calculate the viral coefficient by dividing the number of activated users (refer to Step 4) by the average number of visitors (refer to Step 1). If you have 200 activated users and 100 average visitors, the viral coefficient is 2.

A coefficient lower than 1 indicates a standstill. Your goal is a viral coefficient that is significantly higher than 1.

**TIP**

Don't exaggerate with the key figures; otherwise, you'll lose track. Select only a limited amount from the possible key figures. Focus on just a few figures — the key performance indicators (KPI).

# Learning from Test Results

After you have carried out interviews or examined the online behavior of your target users, the next priority is determining the learning effect of the results. In addition to checking the individual assumptions or the viability of your idea, you can glean even more information from customer feedback. Ask the following questions to examine the result from contact with your target users:

>> What things were evaluated positively?

>> What were the concerns?

>> What was a surprising customer statement?

>> Did the customer display any emotions, and if so, what kind?

>> What suggestions were made?

>> What insights and feedback did the idea concept receive?

>> What can be learned from this?

From the results of your interviews or online studies, determine which statements have great significance for your design thinking project. Try to implement the feedback with the next prototype.

**TIP**

The customer feedback may also result in options for variations in the product or service idea. Based on the results, think about whether other variants of the product, service, or business model might be requested. Ask yourself in what respect the idea could be varied. Then check how extensive other variants would be and whether they're feasible and economically viable.

If your assumptions aren't confirmed or if your observations and surveys show ambiguous results, you might need to return to an earlier stage in the design thinking process. If your assumptions regarding the problems or needs of your target users aren't confirmed, you should review your task. (For more on how to carry out this review, see Chapter 9). If you get different results from your potential customers, it's possible that your target users aren't forming a consistent group. Reconsider the description of your target users (see Chapter 7 for more on this topic), focus on a subgroup, and perform the tests again. If your idea for a solution isn't approved, you should develop a new idea. (See Chapters 10 and 11 for more on how to carry out this task.) If the potential customer can't picture your idea, you should create a new prototype. (For more on prototypes, see Chapter 13.)

Needing to come up with a new description of your target users, a new examination of their problems or needs, or the development of a new idea or prototype doesn't amount to failure. Quite the contrary: You avoid focusing on the wrong target users or the wrong problem using a bad idea. You avoid high investments in the implementation of a product, service, or business model that the potential customer won't approve. Design thinking thrives on feedback from the previous phases. You learn from the failure, change the idea according to the feedback from your target users, create an improved prototype, and then perform new tests. With this approach, you're sure to gradually reach a promising product, service, or business model innovation.

# The Part of Tens

Ten success factors for correctly preparing for, completing, and following up on interviews.

Ten success factors for proceeding strategically, laying the foundations for success, and responding to objections.

IN THIS CHAPTER

» Planning and completing
  interviews correctly

» Learning from discussions

» Tackling surveys using different
  formats

# Chapter **15**

# Ten Success Factors for Interviews

S haring information with your target users is an essential part of the design thinking process. You can use interviews to learn more about your target users — their wishes as well as their problems. You'll get decisive feedback and new suggestions for your idea for a solution. To succeed with design thinking, it's important that you plan and complete interviews quickly and efficiently. In this chapter, you'll find ten factors for successfully carrying out interviews.

## Ensuring Good Preparation

Walk through the situation in your mind before the interview. Look at the previous information about the person with whom you want to speak. Think about their character, problems, and needs. You can find information about their educational background, publications, lectures, or job descriptions through social networks or Internet research.

A good way to prepare is to practice the interview with friends or colleagues in advance. Before you start, test whether your questions are clear. You should check each question to see whether it will help you reach your goals and whether it should be shortened or deleted. The less you ask, the better.

TIP

For structuring and for an efficient and effective interview, create a binding interview guide — it lists the essential assumptions in the form of questions. (For more on the individual assumptions you have to know about, see Chapter 14.)

Prepare so that you can adhere to the schedule. You should prioritize your questions and ask them in that order so that you can at least test your key assumptions if time is short. Consider the focus of the interview in advance so that you can concentrate on it.

# Finding the Right Entry

During your initial contact with people you don't know, you should emphasize that this isn't a sales pitch but that you're looking for advice and need that person's evaluation. It's often surprising how many people are glad to help you, even when time is short, because they feel flattered or consider the problem relevant. Communicate at the beginning that the conversation will take only a few minutes (from 5 minutes to no more than 20 minutes). Describe the topic in two or three sentences. Start by asking about their personal preferences or their own experiences with the topic. This question can be an icebreaker.

# Taking Notes Correctly

Before starting to test your assumptions or your prototype, think about how you want to record the customer feedback (logging, filming). In principle, you shouldn't use recording devices in interviews with people you don't know. The interview partners hold back more when they're being recorded. Asking for their consent to be recorded isn't a good way to start the interview. You can also attend with another teammate. One person asks, and the other takes notes. However, this can also have a deterrence effect and is cost- and time-intensive.

Notes are certainly helpful for phone interviews, but they can prove to be more hindrance than help in personal interviews. Avoid using a laptop in personal conversations, because it creates a protective "shield" between you and your interview partner. Tablets are more practical. When you take notes, you should be aware that you'll pay less attention to the interview partner at that time. You might miss the gestures and facial expressions of your discussion partner. On the whole, the interview can seem less natural with a recording.

You can take the notes electronically or per handwriting, using notepads, sticky notes, or index cards to write on. The advantage of using sticky notes and index cards is that you can rearrange them and order them on a wall. While taking notes either during or after the interview, you can mark the results with simple symbols to highlight interesting statements. Quote important (especially the emotional) statements word-for-word. You can use emojis so that you can capture the type of emotions (annoyance, worry, frustration, curiosity, excitement). Putting down in writing the scope and type of emotions can provide important information.

## Listening Actively

Listen more, talk less. The interview partner should speak 80 percent of the time; the person asking questions, 20 percent. During the conversation, confirm the discussion partner's statements by nodding affirmatively, asking additional questions in case of ambiguities, and occasionally summarizing the contents with your own words. Maintain eye contact, but don't hide behind a laptop. Avoid judging your discussion partner and their statements during the course of the interview. When talking, don't consider what you could do with the information. Focus on what and how your interview partner says something. Evaluate and utilize the information only after the discussion ends.

## Paying Attention to Emotions

Pay attention to the language (volume, speech rhythm, melody, emphasis), gestures, and facial expressions during the conversation. Contradictions between what is said and how it is said can be particularly useful for the subsequent analysis. During each interview, your attention should be not just on the content-specific claims but also on surprising and emotional statements. Emotions are expressed in the content of what is being said as well as in the choice of words, pitch, gestures, and facial expressions. Emotions can show annoyance, worries, frustration, curiosity, or excitement, for example.

## Always Following Up

Never assume something that your discussion partner might mean in a statement. Never take anything for granted. Ask what your interview partner means or understands. Ask for an explanation if you don't know the alleged reason or if you yourself consider something self-explanatory.

Consider every statement with skepticism. Use statements of a questionable nature as an opportunity to ask more or confront other people with this statement. You should be flexible during the discussions. If the customer talks about something with a certain amount of emotion or reports a failed search for a solution and the problem doesn't correspond to your original approach, ask about details to better understand the issue. This way, you might discover a new business idea and might also have to change direction, or *pivot*, with your original idea.

# Concluding Discussions Successfully

The last impression is the one that's remembered, which is why you should finish your discussion with a positive send-off. When the interview is finished, always express thanks and provide information about the next steps — what you'll do with the information, in other words. Keep in mind that your interview partner is a potential customer and, as an influencer, can recommend your innovation to others after the market launch. It might be useful if you end the interview by asking whether you may contact the potential customer for additional questions or if there is interest in your providing information about the subsequent product launch to your interview partner. Ask whether the interview partner might be able to recommend others.

# Completing a Sufficient Number of Interviews

You know that you have conducted a sufficient number of interviews when you recognize a clear response pattern. The broader your potential target group, the more interviews you must carry out. If you have a small target group, five to ten interviews might be enough for you to recognize a clear pattern. The number of interview partners depends on the size of the planned target market. If no clear response patterns emerge after a large number of interviews, you should critically consider the selection of your target group again (Who are our customers, really?) or revise your questions (Which problems or needs do the customers actually have?).

# Postprocessing Interviews

After the interviews, always follow up by documenting the most important events during the conversation as well as the significant results. For your personal post-processing, you can ask yourself the following questions:

>> What went well and functioned smoothly during the interview?

>> What didn't go so well?

>> What were the high and low points of the interview?

>> Was anything unclear during the interview?

>> What did you achieve with the discussion? What didn't you achieve?

>> What do you have to do differently during the next interview?

>> How can you ensure that the next interview will go (even) better?

You can learn for the next interview from your answers to these questions. Take time for postprocessing, because you're sure to benefit from it.

# Using Every Opportunity

Use every opportunity for exchanges with your target users. It's never too early to start with interviews in the design thinking process. Only by inviting early feedback and suggestions from your potential customers can you get the information you need for your own work.

Create a list with the top three questions you will use during spontaneous meetings with your potential customers. This means you will always be prepared in discussions with interesting people and will use them effectively to learn.

If you have no opportunity for a personal conversation, utilize information and communication technologies. In video chats, you can follow the gestures and facial expressions of your discussion partner. This method is recommended for technically savvy customers. You can share additional information with each other electronically. Instant messaging can be used for customers who don't like verbal communication or video transfers. In instant messaging, messages are transmitted immediately via a software program. Just be aware that the instant messaging approach can lead to people misinterpreting each other's statements, even when emojis are used.

If a time delay is acceptable during the exchange of questions and answers, you can also use emails. This is a way to survey customers in distant places and other time zones. Your interview partners can respond to your questions at a time that's suitable for them.

You can gain systematic feedback about your assumptions and ideas by using online surveys with a questionnaire. Although the response rate is often low for an online survey, it's a quick way to solicit quantifiable statements. A few free software solutions are available for the implementation.

Keep in mind the limits of digital media when it comes to surveys. People's response behavior is influenced by electronic recordings or transmissions. You won't get confidential information. The gestures and facial expressions are lost. Emotions are suppressed. That's why you should make the effort to visit your target users onsite and engage in personal discussions without much technical support. Analog is the new digital. On a graffiti wall, users anonymously express their impressions about a product or service on a blank sheet of paper onsite. Make a pen available and ask open questions about how the customer felt about the service, location, or product after using the product or service:

>> What was good?

>> What annoyed you?

>> What could be improved?

This method is a good choice for situations in which personal surveys aren't possible or where you might influence the answer by being present.

Chapter **16**

# Ten Success Factors for Implementing Your Idea

Design thinking isn't something you do just once. It's not enough for you to set up a project and then fail to take further measures. Design thinking must become a component of the company's culture of innovation. That's the only way for sustainable success to succeed in a dynamically changing environment. You can achieve competitive advantages by taking advantage of the agile, creative, and flexible recognition and utilization of entrepreneurial opportunities. Be sure to consider an organization's entire culture of innovation.

A company's structure, business strategy, processes, and leadership style, plus the competencies of its employees, shape the culture of innovation. They are the Five Big Factors of innovation. In this chapter, you can read about ten factors for shaping the culture of innovation and successfully implementing design thinking.

## Prepare the Structures

The approaches of design thinking may be different from the usual business processes at a company — processes characterized by routine and standard tasks. A culture that orients itself toward efficiency is predominant in business processes. It is evident in the avoidance of mistakes and frequent task changes, in that employees follow formal rules for carrying out individual tasks and that controls are always performed when services are provided.

Design thinking requires an innovation orientation, where mistakes are desirable for the purpose of learning and improvements. The employees are given breathing room and encouraged to act autonomously. If a conflict takes place between an efficiency orientation and an innovation orientation at your company, you should organizationally separate the innovation activities from the routine processes.

The separation can be carried out through a project, a different organizational business unit, or an independent subsidiary. Apply the principles of design thinking for the project, the separate business unit, or the independent subsidiary for which you're carrying out the innovation activities. You'll tolerate mistakes, involve customers in the process at an early stage, design creative workspaces, rely on variety in the team, and handle changes in an agile and flexible manner. (For more on these principles, see Chapter 2.)

If you organizationally separate your company's business processes from its innovation activities, you should ensure that the two areas don't get excluded or isolated from each other over time. This would make the coordination between the two areas more difficult — so difficult, in fact, that an idea for innovation may not even find approval in the other unit in charge of successfully implementing it. Conduct regular discussions to coordinate. Switch employees between the departments. Form a steering panel composed of employees from both areas that would be responsible for the coordination and exchange of information.

# Encourage Collaboration and Communicate Openly

Open and efficient collaboration and communication at an organization are decisive success factors in the development of innovations. Design thinking processes thrive on an interdepartmental and interdisciplinary exchange between those involved, an exchange founded on mutual appreciation between different departments and operational functional areas. The collaboration in design thinking projects takes place in teams. Managers have to take on diverse and challenging tasks to promote team development. One model for describing the phases of successful team development was proposed by the American psychologist Bruce Tuckmann, who characterized the team development cycle as a move from forming to storming to norming to performing to adjourning. The next few sections look at that model in some detail.

# Complete the forming phase in a positive way

During the *forming* phase of team development, team members must become accustomed to their roles. A high level of uncertainty is pervasive in the team at its initial formation, so you, as a manager or project manager, must pay attention to these guidelines:

>> **Give the team members time to get to know each other.** Each person in the team should be able to introduce themselves in a relaxed manner. A traditional method for introductions at the beginning of a new project or workshop is to have each participant state their name, position, and educational background in a single sentence. In another sentence, the participants can also talk about their motivations, wishes, and expectations for the project or workshop. One casual introduction method that fits design thinking is to lay out pictures or objects. Each participant should select an image or object and explain why they picked it and what they associate with it. This might involve professional experiences, or it might be personal stories.

>> **Give the team members a proper orientation.** Tell them the reasons for the project and its goals, and explain the basic conditions (contribution to the corporate strategy, budget specifications, timeframe).

>> **Clarify the participants' questions and jointly plan goals, tasks, and processes.** For more on this clarification process, see Chapter 4.

>> **Define the responsibilities and tasks in the team and coordinate how to report about results.** Organize regular and frequent meetings in the beginning. (For more on defining responsibilities and tasks, see Chapter 5.)

# Master the storming phase

During the *storming* phase, team members get to know each other better and become more self-confident. With that self-confidence come the first "storms" (hence the term *storming*), where people start to push against boundaries as the collaboration process proceeds. This can be reflected by a sense of impatience and frustration caused by a lack of initial success and can cause conflicts in the team. As a manager or project manager, you should react this way:

>> **Facilitate quick wins during the project work.** To do this, select tasks that the team can work on quickly and easily.

>> **Avoid excluding anyone during meetings.** Instead, encourage everyone to participate verbally when experiences are shared.

>> **Promote knowledge sharing.** To ensure open communication, provide all team members with the necessary resources:

- *Hardware:* Computer, phone system, mobile communications
- *Software:* Collaboration programs to exchange messages, task lists, and shared documents and to hold videoconferences

>> **Further a culture that welcomes open discussion and doesn't shy away from conflict.** Directly address themes and conflicts, and discuss them with those involved.

## Support the norming phase

During the *norming* phase — the phase where people start to resolve their differences, appreciate their colleagues' strengths, and respect your authority as a leader — you'll see a growing development of clear role distributions in the team along with collaboration standards. The team spirit starts to grow. As a manager or project manager, you can support the process this way:

>> **Establish trust.** Report about relevant information, and promote and demand mutual feedback about the team's completed work.

>> **Support the team in formulating rules for the collaborative process.** Even unwritten rules must be spoken about and, preferably, set in writing. (For more on collaborations, see Chapter 5.)

>> **Give the team orientation.** Set the goal of documenting interim results of the project work.

In this phase, the manager or project manager assumes the role of a moderator or coach.

## Use the performing phase efficiently

In the *performing* phase, the team moves into the phase of its highest productivity and is optimally established. In this phase, the task of the manager is to

>> **Encourage self-organization in the team.** Hold back and don't assign tasks.

>> **Observe changes in the project environment and inform the team about new developments.** Influencing factors from the environment for the project can include new legal requirements, technological inventions, changed customer requirements, or a new company strategy. (For more on analyzing external influences, see Chapter 6.)

>> **Ensure resource distribution.** Make sure that the necessary resources at the company (personnel, equipment, capital) are available over the long term.

>> **Communicate.** Share the successes of the team with the outside world.

## Successfully prepare the adjourning phase

Often, not enough attention is paid to the *adjourning* phase, where a team is disbanded. An organized conclusion affects the ongoing project as well as future projects. The participants often form an overall impression just from the ending. If the conclusion is well-organized and satisfactory, the entire project will be rated positively: As a manager or project manager, you can help your team in the following manner:

>> **Perform a review with the team.** Address how the project worked out and what can be deduced for the future (postmortem).

>> **Document the results.** Describe experiences from the project.

>> **Praise the team's work and performance.** Celebrate the conclusion with good food and drinks.

>> **Give the individual employees personal feedback about their contribution to the team.** Engage yourself to ensure that team members find an interesting new job at the company after the project ends.

# Create a Sense of Urgency

You can create a sense of necessity and urgency to change the corporate culture if you initiate a blunt analysis of the current situation and the future challenges at the company. The past has shaped the corporate culture, which is why the company situation should be analyzed with a look back. The following questions will help you analyze the current situation of the corporate culture:

>> How would one describe our culture of innovation?

>> What makes us particularly innovative? Where are we weak?

>> From the perspective of our customers/employees, what is it exactly that we stand for?

>> How do we deal with each other and with external parties?

>> Which principles shape our actions?

>> What do we want to achieve with our culture of innovation? What don't we want to achieve?

>> What suits us? What doesn't?

>> How do we have to organize ourselves to reach our goals in the best possible way?

>> What has to be changed? How do we develop our company further?

These questions can essentially be answered in different constellations of discussions. These are discussions between the company management and stakeholders (investors, customers, suppliers), employee conversations, informal discussion rounds, or workgroups and workshops focused on the culture of innovation. In these discussions, it's already important that the necessity and urgency of changes in the culture of innovation are shown and that the contribution of design thinking is emphasized.

# Establish a Leadership Coalition

To sustainably establish the principles and methods of design thinking at the entire company, you need people who will support you in this change. These people must be credible and have high levels of recognition at the company. Assume that a company has 20 percent supporters and 20 percent opponents of a change. The remaining 60 percent are undecided about changes.

In personal discussions and meetings, you will recognize who wants to support you when it comes to your project. Pay attention to those who follow your explanations on design thinking with interest and want to know more. Select people from different areas (research, production, marketing, sales, controlling) and various hierarchical levels.

Supporters who can establish a leadership coalition for change are necessary at all hierarchical levels and in all affected areas. When it comes to changing the culture of innovation at the company, the leadership coalition should range across all departments and hierarchies.

The main tasks of the leadership coalition include participation in the strategy development and implementation planning for design thinking projects. This leadership coalition can become an early warning agency for resistance at the company and at the same time spread the opportunities of design thinking throughout the company. The representatives of the leadership coalition are responsible for supporting the participants within the framework of the company's design thinking projects.

# Communicate a Vision for the Culture of Innovation

It's important to have open communication at the company about the new culture of innovation that encompasses the principles and methods of design thinking. It is top management's task to emphasize the necessity and urgency of change at the company at every opportunity and to explain the principles of design thinking. The members of the leadership coalition must exemplify the change as role models and be opinion leaders in communicating the benefits of a design thinking approach. The communication should be carried out in a pictorial language and reflect these benefits for the company. Check whether the principles and methods of design thinking were understood.

Ask the following questions to determine whether there has been sufficient communication about the vision:

>> Did the employees understand the goals of the change?

>> Do the affected persons know the reason for the change?

>> Do the employees understand the benefits of design thinking?

>> Do the employees know the principles and methods of design thinking?

If you discover a lack of information among the employees, you have to hold conversations or workshops on design thinking.

# Establish a Company Culture Tolerant of Mistakes

Design thinking can lead to mistakes. Not every assumption about the problems and wishes of your target users will be confirmed. Not every idea is successful. Not every prototype is evaluated positively by customers. From these mistakes, you can learn what the potential customer's problem actually is, which idea is feasible, and which prototype will be appealing to the customer.

You should utilize mistakes for your learning progress not just at a project level — you also have to develop a culture that tolerates mistakes and works to learn from them at the company level. (For more on handling mistakes at the project level, see Chapter 3.)

Employees must be able to speak openly and honestly about mistakes across the entire company. When you introduce a culture of mistakes, managers function as role models. Managers must stand by their own mistakes and report how they felt about these and, above all, what they learned from them. Honesty and openness aren't weaknesses. They are important values that increase the credibility of a manager. As a manager, address your own mistakes and report which conclusions you have drawn from these mistakes at every opportunity — in lectures, presentations, interviews in the employee newsletter, and talks with employees.

Start a meeting by describing your own mistakes. Emphasize that mistakes are part of creating innovations and are learning opportunities. This encourages participants to talk about their own mistakes.

When a manager handles employees' mistakes in an objective way so that no one who honestly and openly reports on their mistakes is exposed, this establishes trust while also setting an example. This requires every manager to regularly reflect on their own attitude toward mistakes and behaviors, by answering these questions:

>> How do I define mistakes?

>> As a manager, how do I want to handle the mistakes of employees?

>> How can the employee learn from mistakes? What can I learn from the employees' mistakes? What can the company learn from the mistakes?

The manager's approach to their own mistakes and those of the employees will become known and, in a positive case, can shape the culture of mistakes at the company.

# Broadly Empower Employees

Employees must be informed and empowered on a broad basis so that the new corporate culture can be integrated smoothly into the daily work routine. It's possible to reduce distrust and barriers among the affected employees through discussions and agreements regarding active participation in the design thinking projects. If the existing skills must be expanded and further developed for the culture of innovation, you should carry out advanced training measures in the form of training sessions and workshops. You can offer events on the following topics:

>> **Understanding the principles and methods of design thinking:** For more on these topics, see Chapters 1 and 2.

>> **Being agile in executing projects:** For more on this topic, see Chapters 4 and 5.

>> **Developing empathy toward customer problems.** For more on this topic, see Chapters 6, 7, 8, and 9.

>> **Creatively finding ideas.** For more on these topics, see Chapters 10 and 11.

>> **Evaluating ideas from different perspectives.** For more on this topic, see Chapter 12.

>> **Creating and testing prototypes.** For more on these topics, see Chapters 13 and 14.

On an individual level, include the goals of the culture of innovation in employees' target agreements and, on a company level, in the concept of personnel development. This way, you can reward work on a design thinking project. The culture of innovation thrives on the feedback of the involved and affected employees. As a manager, you should regularly hold discussions with employees about the results of the culture of innovation.

# Overcome Resistance

The novelty of implementing design thinking can cause uncertainty among the participants. A design thinking approach means that previous work methods will change. Changes are perceived as disturbances, annoyances, upheavals, or pointless turbulence. You have to expect resistance when it comes to initiating a design thinking approach. The resistance can have very different effects on the innovation: In the worst case scenario, the innovation will be prevented. There may also be a delay in the innovation process. It's also possible for the original idea to be changed and watered down in the course of the development process.

Treat the resistance constructively. Resistance can also have positive effects and contribute to an improvement of the innovation or the innovation process. Constructive resistance allows you to identify and remedy deficits in your idea at an early stage.

Overcome resistances by recognizing what kinds of barriers there are and where they come from. You can classify resistances as these types of barriers:

>> **Inability:** This barrier is reflected by an inadequate use of resources. Make sure that enough resources are available for innovative projects.

>> **Not knowing:** The knowledge regarding the development and implementation of the innovation is missing or not available throughout the company. Expand the competencies of the employees and offer events about design thinking.

>> **No permission:** If there's no permission, there's no support from the top management. This means design thinking isn't one of the strategic priorities. Employees may not use their working hours for creative work. Convince the top management about the advantages of design thinking. Advocate that the employees gain design freedom to pursue creative approaches and that they may carry out the first projects within an initially limited budget.

>> **Not wanting:** Examples of this type of barrier include persistence effects about the status quo as well as a lack of willingness to learn or change. Form a leadership coalition with other employees, which will communicate the usefulness and principles of a design thinking approach throughout the company.

# Counter Objections

An obvious manifestation of resistances and barriers is the communication of *killer phrases*, which are unsubstantiated claims or expressed biases that indicate rejection. Here are some typical killer phrases:

>> "We don't need anything like that."

>> "This can't work."

>> "That might happen in theory."

You can invalidate killer phrases by asking for the reasons behind the claims and requesting evidence for the statements. Table 16-1 summarizes a few questions and statements you can use to invalidate killer phrases. Also display the killer phrases in a clearly visible way in communal spaces and at workshops. No one should use these phrases during teamwork.

**TABLE 16-1**     **Invalidating Killer Phrases**

| Killer Phrase | Your Reply |
|---|---|
| "We don't need anything like that." | Ask what would happen with the company if it canceled all efforts toward innovation (the do-nothing scenario). Doing nothing will be punished by customers and competitors. |
| "This can't work." | Ask why it wouldn't work and whether is the speaker has proof of this. |
| "What's the purpose of that?" | Explain the principles of design thinking (for more on this topic, see Chapter 2) and the approach (for more on this, see Chapter 1). |
| "That might happen in theory." | Give examples. The first computer mouse and the first ergonomic toothbrush were developed according to the principles of design thinking. (You can find more examples in Parts 1 and 2 of this book.) |
| "This isn't a priority for us at the moment." | Point out changes in the areas of technology, society, and the economy that require a fast response. |
| "This can't be financed." | Suggest starting with a small project that has a limited budget. The progress of the project can be checked after a milestone. |
| "Interesting — let's discuss this sometime." | Prevent getting put off. Arrange an appointment with decision-makers in the near future so that you can discuss this. |
| "Yes, but . . ." | "Yes, but . . ." is a common way to start a general rejection. Ask the person to specifically address the proposal. Ask how you can improve the proposal. |

# Curb Euphoria

A positive attitude toward design thinking is beneficial for the success of the project. However, expectations that are too high can be dangerous for an idea's implementation. As a result of the euphoria, design thinking might be understood as creative rubbish, if there's a constant development of new ideas that aren't tested for feasibility or economic viability or transferred into a functional prototype.

TIP

Euphoria in a team may result in hastily rushing into decisions — you should avoid this situation. Evaluate the ideas and select the most promising suggestions. (For more on how to evaluate ideas, see Chapter 12.) Implement selected ideas as a prototype, and test it with your customers. (For more on prototypes, see Chapters 13 and 14.)

In a design thinking team, euphoria can lead to negative group thinking (groupthink). If the team overestimates itself, it reduces the willingness of others outside the group to recognize and consider perspectives and ideas. At every phase of the design thinking process, critically check whether the necessary competencies are present in the team and integrate other partners — representatives of suppliers, research institutes, and universities, for example, or other external advisers.

# Index

## Numerics

3-point estimate, 73
5 P's of design thinking, 11
5 Whys technique, 106
404 web page, 237
635 method, 195, 201–204

## A

A/B testing, 250
abstraction principle, 21, 185
action research, 145
action steps/behaviors, 156
Active, in RACI matrix, 80–81
active listening, 259
active problem/need, 243
actual competencies, 55, 56
adaptability, as a criteria, 22, 215, 220–221
adjourning phase, 267
adjusting
   encouraging willingness to change, 45
   perspectives, 205–207
   tasks, 115
advantages, evaluating for ideas, 213–214
agile approach, 66
aging population, 96–97
Airbnb, 40, 238
alignment with trends, as criteria for measuring
      product appeal/competitiveness, 223–224
Ambitious, in SMART criteria, 62–63
analogy method/principle, 21, 184–185, 198
analysis
   artifacts, 153, 154–155
   benefit, 221–226
   means-ends, 170–172
   of needs as tasks, 166–172
   of secondary material, 120
   of weak areas in customer journey, 134

analysis grid, 113
anonymous brainstorming/writing, 199
applying
   consistent observational methodologies,
      153–158
   principle of self-organization, 81
appreciation, of work, 57
arousing curiosity, 45–48
arranging workshops, 85–89
artifacts analysis, 153, 154–155
asking
   for creative freedom, 49
   good questions, 248–249
   questions correctly, 249–250
   for support, 27, 48
association principle, 20
associative principle, 184
assumptions
   checking about problems/needs, 243–245
   checking about target users, 242–243
   testing, 241–253
   testing about idea benefits, 245–246
attitudes, ensuring positive, 43–45
attribution error, 152
auxiliary materials, as a resource, 72

## B

B2B (business-to-business), 123
bar graphs, creating, 71–72
barriers, evaluating for ideas, 213–214
Basic customer requirements, in Kano model, 173
behavioral mapping and tracking, 153, 155
benefit analysis, 221–226
benefits, of experiments, 228
bias, 119
big brainstorming, 201
bisociation, 184

black hat, in Six Hats method, 209

blindstorming, 200

blue hat, in Six Hats method, 208

bodystorming, 200

brain activity, recording, 143

brainprinting, 199

brainshaping, 200

brainstation, 200

brainstorming
  about, 11, 196–197
  generating ideas by, 196–204
  improving flow of ideas, 197–199
  variants in, 199–201
  written, 201–204

brainwalking, 200

brainwriting, 201–204

break areas, 91

breaking the rules, 205

breathing, recording, 143

British Design Council, 16

budget planning, 74–75

Buffer app, 238

buffer times, 71

Burbn app, 231

business models, designing, 13

business scalability, as a criteria, 215, 218–219

business units, as internal stakeholders, 112

business viability, as a criteria, 22, 215, 218–219

business-to-business (B2B), 123

buyer role, 164

buying center, 164

# C

card sequence, 213

CERN (European Organization for Nuclear Research), 32–33

challenges, presenting tasks as, 46

changing
  encouraging willingness to change, 45
  perspectives, 205–207
  tasks, 115

characterizing customers using Persona method, 122–125

Cheat Sheet (website), 4

checkers, 158

checklists, evaluating ideas with, 215–221

choosing
  creativity techniques, 190–193
  evaluation methods, 211–212
  ideas, 212–213, 226
  interviewees, 247–248
  most important wishes/problems, 172–174
  problems, 172–174
  solutions, 22
  wishes, 172–174

Christensen, Clayton (professor), 165

clarifying
  communication within teams, 81–84
  responsibilities, 50
  tasks in prototype phase, 228–229
  tasks in test phase, 241–246
  what the task is, 100–101
  when the problem/wish occurs, 103
  where the problem/wish occurs, 103
  who has the problem/wish, 101–103
  why the problem/wish occurs, 103–106

clients, internal, as internal stakeholders, 112

climate, of common spaces, 91

closing knowledge gaps, 107

cognitive dissonance, 151

cognitive empathy, 117–118

collaboration
  encouraging, 264–267
  with experts, 183

collecting
  information, 120–121
  task information, 18

collective-notebook method, 203–204

common spaces, designing, 89–91

communication
  clarifying within teams, 81–84
  compared with documenting, 83

defining practices for, 25
goals, 63–64
in performing phase, 267
principles, 14–15
promoting with common spaces, 89–90
quality of, mystery shopping and, 158
setting up rules for, 83–84
vision, 44–45, 269
company culture, establishing, 269–270
compare the incomparable, 205
comparing
avoiding, 162
target and actual competencies, 56
user behavior, 250
competencies
actual, 55, 56
checking, 56
finding, 54–57
searching in areas of, 98–99
target, 55, 56
competitors
as external stakeholders, 111
monitoring, 182
complexity, as criteria for measuring feasibility, 223
concluding discussions in interviews, 260
concurrent think-aloud, 150
conditions, creating ideal, 43–57
conducting decision-making efficiently, 51–52
conferences, participating in, 183
confirmation bias, 228
confrontation principle, 21, 184–185
construction materials, 88
consultations, quality of, mystery shopping and, 158
Consulted, in RACI matric, 80–81
contact effect, 151
contrast effect, 152
control, as a benefit of clear goal definition, 60
conventional wisdom, questioning, 185–186
convergent phase, 15–16

conversion rate, 251
cooperative partners, as external stakeholders, 111
copyright, brainstorming and, 195
correcting pivots, 231
costs
development, 223
types of, 74
Could have, in MoSCoW ranking, 66
countering objections, 272–273
creating
bar graphs, 71–72
company culture, 269–270
culture of innovation, 14
goals, 61–62
ideal conditions, 43–57
ideas by brainstorming, 196–204
leadership coalition, 268–269
matrix of responsibility, 80–81
with openness, 118–119
sense of urgency, 267–268
services, 12–13
teams, 24–25, 78–81
trust, 266
visions for project, 44
creative freedom, asking for, 49
creative principles, 184–185
creative process, mastering the, 179–180
creative workspaces, 39–40
creativity
overcoming obstacles to, 188–190
promoting with common spaces, 89–90
selecting techniques, 190–193
success factors for increasing, 185–190
criteria
about, 22
weighing, 225–226
critic role, 206–207
critical incident technique, 134
criticism, in brainstorming, 195
cultural fit, as a criteria, 22, 215, 217, 223

culture of innovation, 269

curiosity

  arousing, 45–48

  training, 47–48

customer journey

  about, 122

  analyzing weak areas in, 134

  discovering problems/improvements in, 131–136

  phases of, 130–131

  using, 129–130

customer orientation, 30–31

customer satisfaction, Kano model and, 173

customer service, digitization options for, 86

customer-benefits matrix method, 135

customers

  characterizing using Persona method, 122–125

  as external stakeholders, 111

  involving in developing solutions, 182

# D

de Bono, Edward (creativity researcher), 207

decision-maker role, 164

decision-making unit (DMU), 164

decisions

  conducting decision-making efficiently, 51–52

  enabling in design thinking process, 49–52

  following up on, 52

  preparing efficiently, 50–51

decomposition principle, 20, 184

defining

  communication practices, 25

  mistakes, 53

  project goals, 60–64

  roles on teams, 80

  tasks, 19–20, 99–106

  team roles, 25

Defining the Question phase, 17

definition, 160

delivery, quality of, mystery shopping and, 158

demographic shift, 96–97

demonstrating, compared with presenting, 238–239

departments, as internal stakeholders, 112

design brief, 49, 60

design thinking. *See also specific topics*

  about, 9–11

  basics of, 14–24

  5 P's of, 11

  principles of, 29–41

  process of, 16–17

  starting, 24–27

  uses for, 12–14

designing

  business models, 13

  common spaces, 89–91

  organizational innovations, 13–14

  prototypes, 227–239

  social innovations, 13–14

desirability, as a criteria, 215, 217–218

desired goals, 61

determining

  adaptability, 220–221

  feasibility, 215–216

  point of view, 175–176

  problems of target users, 168–169

  project reporting format, 82

  target competencies, 55

  work packages from user perspective, 66–67

developing

  empathy, 36–37

  goals, 62–63

  ideas, 179–193, 195–209

  products, 12

  prototypes, 22–23

  questions, 161–162

  tasks, 162–163

  work packages from user perspective, 66–67

Developing Prototypes phase, 17

development costs, as criteria for measuring feasibility, 223

development period, as criteria for measuring feasibility, 222 didactic brainstorming, 201

differentiation advantages, as criteria for measuring product appeal/competitiveness, 224

digital prototypes, 23, 237–238

digitization
about, 98
for customer service, 86

discounting your own ideas, 119

discussions, concluding in interviews, 260

disruptive innovation, 170

divergent phase, 15–16

diversity
ensuring on teams, 39
for evaluations, 212
in teams, 15, 78–79

DMU (decision-making unit), 164

documenting, compared with communicating, 83

"do-nothing" scenario, 45

dot-voting, 22, 213

Double Diamond Process Model, 16

drawings, for prototypes, 23

dreamer role, 206

Dropbox, 38

d.school, 16–17

Dummies (website), 4

## E

ecology trends, 97

economic influences, 108–109

Edison, Thomas, 186–187

education trends, 97

effectuation approach, 99

effort, minimizing, 230–231

electronic brainstorming, 200

Ellis, Sean (start-up coach), 246

emotional jobs, 165

emotions, in interviews, 259

empathic design, 118

empathy
about, 15
analyzing weak areas in customer journey, 134
collecting information, 120–121
defined, 117
developing, 36–37
evaluating information, 121–136
importance of, 117–118
proceeding with, 118–120

empathy map
about, 122
using, 125–128

employees
empowering, 270–271
as internal stakeholders, 112
skills/knowledge, taking advantage of, 181

empowering employees, 270–271

enabling decisions in design thinking process, 49–52

encouraging
collaboration, 264–267
self-organization, 266
willingness to change, 45

enlarging tasks, 115

ensuring
diversity on teams, 39
positive attitudes, 43–45
resource distribution, 267
sustainability, 220

Enthusiasm customer requirements, in Kano model, 173

entries, finding for interviews, 258

environment
flexibility of, 90–91
quality of, mystery shopping and, 158

environmental barriers, overcoming, 188

environmental influences, evaluating, 108

Epperson, Frank, 39

equipment, providing, 88–89

errors, tolerating, 52–54, 232, 269–270

establishing
  company culture, 269–270
  culture of innovation, 14
  leadership coalition, 268–269
  trust, 266
estimating
  fit, 217
  influences on tasks, 108–113
  required time, 71
euphoria, curbing, 273
European Organization for Nuclear Research (CERN), 32–33
European Patent Office (website), 183
evaluating
  advantages for ideas, 213–214
  barriers for ideas, 213–214
  diversity for, 212
  environmental influences, 108–111
  ideas, 211–226
  ideas with checklists, 215–221
  information, 121–136
  patent information, 183
  publications, 183
  task information, 18
  user behavior with key figures, 251–252
Example icon, 4
experiences, 121
experiments
  about, 121
  benefits of, 228
  with ideas, 187
experts, collaborating with, 183
explanatory videos, 236
expression of ideas, free, brainstorming and, 196
external observations, 144–145
external stakeholders, 111–112
eye-tracking systems, 143

**F**

Fab.com, 99
failure, learning from, 15, 38–39, 232
fake door web page, 237

fear, overcoming, 47
feasibility
  assessing, 222–223
  as a criteria, 22, 215–216
  determining, 215–216
feedback, user, 174
feedback loop, 242
female shift in society trends, 97
finding
  competencies, 54–57
  entries for interviews, 258
  evaluation criteria, 222–224
  lead users, 32–35
  problems/improvements in customer journey, 131–136
  search areas, 95–99
  solutions, 20–21
  tasks, 159–163
Finding and Selecting Ideas phase, 17
Fisher, Gary, 33
fit
  as a criteria, 22
  estimating, 217
5 P's of design thinking, 11
5 Whys technique, 106
five-finger method, 213
Fleming, Alexander (bacteriologist), 38
flexibility
  of environment, 90–91
  of process, 15, 40–41
  quality of, mystery shopping and, 158
following principles, 14–15
following up
  after interviews, 259–260
  on decisions, 52
Food on Your Table platform, 239
Ford, Henry, 32
form-and-design materials/tools, 88
forming phase, 265
formulating
  empathy, 36–37
  goals, 62–63

ideas, 179–193, 195–209

products, 12

prototypes, 22–23

questions, 161–162

tasks, 162–163

work packages from user perspective, 66–67

404 web page, 237

freemium principle, 13

functional fixedness, 32

functional jobs, 165

functional value questions, 172

## G

galvanic skin response (GSR) measurements, 143

Gantt, Henry Laurence, 71

Gantt chart, 71–72

Gascoigne, Joel (Buffer app founder), 238

General Electric Healthcare, 12

globalization, 96–97

Go decision, 52

goals

communicating, 63–64

compiling, 61–62

formulating, 62–63

ordering, 61–62

weighing, 62

Goldberg, Jason, 99

golden mean effect, 153

gold-plating, 170

Google Glass, 36

Google Patents search engine (website), 183

green hat, in Six Hats method, 208–209

Groupon, 239

GSR (galvanic skin response) measurements, 143

## H

Halo effect, 151

Hasso Plattner Institute of Design, 16–17

Hawthorne effect, 151, 155

headstand, 201

health trends, 97

holding workshops, 86–88

hypothesis, 241

## I

IBM, 239

icons, explained, 4

ideas

boosting flow of, 197–199

creative principles, 184–185

developing, 179–193, 195–209

evaluating, 211–226

evaluating advantages for, 213–214

evaluating barriers for, 213–214

evaluating with checklists, 215–221

experimenting with, 187

generating by brainstorming, 196–204

illustrating, 37–38

implementing, 263–273

mastering creative process, 179–180

opening up sources for new, 181–183

selecting, 212–213, 226

selecting creativity techniques, 190–193

success factors for increasing creativity, 185–190

testing, 241–253

testing assumptions about benefits of, 245–246

ideation, 180

identifying

knowledge gaps, 106–107

stakeholders, 108, 111–113

target user wishes, 169–170

IKEA, 186

illumination, 180

illustrating

ideas, 37–38

tasks, 115

image effect, as criteria for measuring product appeal/competitiveness, 224

imaginary brainstorming, 200

imagination principle, 21, 185

impartiality, 119

implementation
    of ideas, 263–273
    probability of, 222
improvements, discovering in customer journey, 131–136
improving flow of ideas, 197–199
inability, as a barrier, 272
incomparable, compare the, 205
incremental progress, planning work packages for, 65
individual-centered mapping, 155
individualization trends, 97
influencer role, 164
influences, estimating on tasks, 108–113
information
    collecting, 120–121
    evaluating, 121–136
Informed, in RACI matrix, 80–81
initiator role, 164
innovation
    culture of, 269
    establishing culture of, 14
innovation factory, 40
Instagram, 231
instrumental value questions, 172
intelligent mistakes, 54
interest groups, as external stakeholders, 112
internal stakeholders, 112
Internet resources
    Cheat Sheet, 4
    Dummies, 4
    European Patent Office, 183
    Google Patents search engine, 183
    US Patent Office, 183
interviewees, selecting, 247–248
Interviewer effect, 151, 155
interviews
    success factors for, 257–262
    testing with, 247–250
investors, as external stakeholders, 112
Ishikawa, Kaoru, 103
Ishikawa diagram, 103–106

**J**

jobs-to-be-done concept, 174
Juicero, 30

**K**

Kamprad, Ingvar (IKEA founder), 186
Kano, Noriaki (doctor), 173
Kano model, 173
Kekulé, Friedrich August (chemist), 185
Kennedy, John F., 44
key figures, evaluating user behavior with, 251–252
Kickstarter, 40
killer phrases, 272–273
knowledge, employee, 181
knowledge gaps, 106–107
knowledge map, 181
knowledge sharing, promoting, 266
knowledge trends, 97

**L**

landing page, 238
latent problem/need, 244
lead users
    about, 14, 182, 248
    finding, 32–35
    involving, 35–36
leadership coalition, establishing, 268–269
learning
    from failure, 15, 38–39
    from test results, 252–253
    two-legged, 38
legal influences, 109
Lego, 40
Levitt, Theodore (professor), 165
Liip app, 13–14
listening actively, in interviews, 259
little technique, 201
logical fallacies, 152
"Lorem ipsum" texts, 237

## M

Machine category, in Ishikawa diagram, 104
machines, as a resource, 72
Man category, in Ishikawa diagram, 104
management, as internal stakeholders, 112
Management category, in Ishikawa diagram, 105
mandatory goals, 61
market entry barriers, as criteria for rating market attractiveness, 224
market growth rate, as criteria for rating market attractiveness, 224
market pull, 98
market research, traditional, 31–32
market segment, searching in, 96–98
market size, as criteria for rating market attractiveness, 224
Massachusetts Institute of Technology (MIT), 33, 229
Material category, in Ishikawa diagram, 104
materials
  providing, 88–89
  as a resource, 72
matrix of responsibility, creating, 80–81
McDonald, Dick, 13, 186
McDonald, Mac, 13, 186
McDonald's, 13
me spaces, 26
means-ends analysis (MEA), 170–172
Measurable, in SMART criteria, 62
Measurement category, in Ishikawa diagram, 105
media, as external stakeholders, 112
mental models, 153, 156–157
Method category, in Ishikawa diagram, 105
methods, of design thinking, 11
midlevel value (MV), 73
mildness effect, 153
mind maps, 191–192
minimizing effort, 230–231
minimum viable product (MVP), 229–230
mistakes, tolerating, 52–54, 232, 269–270
MIT (Massachusetts Institute of Technology), 229
mock-ups, 238
model constructions, for prototypes, 23

modeling clay, 89
models
  business, 13
  Kano, 173
  mental, 153, 156–157
moments of truth, 133
Money category, in Ishikawa diagram, 105
monitoring competitors, 182
moonshot thinking, 44
morphological box, 184, 192–193
MoSCoW ranking, 66
Mother Nature category, in Ishikawa diagram, 105
motivation, as a benefit of clear goal definition, 60
Must have, in MoSCoW ranking, 66
MV (midlevel value), 73
MVP (minimum viable product), 229–230
mysery shopping, 153, 156–158
mystery call, 156

## N

needs
  analyzing as tasks, 166–172
  checking assumptions about, 243–245
  recognizing for target users, 165–166
negative words, 161
net promoter score (NPS), 246
networking, 188
new work trends, 97
no permission, as a barrier, 272
non-goals, 61
norming phase, 266
not knowing, as a barrier, 272
not wanting, as a barrier, 272
notes, taking correctly in interviews, 258–259
NPS (net promoter score), 246
numbers, of interviews, 260

## O

object brainstorming, 200
objections, countering, 272–273

observations
   about, 120–121, 137
   applying consistent methodologies for, 153–158
   avoiding errors, 151–153
   of customers for developing solutions, 182
   of everything/everyone, 187
   mental model diagrams, 156–157
   preparing, 139–145
   systematic, 145–153
   of target users, 18–19
   using, 137–138
Observing Customers phase, 17
offering team-oriented/creative workspaces, 39–40
online studies, testing with, 250–252
open questions, 245
openness, creating with, 118–119
operating materials, as a resource, 72
opportunities, with target users, 261–262
optimistic value (OV), 73
ordering goals, 61–62
organizational innovations, designing, 13–14
orientation, as a benefit of clear goal definition, 60
OV (optimistic value), 73
overcoming
   fear, 47
   obstacles to creativity, 188–190
   psychological blocks, 189–190
   resistance, 271–272
   sociological blocks, 188–189
overengineering, 30, 170
overfilled, 170
overhead, 74
owners, as external stakeholders, 112

## P

Page Not Found error message, 237
participating
   in conferences, 183
   in trade fairs, 183
passive problem/need, 244

patent information, evaluating, 183
people
   focusing on, 30–31
   as one of 5 P's of design thinking, 11
   as a resource, 72
Performance customer requirements, in Kano model, 173
performing
   stories, 236–237
   team reviews, 267
performing phase, 266–267
periphery effect, 152–153
persona, 102–103
Persona method, 19, 113, 122–125, 164, 228, 234
personal jobs, 165
personnel, as a resource, 72
perspectives, changing, 205–207
pessimistic value (PV), 73
PESTEL (political, economic, social, technological, environmental and legal spheres of influence) method, 108–113
phone interview, 247
photo collages, for prototypes, 23
physical barriers, overcoming, 188
pinboard, 235–236
pivots, 231
place-centered mapping, 155
Places, as one of 5 P's of design thinking, 11
planning
   for budget, 74–75
   project work, 25–26
   projects, 59–75
   for resources, 72–74
   sequence, 70–72
   work packages, 64–70
Pluses, Potentials, Concerns, and Overcoming concerns (PPCO), 213–214
PO (provocative operation), 205
point of view, determining, 175–176
political, economic, social, technological, environmental and legal spheres of influence (PESTEL method), 108–113

political influences, 108

politics, as external stakeholders, 112

postprocessing interviews, 261

power-of-ten technique, 115

PPCO (Pluses, Potentials, Concerns, and Overcoming concerns), 213–214

Practices, as one of 5 P's of design thinking, 11

pre-mortem, 201

preparing

  decisions efficiently, 50–51

  for interviews, 257–258

  observations, 139–145

  structures, 263–264

  workshops, 85–86

prescribing solutions, 161

presenting

  compared with demonstrating, 238–239

  tasks as challenges, 46

  tasks as rewards, 46

  tasks in comprehensible fashion, 47

preventing

  euphoria, 273

  search field errors, 160–161

primary effect, 151

principles

  abstraction, 21, 185

  analogy, 21, 184–185, 198

  association, 20

  associative, 184

  communicating, 14–15

  creative, 184–185

  of design thinking, 29–41

  following, 14–15

  as one of 5 P's of design thinking, 11

probability of implementation, as criteria for measuring feasibility, 222

problem space, 15

problems

  checking assumptions about, 243–245

  determining for target users, 168–169

  discovering in customer journey, 131–136

  reasons for, 170–172

  redefining, 159–176

  selecting, 172–174

  solving, 195–196

process

  enabling decisions in dseign thinking, 49–52

  flexibility of, 15, 40–41

  as one of 5 P's of design thinking, 11

product development, 12

production factory, 40

products, simplifying, 186

project reporting, 82

projects

  creating vision for, 44

  defining goals for, 60–64

  determining reporting format for, 82

  planning, 59–75

  planning work, 25–26

promoting knowledge sharing, 266

prototype phase, clarifying tasks in, 228–229

prototypes

  about, 227

  benefit of experiments, 228

  clarifying tasks in prototype phase, 228–229

  clarity of ideas, 233–239

  designing, 227–239

  developing, 22–23, 229–232

  digital, 237–238

  tangible nature of ideas, 233–239

  using different, 232–233

  using efficiently, 229–232

providing equipment/materials, 88–89

provocation technique, 21, 205

provocative operation (PO), 205

psychological blocks, overcoming, 189–190

psychological value questions, 172

publications, evaluating, 183

pupil reactions, recording, 143

PV (pessimistiv value), 73

## Q

quantity preceds quality, brainstorming and, 196
question storming, 201
questions
  asking correctly, 249–250
  asking good, 248–249
  formulating, 161–162
  open, 245
  suggestive, 249

## R

RACI matrix, 80–81
random-word technique, 204
raw materials, as a resource, 72
realist role, 206
Realistic, in SMART criteria, 63
realistic value (MV), 73
receiving creative freedom, 49
recency effect, 151
recognizable benefit, as criteria for measuring
   product appeal/competitiveness, 223
recognizing needs of target users, 165–166
recommender role, 164
red hat, in Six Hats method, 209
redefining problems, 159–176
redefinition, 160
reformulating tasks, 114–115
resistance, overcoming, 271–272
resource distribution, ensuring, 267
resource planning, 72–74
resources
  planning for, 72–74
  types of, 72
responsibilities, clarifying, 50
Responsible, in RACI matric, 80–81
results, sharing, 120
retrospective think-aloud, 150
reversal, 205
reverse brainstorming, 201
reverse engineering, 182
reversing tasks, 115

rewards, presenting tasks as, 46
Ries, Eric (author), 229–230
role effect, 151
role-playing games, for prototypes, 23, 236–237
roles, defining on teams, 80
rolestorming, 200
Rosenthal effect, 151
Rosso, Manuel (app founder), 239
rules, breaking the, 205

## S

saboteur role, 164
safety, feeling of, 234
scalability, as a criteria, 22, 215, 218–219
Schrage, Michael, 229
science, as external stakeholders, 111
scrutinization, 48
Sean Ellis test, 246
search areas, finding, 95–99
search fields
  about, 95–96
  preventing errors with, 160–161
searching
  in areas of competence, 98–99
  in market segment, 96–98
  in technology area, 98
secondary aspects, 64
secondary material, analysis of, 120
security, feeling of, 234
security trends, 98
selecting
  creativity techniques, 190–193
  evaluation methods, 211–212
  ideas, 212–213, 226
  interviewees, 247–248
  most important wishes/problems, 172–174
  problems, 172–174
  solutions, 22
  wishes, 172–174
selective perception, 153

self-organization
  applying principle of, 81
  encouraging, 266
sense of urgency, creating, 267–268
sequence planning, 59, 70–72
service creation, 12–13
services, simplifying, 186
setup
  communication rules, 83–84
  steering committee, 50
shadowing, 145
shareholders, as external stakeholders, 112
sharing results, 120
Shellhammer, Bradford, 99
shop committee, as internal stakeholders, 112
Should have, in MoSCoW ranking, 66
show effect, 152
shrinking tasks, 115
significance for customer, as criteria for
    measuring product appeal/
    competitiveness, 223
silent shopping, 156–158
similarity effect, 152
simplification principle, 21
simplifying
  products, 186
  services, 186
Six Hats method, 207–209
635 method, 195, 201–204
skills, employee, taking advantage of, 181
SMART criteria, 62–63
social influences, 109
social innovations, designing, 13–14
social jobs, 165
sociological blocks, overcoming, 188–189
solution space, 15
solutions
  finding, 20–21
  including customers in developing, 182
  prescribing, 161

quality of, mystery shopping and, 158
selecting, 22
testing, 23–24
solving problems, 195–196
sources, for ideas, 181–183
Specific, in SMART criteria, 62
speedstorming, 200
stakeholder analysis, 111–113
stakeholders
  external, 111–112
  identifying, 108, 111–113
  internal, 112
Stanford University, 13, 16–17
starting design thinking, 24–27
status, sense of, 234
steering committee, setting up, 50
step-by-step brainstorming, 199
sticky effect, 152
stimulation, sense of, 234
Stop decision, 52
stop-and-go brainstorming, 200
stories
  performing, 236–237
  for prototypes, 23
  telling, 233–235
  visualizing, 235–236
storming phase, 265–266
storyboarding, 235–236
storytelling, 233–235
strategic fit, as a criteria, 22, 215, 217, 223
strategic significance, as criteria for measuring
    support, 223
streamlining, 186
strictness effect, 153
structured association, 184
structures, preparing, 263–264
success, making chances for measurable, 221–226
suggestive questions, 249
superiority, sense of, 234
supplied parts, as a resource, 72

suppliers
  as external stakeholders, 111
  surveying, 182
support, asking for, 27, 48
surveying
  customers, 182
  suppliers, 182
surveys, 120
sustainability, as a criteria, 22, 215, 220
sustainability of competitive advantage,
    as criteria for measuring product
    appeal/competitiveness, 224
sustainability trends, 97
Swinmurn, Nick (Zappos founder), 187
synergy effect, as criteria for measuring
    support, 223
synthesis, 19
systematic observations, 145–153

# T

target competencies
  compared with actual competencies, 56
  determining, 55
target users
  about, 159
  checking assumptions about, 242–243
  determining problems of, 168–169
  finding tasks, 159–163
  focusing on, 163–164
  identifying wishes of, 169–170
  Kano model, 173
  observing, 18–19
  opportunities with, 261–262
  recognizing needs of, 165–166
task boards, 67–70
tasks
  about, 95
  analyzing needs as, 166–172
  changing, 115
  clarifying in prototype phase, 228–229
  clarifying in test phase, 241–246
  clarifying what it is, 100–101

clarifying when the problem/wish occurs, 103
clarifying where the problem/wish occurs, 103
clarifying who has the problem/wish, 101–103
clarifying why the problem/wish occurs,
    103–106
closing knowledge gaps, 107
collecting information, 18
defining, 19–20, 99–106
enlarging, 115
estimating influences on, 108–113
evaluating information, 18
finding, 159–163
finding search areas, 95–99
formulating, 162–163
identifying knowledge gaps, 106–107
illustrating, 115
presenting as challenges, 46
presenting as rewards, 46
presenting in comprehensible fashion, 47
reformulating, 114–115
reversing, 115
shrinking, 115
trying new, 47–48
team directory, 81
team diversity, 15
team-oriented workspaces, 39–40
teams
  about, 77
  adjourning phase, 267
  applying principle of self-organization, 81
  arranging workshops, 85–89
  assembling, 24–25, 78–81
  clarifying communication within, 81–84
  defining roles in, 25, 80
  designing common spaces, 89–91
  diversity in, 78–79
  ensuring diversity on, 39
  forming phase, 265
  norming phase, 266
  performing phase, 266–267
  storming phase, 265–266
  T-shaped individuals, 78–79

technological influences, 109

technology area, searching in, 98

Teflon, 38

telling stories, 233–235

terminal value questions, 172

test phase, clarifying tasks in, 241–246

testing
  A/B, 250
  assumptions, 241–253
  assumptions about idea benefits, 245–246
  assumptions about problems/needs, 243–245
  assumptions about target users, 242–243
  competencies, 56
  ideas, 241–253
  with interviews, 247–250
  learning from test results, 252–253
  with online studies, 250–252
  solutions, 23–24

Testing Assumptions phase, 17

think-aloud technique, 150

3-point estimate, 73

thumb method, 213

time
  buffer, 71
  estimating required, 71
  quality of management of, mystery shopping and, 158

Time-bound, in SMART criteria, 63

Tip icon, 4

tolerating
  errors, 232
  mistakes, 52–54, 269–270

touchpoints
  in customer journey, 131–136
  defined, 157

trade fairs, participating in, 183

traditional market research, 31–32

training curiosity, 47–48

trends, 97–98

trigger questions, 197

trust, establishing, 266

T-shaped individuals, 78–79

tuning questions, 197

Twitter, 231

two-legged learning, 38

"two-pizza rule," 78

## U

Understanding the Problem phase, 16

urbanization trends, 97

urgency, sense of, 267–268

US Patent Office (website), 183

user behavior
  comparing, 250
  evaluating with key figures, 251–252

user feedback, 174

user perspective, formulating/determining work packages from, 66–67

user role, 164

user story, 175

user-friendliness, 115

users, as external stakeholders, 111

## V

value proposition, as criteria for measuring product appeal/competitiveness, 223

variants, in brainstorming, 199–201

verification, 180

verifying
  communication within teams, 81–84
  responsibilities, 50
  tasks in prototype phase, 228–229
  tasks in test phase, 241–246
  what the task is, 100–101
  when the problem/wish occurs, 103
  where the problem/wish occurs, 103
  who has the problem/wish, 101–103
  why the problem/wish occurs, 103–106

viability, as a criteria, 215, 218–219

video conferences, 51

virtual meetings, 51

vision
  communicating, 44–45, 269
  creating for projects, 44
visual brainstorming, 199
visual storytelling, 235–236
visualizing stories, 235–236
voice frequency analyses, 143
von Hippel, Eric (professor), 33

# W

Walt Disney method, 205–207
Warning icon, 4
we spaces, 26, 89–90
websites
  Cheat Sheet, 4
  Dummies, 4
  European Patent Office, 183
  Google Patents search engine, 183
  US Patent Office, 183
weighing
  criteria, 225–226
  goals, 62
weighting evaluation criteria, 222–224
what-if technique, 198
white hat, in Six Hats method, 208
wicked problems, 195–196
wireframes, 237–238
wishes
  identifying for target users, 169–170
  reasons for, 170–172
  selecting, 172–174
  selecting most important, 172–174
wishful thinking, 205
*Wizard of Oz* minimum viable product, 239
Won't have this time, in MoSCoW ranking, 66
work environment, 26–27
work packages
  about, 25
  planning, 64–70
  using task boards, 67–70
workshops
  arranging, 85–89
  holding, 86–88
  preparing, 85–86
workspaces
  creative, 15, 39–40
  team-oriented, 15, 39–40
writing, from user's perspective, 162
written brainstorming, 201–204

# Y

yellow hat, in Six Hats method, 209
Yellow Pages, 181
yes-and technique, 195

# Z

Zappos, 187
Zero Defects approach, 38
Zuckerberg, Mark, 32

# About the Author

**Dr. Christian Müller-Roterberg** has years of experience in implementing design thinking projects in collaboration with a number of different companies. He works on projects with leading international industries and service companies as well as numerous start-ups. He is a professor in the areas of technology, innovation management, and entrepreneurship at the Ruhr West University in Mülheim, where he gives lectures, leads tutorials, and holds seminars. He also advises companies and holds corporate workshops, using methods such as design thinking, the lean start-up approach, and the business model canvas. He has authored several books and more than 30 German- and English-language publications in the field of innovation management and entrepreneurship.

In his professional life, Christian has been actively involved in several start-up projects and performed the due diligence audit for the IPO of a start-up company. He has also worked at Germany's Federal Ministry of Education and Research, where he oversaw the funding of research projects, particularly with respect to start-ups and cooperation between business and science. Preceding this, he was in charge of technology transfer at the Charité University Hospital in Berlin, where he advised corporate management and consulted on the topic of patents. He completed a correspondence course in the field of industrial property rights and is also a qualified internal auditor in the area of quality management.

Christian's doctoral thesis in business was completed at the Technical University of Hamburg at the Institute for Technology and Innovation Management. The topic dealt with the levels of cooperation between large corporations and start-up companies in the areas of research and development. He spent several months in Japan at the Toyohashi University of Technology to complete a study on entrepreneurship activities in Japan.

Christian received his undergraduate degree from the Technical University of Braunschweig and spent a year at the Massachusetts Institute of Technology (MIT) in the USA for his master's thesis. You can find more information about him at www.innovationsratgeber.de.

# Dedication

For Gertrud and Bernhard.

For Kerstin, Leonard, and Maximilian.

Thank you for the joyful path that you all take — and will continue to take — with me.

Thanks for the loving hands that always help me so much.

Thank you for your love and support.

# Author's Acknowledgments

I'm especially grateful to Ms. Anna Freihöfer-Gamrad, scientific staff member at the Ruhr West University, who edited the initial drafts of the individual chapters with a great deal of commitment, professional expertise, precision, and poise. I would also like to thank Mr. Simon Berndt, scientific assistant at the Ruhr West University, for his supporting research and formatting work on the images.

Many thanks also to the fantastic team at John Wiley & Sons: Ms. Inken Bohn, who, entirely in line with design thinking, gave me fast and competent feedback. Also, thank you to Steve Hayes, Paul Levesque, and Becky Whitney, who did an extraordinary job bringing out the book in the unique *For-Dummies* style. Last but not least, I'd like to express my gratitude to the other helping hands in the background, who contributed their expertise so that this book can become the guide that we have hoped for together.

## Publisher's Acknowledgments

**Acquisitions Editor:** Steve Hayes

**Special Help:** Inken Bohn

**Senior Project Editor:** Paul Levesque

**Copy Editor:** Becky Whitney

**Editorial Assistant:** Matthew Lowe

**Sr. Editorial Assistant:** Cherie Case

**Production Editor:** Magesh Elangovan

**Cover Image:** © ismagilov/Getty images